Facebook Nation

Newton Lee

Facebook Nation

Total Information Awareness

 Springer

6/11/13
WW
84.15

Newton Lee
Newton Lee Laboratories, LLC
Tujunga, CA
USA

ISBN 978-1-4614-5307-9   ISBN 978-1-4614-5308-6   (eBook)
DOI 10.1007/978-1-4614-5308-6
Springer New York Heidelberg Dordrecht London

Library of Congress Control Number: 2012945480

Springer Science+Business Media New York 2013

Printed on acid-free paper

Springer is part of Springer Science+Business Media (www.springer.com)

Dedicated to my beloved one in a million among billions of cybercitizens

Contents

About the Book

President Barack Obama, in his 2011 State of the Union Address, called America "the nation of Edison and the Wright brothers" and "of Google and Facebook." U.S. Chief Information Officer, Steven VanRoekel, said that America has become a "Facebook nation" that demands increased transparency and interactivity from the federal government.

Facebook as a nation in 2012 would be the third largest country in the world with over 955 million citizens, after China and India. This book portrays the social media eco-system as a world of increasing Total Information Awareness, which is essentially a civilian version of the controversial Total Information Awareness program unveiled in 2002 by the Defense Advanced Research Projects Agency (DARPA) at the U.S. Department of Defense.

Back in the 1960s, DARPA initiated and funded the research and development of Advanced Research Projects Agency Network (ARPANET) that went online in 1969. The success of ARPANET gave rise to the global commercial Internet in the 1990s and the new generation of Fortune 500 companies today including Amazon.com, Google, eBay, and Yahoo!. As if life comes to full circle in the twenty-first century, private businesses and the ubiquity of social networks such as Facebook, Google+, Twitter, and YouTube are creating the technologies and infrastructures necessary for the DARPA-proposed Total Information Awareness program.

WikiLeaks founder Julian Assange called Facebook "the most appalling spying machine that has ever been invented." Indeed, military and civilian technologies have interwoven into every fabric of our society, as Facebook co-founder and CEO Mark Zuckerberg said, "We exist at the intersection of technology and social issues."

This book offers discourse and practical advice on the privacy issue in the age of big data, the rise of Facebook nation, and Total Information Awareness.

Part I
Prologue

Chapter 1
From 1984 to Total Information Awareness

Information is the oxygen of the modern age. It seeps through the walls topped by barbed wire, it wafts across the electrified borders, the Goliath of totalitarianism will be brought down by the David of the microchip.
— President Ronald Reagan (June 14, 1989)

We exist at the intersection of technology and social issues.
— Facebook co-founder and CEO Mark Zuckerberg
(September 22, 2011)

1.1 President Ronald Reagan in 1984

In April 1984, President Ronald Reagan signed the National Security Decision Directive (NSDD) 138: Combating Terrorism, which authorized the increase of intelligence collection directed against groups or states involved in terrorism [1]. I was a graduate student at Virginia Tech majoring in computer science with specialization in artificial intelligence (AI). A year earlier in January 1983, I received a surprise letter from the White House signed by President Reagan himself. The 4-page letter opened with "Dear Mr. Lee: I am grateful to you, more than I can express in a letter, for your wonderful support of our Congressional Committee." Although I was neither a registered Republican nor Democrat, I was truly delighted by the President's letter.

In the summer of 1984, then Virginia Tech professor Dr. Timothy Lindquist introduced me to Dr. John F. Kramer at the Institute for Defense Analyses (IDA), a nonprofit think tank serving the U.S. Department of Defense (DoD) and the Executive Office of the President [2]. Partly motivated by President Reagan's letter, I accepted the internship and became a research staff member at IDA. My first summer project was to assist in the drafting of the Military Standard Common APSE (Ada Programming Support Environment) Interface Set (CAIS) [3]. My second project in the winter semester was to design a counter terrorism software program for a multi-agency joint research effort involving the Defense Advanced Research Projects Agency (DARPA), National Security Agency (NSA), and Federal Bureau of Investigation (FBI).

As a co-pioneer of artificial intelligence applications in counter terrorism, I helped develop a natural language parser and machine learning program to digest news and articles in search of potential terrorist threats around the globe. Employing

N. Lee, *Facebook Nation*, DOI: 10.1007/978-1-4614-5308-6_1,
© Springer Science+Business Media New York 2013

psychology and cognitive science, the prototype system thinks like a human in constructing small-scale models of reality that it uses to anticipate events [4]. The knowledge representation and data structures were based on "A Framework for Representing Knowledge" by MIT Artificial Intelligence Lab researcher Marvin Minsky [5].

I joined AT&T Bell Laboratories in 1985 to further my research on artificial intelligence and expert systems. At Bell Labs, I conceived Dynamic Mental Models (DM2) as a general algorithm that combines analytical models and experiential knowledge in diagnostic problem solving, regardless of the problem domains [6]. The algorithm mimics a human expert in formulating and using an internal, cognitive representation of a physical system during the process of diagnosis. In 1989, the U.S. Army Research Office studied DM2 for use in diagnostic support of complex modern weapons systems with encouraging results [7].

Inspired by Steve Jobs' revolutionary NeXT machines, I switched my focus to multimedia applications in 1989. Integrating AI, expert systems, natural language processing, and hypermedia, I developed on the NeXT Computer the world's first annotated multimedia Online Public Access Catalog (OPAC) at Virginia Tech and the U.S. National Agricultural Library [8].

Despite NeXT's limited commercial success, its NeXTSTEP operating system and object-oriented programming had a wide-ranging impact on the computer industry. Tim Berners-Lee at the European Organization for Nuclear Research (CERN) used a NeXT Computer in 1991 to create the first web browser and web server [9]. NeXT also gained popularity at U.S. federal agencies including the Naval Research Laboratory (NRL), National Security Agency (NSA), Defense Advanced Research Projects Agency (DARPA), Central Intelligence Agency (CIA), and National Reconnaissance Office (NRO) [10].

In 1996, I switched my focus again, this time to the World Wide Web, when I joined Disney Online to build games, websites, social media, and search technology for The Walt Disney Company. Disney is an early adopter of the Internet as well as online communities. In 2000, I led a team in creating Disney Online Chat Studio and multiplayer games where children could engage in safe chats and send prescreened messages to one another [11].

It was at Disney where I met Dr. Eric Haseltine whom I invited to my Disney Online Technology Forum in 2001 to give a talk on how a human brain reacts neurologically to stories. After the 9/11 terrorist attacks, Haseltine left his position as Executive Vice President of R&D at Walt Disney Imagineering to join the National Security Agency (NSA) as Director of Research in 2002. From 2005 to 2007, Haseltine was Associate Director for Science and Technology at the newly established Office of the Director of National Intelligence (ODNI). In collaboration with Georgetown University researchers, [12] Haseltine and his successor Steve Nixon at ODNI oversaw the development of Argus, a biosurveillance AI program that monitors foreign news reports and other open sources looking for anything that could provide an early warning of an epidemic, nuclear accident, or environmental catastrophe [13].

Fig. 1.1 Official seal of the information awareness office (*IAO*)

1.2 Total Information Awareness

In an April 2002 statement, Dr. Tony Tether, then director of Defense Advanced Research Projects Agency (DARPA), informed the U.S. Senate Committee on Armed Services about the new establishment of the Information Awareness Office (IAO) headed by controversial ex-Navy Admiral John Poindexter, former U.S. National Security Advisor to President Ronald Reagan (See Fig. 1.1). IAO's charter was to "develop the information systems needed to find, identify, track, and understand terrorist networks and vastly improve what we know about our adversaries"[14]. IAO was responsible for the Evidence Extraction and Link Discovery program, Wargaming the Asymmetric Environment program, and Total Information Awareness (TIA) program.

The American public was startled on November 9, 2002 by *The New York Times* headline: "Pentagon Plans a Computer System That Would Peek at Personal Data of Americans" [15]. Total Information Awareness (TIA) prompted privacy concerns that the system would provide intelligence analysts and law enforcement officials with instant access to information collected from personal emails, phone calls, credit card records, medical records, banking transactions, travel documents, and other sources without any requirement for a search warrant.

In a March 2003 statement to the U.S. House of Representatives Armed Services Committee, Tether attempted to pacify the controversy by affirming that DRAPA's Information Awareness programs, including TIA, were not developing technology to maintain dossiers on every U.S. citizen or to assemble a giant database on Americans. Instead, TIA was designed as an experimental, multi-agency prototype network that enables law enforcement to collaborate, "connect the dots", and prevent terrorist attacks [16]. In spite of DRAPA's final attempt to justify TIA by renaming Total Information Awareness to Terrorism Information Awareness [17], the U.S. Congress eliminated the funding for TIA and terminated the Information Awareness Office (IAO) in August 2003 [18].

However, TIA did not end in 2003. In March 2008, a *Wall Street Journal* article reported that the National Security Agency (NSA) has been building essentially the same system as TIA. The article reads, "According to current and former intelligence officials, the spy agency now monitors huge volumes of records of domestic emails and Internet searches as well as bank transfers, credit card transactions, travel and telephone records…. The NSA uses its own high-powered version of social-network analysis to search for possible new patterns and links to terrorism" [19]. The American Civil Liberties Union (ACLU) responded by accusing the NSA of reviving TIA to be an "Orwellian" domestic spying program [20].

Earlier in January 2008, Pulitzer Prize-winner Lawrence Wright wrote in *The New Yorker* an in-depth article about the U.S. intelligence community focusing on the Office of the Director of National Intelligence (ODNI) and the necessity for interagency communications—something that TIA was meant to facilitate. Wright observed, "The fantasy worlds that Disney creates have a surprising amount in common with the ideal universe envisaged by the intelligence community, in which environments are carefully controlled and people are closely observed, and no one seems to mind" [21].

While the Disney universe is confined to its theme parks and certain visiting hours, social networks such as Facebook, Google+, Twitter, and YouTube are reaching more than 955 million people worldwide 24/7 in their workplaces, schools, homes, and even on the go with their mobile devices. The social networks are leading the way towards Total Information Awareness.

Looking back to the 60's, DARPA initiated and funded the research and development of Advanced Research Projects Agency Network (ARPANET) that went online in 1969 [22]. The success of ARPANET gave rise to the global commercial Internet in the mid-1990s and the new generation of Fortune 500 companies today including Amazon.com, Google, eBay, and Yahoo!.

As if life comes full circle in the twenty first century, private businesses and the ubiquity of social networks such as Facebook, Google+, Twitter, and YouTube are creating the technologies and infrastructures necessary for the DARPA-proposed Total Information Awareness program. Facial recognition, location tracking, ambient social apps on GPS-enabled devices, Google Street View, digital footprints, and data mining are some key elements in information awareness. In fact, the homepage of DARPA conspicuously displays the icons of Facebook, Twitter, Google+, YouTube, et al. (See Fig. 1.2).

On March 29, 2012, the Obama administration announced more than $200 million in funding for "Big Data Research and Development Initiative" [23]. Information Innovation Office has replaced the Information Awareness Office [24]. The first wave of agency commitments includes National Science Foundation (NSF), National Institutes of Health (NIH), Department of Energy (DOE), U.S. Geological Survey, and Department of Defense (including DARPA) [25]. Not to imply that DARPA intends to resurrect the Total Information Awareness program, but the DARPA-proposed Anomaly Detection at Multiple Scales (ADAMS) program is one of several key technologies that are directly applicable to Total Information Awareness [26].

Fig. 1.2 Homepage of *DARPA* showing Facebook, Twitter, Google+, YouTube, et al

The U.S. government has also been learning from private businesses who often share customers' data to make a profit. Letitia Long, Director of the National Geospatial-Intelligence Agency (NGA) described the shift across the post-9/11 intelligence community as the transition from a "need-to-know" atmosphere to a "need-to-share and need-to-provide" culture [27].

WikiLeaks founder Julian Assange said in a May 2011 interview, "Facebook in particular is the most appalling spying machine that has ever been invented. Here we have the world's most comprehensive database about people, their relationships, their names, their addresses, their locations and their communications with each other, their relatives, all sitting within the United States, all accessible to US intelligence" [28].

Indeed, military and civilian technologies have interwoven into every fabric of our society, as Facebook co-founder and CEO Mark Zuckerberg said at the 2011 annual f8 conference, "We exist at the intersection of technology and social issues" [29].

President Barack Obama, in his 2011 State of the Union Address, called America "the nation of Edison and the Wright brothers" and "of Google and Facebook"[30]. This book offers discourse and practical advice on the privacy issue in the age of big data, the rise of Facebook nation, and Total Information Awareness.

References

1. United States White House Office. (April 26, 1984). National Security Decision Directive 138: Combating Terrorism. Homeland Security Digital Library. https://www.hsdl.org/?abstract&did=440725
2. Institute for Defense Analyses. (Retrieved January 1, 2002). IDA's History and Mission. https://www.ida.org/aboutus/historyandmission.php
3. Ada Joint Program Office. (1985). Military Standard Common APSE (Ada Programming Support Environment) Interface Set (CAIS). Defense Technical Information Center. http://books.google.com/books/about/Military_Standard_Common_APSE_Ada_Progra.html?id=EjEYOAAACAAJ
4. Carik, Kenneth. (1943) The Nature of Explanation. Cambridge University Press, UK. http://www.cambridge.org/us/knowledge/isbn/item1121731/?site_locale=en_US
5. Minsky, Marvin. (June 1974). A Framework for Representing Knowledge. MIT AI Laboratory Memo 306. http://web.media.mit.edu/~minsky/papers/Frames/frames.html
6. Lee, Newton S. (June 1988). DM2: an algorithm for diagnostic reasoning that combines analytical models and experiential knowledge. International Journal of Man-Machine Studies. Volume 28, Issue 6, pp. 643-670. http://www.sciencedirect.com/science/article/pii/S002073738880066X
7. Berwaner, Mary. (October 30, 1989). The Problem of Diagnostic Aiding. The Defense Technical Information Center. www.dtic.mil/cgi-bin/GetTRDoc?AD=ADA239200
8. Lee, Newton S. (November 1990). InfoStation: A multimedia access system for library automation. The Electronic Library. Volume 8, Issue 6, pp. 415–421.
9. Berners-Lee, Tim. (Retrieved January 1, 2012). The WorldWideWeb browser. World Wide Web Consortium (W3C). http://www.w3.org/People/Berners-Lee/WorldWideWeb.html
10. McCarthy, Shawn. (March 6, 1995). Next's OS finally is maturing. (NextStep Unix operating system). Government Computer News. p. 46.
11. Lee, Newton; Madej, Krystina. (May 2012). Disney Stories: Getting to Digital. Springer, New York.
12. Wilson, James M. V, MD. (October 4, 2007). Statement by James M. Wilson V, MD, Research Faculty at Georgetown University, before the Senate Homeland Security & the Federal Workforce, and the District of Columbia. The U.S. Senate. http://www.hsgac.senate.gov//imo/media/doc/WilsonTestimony.pdf
13. U.S. News & World Report. (November 3, 2006). Q&A: DNI Chief Scientist Eric Haseltine. U.S. News & World Report http://www.usnews.com/usnews/news/articles/061103/3qahaseltine_print.htm
14. Tether, Tony. (April 10, 2002). Statement by Dr. Tony Tether, Director of Defense Advanced Research Projects Agency, submitted to the United States Senate Armed Services Committee. The U.S. Senate. http://armed-services.senate.gov/statemnt/2002/April/Tether.pdf
15. Markoff, John. (November 9, 2002). THREATS AND RESPONSES: INTELLIGENCE; Pentagon Plans a Computer System That Would Peek at Personal Data of Americans. The New York Times. http://www.nytimes.com/2002/11/09/us/threats-responses-intelligence-pentagon-plans-computer-system-that-would-peek.html
16. Tether, Tony. (March 27, 2003). Statement by Dr. Tony Tether, Director of Defense Advanced Research Projects Agency, submitted to the U.S. House of Representatives. Defense Advanced Research Projects Agency. http://www.darpa.mil/WorkArea/DownloadAsset.aspx?id=1778
17. Defense Advanced Research Projects Agency. (May 20, 2003). Report to Congress regarding the Terrorism Information Awareness Program. http://epic.org/privacy/profiling/tia/may03_report.pdf
18. 108th Congress. (2003). House Report 108-283 - MAKING APPROPRIATIONS FOR THE DEPARTMENT OF DEFENSE FOR THE FISCAL YEAR ENDING SEPTEMBER 30, 2004, AND FOR OTHER PURPOSES. The Library of Congress. http://thomas.loc.gov/

cgi-bin/cpquery/?&sid=cp108alJsu&refer=&r_n=hr283.108&db_id=108&item=&&sid=cp
108alJsu&r_n=hr283.108&dbname=cp108&&sel=TOC_309917

19. Gorman, Siobhan. (March 10, 2008). NSA's Domestic Spying Grows As Agency Sweeps Up
Data: Terror Fight Blurs Line Over Domain; Tracking Email. The Wall Street Journal. http://
online.wsj.com/article/SB120511973377523845.html
20. American Civil Liberties Union. (March 12, 2008). Stunning New Report on Domestic NSA
Dragnet Spying Confirms ACLU Surveillance Warnings. ACLU http://www.aclu.org/
technology-and-liberty/stunning-new-report-domestic-nsa-dragnet-spying-confirms-aclu-
surveillance-wa
21. Wright, Lawrence. (January 21, 2008). The Spymaster. Can Mike McConnell fix America's
intelligence community? The New Yorker http://www.newyorker.com/reporting/2008/01/21/
080121fa_fact_wright?currentPage=all
22. Birth of the Internet. (Retrieved January 1, 2012). http://smithsonian.yahoo.com/internethistory.
html
23. Kalil, Tom. (March 29, 2012). Big Data is a Big Deal. The White House. http://
www.whitehouse.gov/blog/2012/03/29/big-data-big-deal
24. Information Innovation Office. (Retrieved April 3, 2012). DARPA. http://www.darpa.mil/
Our_Work/I2O/
25. Office of Science and Technology Policy. Executive Office of the President. (March 29,
2012). Obama Administration Unveils "Big Data" Initiative: Announces $200 Million In
New R&D Investments. The White House. http://www.whitehouse.gov/sites/default/files/
microsites/ostp/big_data_press_release.pdf
26. Executive Office of the President. (March 29, 2012). Big Data Across the Federal
Government. The White House. http://www.whitehouse.gov/sites/default/files/microsites/
ostp/big_data_fact_sheet_final_1.pdf
27. Young, Denise. (Spring 2012). Letitia Long: A Global Vision. Alumna leads intelligence
agency in new era of collaboration. Virginia Tech Magazine. http://www.vtmag.vt.edu/
spring12/letitia-long.html
28. RT. (May 2, 2011). WikiLeaks revelations only tip of iceberg – Assange. RT News. http://
www.rt.com/news/wikileaks-revelations-assange-interview/
29. Bosker, Bianca. (September 22, 2011). Facebook's f8 Conference (LIVE BLOG): Get The
Latest Facebook News. The Huffington Post. http://www.huffingtonpost.com/2011/09/22/
facebook-f8-conference-live-blog-latest-news_n_975704.html
30. Obama, Barack. (January 25, 2011). State of the Union 2011: President Obama's Full Speech.
ABC News. http://abcnews.go.com/Politics/State_of_the_Union/state-of-the-union-2011-
full-transcript/story?id=12759395&page=3

Part II
Privacy in the Age of Big Data

Chapter 2
Social Networks and Privacy

"You have zero privacy anyway. Get over it".
—Sun Microsystems' Scott NcNealy (January 1999)

"If you have something that you don't want anyone to know, maybe you shouldn't be doing it in the first place".
—Google's Eric Schmidt (December 2009)

2.1 Zero Privacy

Scott McNealy, co-founder and CEO of Sun Microsystems for 22 years, told a group of reporters and analysts in January 1999: "You have zero privacy anyway. Get over it" [1]. In December 2009, Google's then-CEO Eric Schmidt said, "If you have something that you don't want anyone to know, maybe you shouldn't be doing it in the first place" [2].

A friend of my wife, in his early 20s, graduated in 2008 from a well-known university with a Master's degree in computer science. Instead of looking for a well-paying job, he prefers to spend most of his time living in a remote countryside without a cell phone and Internet connection. He is a skilled archer who hunts for food in the forest. He is also a self-proclaimed magician (think Tim Kring's *Heroes*, not David Copperfield). He enjoys a life of solitude and privacy. Nevertheless, even an eccentric person like him cannot completely escape the temptation of social networks. He has a Facebook profile with a handful of photos of himself and his handmade enchanted objects. He updates his Facebook page very rarely, but when he does, his small circle of college friends would be glued to the computer screen to find out what he is up to. He has limited social interaction by offering limited glimpse into his life to a limited number of friends. As a result, he enjoys reasonably good privacy.

In the year 2012 when more than two billion people are connected online [3], an Arizona man in Phoenix distrusts technology so much that he refuses to use a phone or computer altogether. In order to communicate with his business partner who lives across town in Phoenix, the Arizona man sends his messages via carrier pigeons [4]. We can call it old fashion or paranoia. The fact is that very few people today are determined to safeguard their own privacy with strong convictions, while the overwhelming majority of people are willing to give up some part of their privacy in exchange for being connected. An old English proverb says, "If you can't beat them, join them."

N. Lee, *Facebook Nation*, DOI: 10.1007/978-1-4614-5308-6_2,
© Springer Science+Business Media New York 2013

Most people have families, friends, and business acquaintances to keep in constant contact through in-person meetings, emails, phone calls, and online social networking services such as Facebook, Google+, and Twitter. Most people enjoy making new friends. However, social interaction inevitably raises the privacy issue. Online social networks only exacerbate privacy concerns. The risk is often outweighed by the consumer's need to communicate, as Facebook CEO and co-founder Mark Zuckerberg said about the new Facebook Timeline feature: "it's an important next step to help you tell the story of your life" [5].

Zuckerberg's message resonated with Robert Scoble, a former technology evangelist at Microsoft best known for his blog Scobleizer. "I make everything public on my Facebook account, and I'm not worried about privacy because the more I share about who I am and what interests me, the more Facebook can bring me content that I care about," said Scoble, "Yes, people have lost jobs because of things they have posted on Facebook, but you can also end up getting jobs and making all kinds of great connections because you've posted about your passions" [6].

2.2 The Pervasiveness of Facebook

Facebook's mission is "to give people the power to share and make the world more open and connected" [7]. Launched in February 2004 by Mark Zuckerberg, Facebook has quickly become one of the most pervasive interpersonal communication tools. One month after its official launch, Facebook expanded from Harvard to Stanford, Columbia, and Yale University. Within one year, in December 2004, Facebook reached nearly 1 million active users [8].

In September 2011, Facebook's chief technology officer Bret Taylor confirmed that Facebook has more than 800 million active users, 350 million of whom use Facebook on mobile devices each month [9]. In February 2012, the Facebook IPO filing revealed that the company has reached 845 million users, 483 million of them use the site every day [10] and 425 million of them access Facebook on mobile devices [11]. In July 2012, Facebook revised the total number of monthly active users to 955 million [12]. Practically one out of every two Americans has a Facebook account. In August 2012, Facebook has approximately 160 million active users in the United States [13].

In May 2011, Americans spent a total of 53.5 billion minutes a month on Facebook, more than Yahoo! (17.2 billion minutes), Google (12.5 billion), AOL (11.4 billion), MSN (9.5 billion), YouTube (9.1 billion), EBay (4.5 billion), Blogger (724 million), Tumblr (624 million), and Twitter (565 million) [14].

A 2011 research from NM Incite, a Nielsen McKinsey company, reveals no surprise that knowing someone in real life is the top reason (82 %) cited for friend-ing someone on Facebook [15]. The second main reason (60 %) is to add friends of their mutual friends online. Other reasons include business networking (11 %), physical attractiveness (8 %), increasing friend count (7 %), and friend everyone (7 %). The so-called "friend collectors" send requests out of curiosity and nosiness, as many Facebook users are afflicted with the oh-so itch-able question, "I wonder what so-and-so is doing now" [16]. Omar. Gallaga, reporter for the *Austin American-Statesman,* admitted his Facebook addiction on *CNN,* "More than just a daily habit, Facebook has become the place where I get important, often surprising glimpses into the lives of the 1,365 people with whom I've chosen to connect. (That's not counting friends-of-friends, for Facebook's tentacles are ever-extended)" [17].

Most people have the unquenchable needs to communicate and share information. As Mark Zuckerberg wrote in his letter for the Facebook IPO filing on February 1, 2012, "We live at a moment when the majority of people in the world have access to the internet or mobile phones—the raw tools necessary to start sharing what they're thinking, feeling and doing with whomever they want" [18].

"People don't want to be talked to, they want to be talked with," said Roy Sekoff, founding editor of *The Huffington Post* [19]. However, the busy lifestyle and fast-paced society have deprived people of the face-to-face quality time among friends, families, and acquaintances. CNN producer Kiran Khalid, a self-admitted social-media addict, tried to disconnect from all electronic communications for five days in December 2011. Her conclusion was that severing her dependency on social networks removed an obstacle to real conversations [20].

Paul Miller, a senior editor for *The Verge,* decided to leave the Internet for a year beginning on May 1, 2012 [21]. "I think there are two kinds of people who live with technology constantly in their face: people who freak out when they're forcefully separated from their devices or connectivity, as if their arm has been cut off, and people who feel really chill when they're forcefully separated from their devices or connectivity, as if they've been let out of prison. I've spoken to many of both kinds as I've prepared for leaving the internet, and thankfully I fall in the latter camp" [22]. Most people, however, cannot survive without their digital fixations.

Facebook is the prolific communication tool that fills the void created by the lack of real face-to-face conversations. As far back as September 2005, *Tech-Crunch* reported that 85 % of college students use Facebook to communicate with friends, both on campus and from their former high schools [23]. Today, it is almost inconceivable for a university student not to have a Facebook page.

Facebook is more convenient than emails and less intrusive than phone calls. Someone may wake up at 3 in the morning, post a new photo and write some comments on Facebook. The information goes out to all their online friends. However, there is no distinction between best friends who can keep a secret, casual friends who may laugh at it, and strangers who either do not care about it or use the information for malicious purposes. "We are close, in a sense, to people who don't necessarily like us, sympathize with us or have anything in common with us," Prof. Jon Kleinberg of Cornell University told *The New York Times.* "It's the weak ties that make the world small" [24].

By satisfying the insatiable desire for communication with others who seem to be willing to listen, people have voluntarily sacrificed some degrees of personal privacy. "Have one's cake and eat it too" does not apply to personal privacy in the world of ubiquitous social networks.

2.3 Facebook and Personal Privacy

"Hacking is core to how we build at Facebook," the company said in a blog post announcing Facebook's 2012 Hacker Cup competition [25]. "Whether we're building a prototype for a major product like Timeline at a Hackathon, creating a smarter search algorithm, or tearing down walls at our new headquarters, we're always hacking to find better ways to solve problems" [26].

In 2003, Mark Zuckerberg hacked into the Harvard computer network and stole private dormitory student ID photos in order to create Facemash, the predecessor to Facebook. Similar to the Hot or Not website founded in 2000 by James Hong and Jim Young, Facemash placed two photos next to each other at a time and asked users to choose the hotter person. Facemash attracted 450 visitors and more than 22,000 photo views in its first day of launch before the website was forced to shut down. Zuckerberg was charged by the Harvard administration with breach of security, violating copyrights and individual privacy [27]. Zuckerberg wrote in an email to *The Harvard Crimson* in November 2003, "Issues about violating people's privacy don't seem to be surmountable. I'm not willing to risk insulting anyone".

Zuckerberg, an ingenious hacker, has been known for meeting with prospective investors wearing pajamas. He remains true to himself and does not answer to anybody. "Mark and his signature hoodie: He's actually showing investors he doesn't care that much; he's going to be him," said Michael Pachter, an analyst for Wedbush Securities. "I think that's a mark of immaturity. I think that he has to realize he's bringing investors in as a new constituency right now, and I think he's got to show them the respect that they deserve because he's asking them for their money" [28].

Although Facebook became a publicly traded company in May 2012, Zuckerberg continues to hold majority control over the company. Firstly, his 23 % shares of Facebook stock carry outsized voting rights that give him 31 % voting power. Secondly, he has "irrevocable proxy" over the voting power of almost 56 % of Facebook's shares held by other stakeholders. The U.S. Securities and Exchange Commission (SEC) asked Facebook in February 2012 to "more fully explain how the risk of Mr. Zuckerberg's control affects … the Class A common stockholders on a short-term and long-term basis" [29].

Based on Zuckerberg's history and his personal attitude towards people's privacy, it came as no surprise that Facebook was charged by the U.S. Federal Trade Commission (FTC) for failing to keep privacy promises and violating federal law—the Federal Trade Commission Act [30]. The FTC eight-count complaint lists a number of instances in which Facebook allegedly made promises that it did not keep [31]. The charges include the following:

1. In December 2009, Facebook changed its website so certain information that users may have designated as private—such as their Friends List—was made public. They didn't warn users that this change was coming, or get their approval in advance.

2. Facebook represented that third-party apps installed by the users would have access only to user information that they needed to operate. In fact, the apps could access nearly all of users' personal data—data the apps didn't need.
3. Facebook told users they could restrict sharing of data to limited audiences—for example with "Friends Only". In fact, selecting "Friends Only" did not prevent their information from being shared with third-party applications their friends used.
4. Facebook had a "Verified Apps" program and claimed it certified the security of participating apps. It didn't.
5. Facebook promised users that it would not share their personal information with advertisers. It did.
6. Facebook claimed that when users deactivated or deleted their accounts, their photos and videos would be inaccessible. But Facebook allowed access to the content, even after users had deactivated or deleted their accounts.
7. Facebook claimed that it complied with the U.S.-EU Safe Harbor Framework that governs data transfer between the U.S. and the European Union. It didn't.

Without putting up a legal fight, Facebook in November 2011 agreed to the proposed settlement [32] that the company is: [33].

- barred from making misrepresentations about the privacy or security of consumers' personal information;
- required to obtain consumers' affirmative express consent before enacting changes that override their privacy preferences;
- required to prevent anyone from accessing a user's material more than 30 days after the user has deleted his or her account;
- required to establish and maintain a comprehensive privacy program designed to address privacy risks associated with the development and management of new and existing products and services, and to protect the privacy and confidentiality of consumers' information; and
- required, within 180 days, and every two years after that for the next 20 years, to obtain independent, third-party audits certifying that it has a privacy program in place that meets or exceeds the requirements of the FTC order, and to ensure that the privacy of consumers' information is protected.

Apart from the accusations from the U.S. government, five Facebook members in California sued Facebook for publicizing their "likes" of certain advertisers on the "sponsored stories" feature without paying them or giving them a way to opt out. In May 2012, Facebook agreed to pay $10 million to charity in settling the would-be class-action lawsuit for violating users' rights to control the use of their own names, photographs, and likenesses [34].

Although Facebook was found liable for many of the online privacy issues, many Facebook users have not been vigilant in safeguarding their own privacy. A May 2010 report by Pew Internet indicated that only two-thirds of Facebook users said they had ever changed the privacy settings to limit what they share with others online [35]. A January 2012 study by *Consumer Reports Magazine* revealed, "Almost 13 million users said they had never set, or didn't know about, Facebook's privacy tools. And 28 % shared all, or almost all, of their wall posts with an audience wider than just their friends" [36].

The official Facebook statistics reports that an average user has 130 online friends [37]. A Georgetown University study shows a much higher number among college students—young adults reported an average of 358 Facebook friends, with young women reporting 401 friends and young men reporting 269 friends [38]. However, according to the GoodMobilePhones survey in January 2011, the average Facebook user does not know one fifth of the people listed as friends on the site [39].

To prove the point, a group of students at Millburn High School in New Jersey created a Facebook account in 2009 for a fictional new student in their school [40]. They named her "Lauren" and gave her a fake profile including a picture of a random high school girl downloaded from the Internet. This "Lauren" requested to be Facebook friends with 200 of her classmates. Only two students messaged "Lauren" to question who she was. Nearly 60 % of the 200 students accepted her friendship, and an additional 55 Facebook users requested "Lauren" to be their friends, even though they obviously did not know her.

In fact, of all the reasons why a Facebook user removes a friend online, 41 % of the answers is: "Don't know him/her well" [41]. Those unknown friends, or rather strangers—a more accurate description, have access to photos and information that are meant for only the intended audiences or trusted friends and families. A February 2012 report from Pew Internet and American Life Project indicates that less than 5 % of users hide content from another user on their Facebook feed [42]. Even if a Facebook user decides to delete uploaded photos for whatever reasons, the "deleted" Facebook photos may still be online indefinitely and are accessible via direct links (URLs) [43].

Indeed, everything posted on the Internet is public. Things that had been taken down from a website may live on forever in *The Internet Archive* that offers permanent storage and free access to over 150 billion archived web pages including texts, images, movies, and documents [44]. Synonymous with the term "Wayback Machine," *The Internet Archive* allows us to see what previous versions of websites used to look like and to visit old websites that no longer exist.

2.4 Facebook, Children, and COPPA

To make matter worse, more than 55 % of parents help their underage children to lie to get on Facebook, violating the site's terms of service that prohibit kids under 13 from joining. A 2011 survey conducted by Harris Interactive shows that one in five parents acknowledged having a 10-year-old on Facebook, 32 % of parents allowing their 11-year-olds and 55 % of parents allowing their 12-year-olds to use Facebook [45]. According to *Consumers Reports* in May 2011, there are at least 7.5 million children under 13 and 5 million children ages 10 and under who are actively using Facebook [46].

Perhaps parents are not the only ones to blame, because children of all ages are facing increasing peer pressure from their friends and schoolmates. "I need your advice," a mother posed a question to Danah Boyd, coauthor of *Why parents help their children lie to Facebook about age: Unintended consequences of the Children's Online Privacy Protection Act*, "My 11-year-old daughter wants to join Facebook. She says that all of her friends are on Facebook. At what age do you think I should allow her to join Facebook?" [47].

Children are also most vulnerable to advertisements. In September 2010, *The Wall Street Journal* investigated 50 popular websites aimed at teens and children and 50 most popular U.S. sites overall [48]. The investigators found that popular children's websites install 30 % more tracking technologies (e.g. cookies and beacons) than do the top U.S. websites [49]. Although the tracking data does not include the children's names, it can include their ages, races, hobbies, online habits, posted comments, likes and dislikes, as well as their general locations such as the cities of residence.

In 1998, the U.S. Congress enacted the Children's Online Privacy Protection Act (COPPA), requiring the Federal Trade Commission (FTC) to regulate commercial websites targeted at children and web operators who have actual knowledge of a child's participation [50]. COPPA requires web site owners to notify parents and obtain their consent before collecting, using, or disclosing children's personal information.

I was a senior staff engineer at Disney Online since 1996. Being a family-oriented company, Disney took COPPA and children's online safety very seriously. We made sure that the Disney websites were COPPA-compliant and addressed COPPA-related issues at the weekly senior staff meetings.

The first-ever Disney MMORPG game *ToonTown Online* debuted in 2003 allows players, most of whom are children, to communicate with other players in *ToonTown* via a free-form chat if and only if the players know each other outside the game world [51]. A "True Friends" verification involving a six-digit secret code is required to gain access to free-form chat.

Online safety for kids is number one in the website design and business decisions at Disney Online. Moreover, Disney is highly selective in accepting advertisements to display on its websites targeted for families and children. When I was a senior producer at Disney Online, I worked closely with strategic partners Google, Yahoo!, and WebSideStory. I had to write special software code to filter out the inappropriate ads before any sponsored ads are displayed among the search results on the Disney websites such as Disney.com and FamilyFun.com.

I left Disney after 10 years in 2006. Disney Online acquired Club Penguin with 700,000 paid users in 2007 [52]. By mid-2011, Club Penguin has 12 million members, essentially becoming the world's largest social network for kids [53]. A combination of games, educational resources, and social networking, Club Penguin presents a fictional world made up of user-created penguins that act as avatars for the millions of kids aged 8–11 in more than 190 countries around the world [54].

After Club Penguin, Disney Online acquired social-gaming company Playdom with 42 million players in 2010 [55]. In May 2011, the Federal Trade Commission charged that Disney's Playdom violated COPPA between 2006 and 2010 when children under the age of 13 were able to register for the site, share their ages and email addresses, all without parental consent. Playdom continued to violate COPPA after the merger with Disney in August 2010. It results in a tarnished reputation and a $3 million fine [56].

"Let's be clear: Whether you are a virtual world, a social network, or any other interactive site that appeals to kids, you owe it to parents and their children to provide proper notice and get proper consent," said Jon Leibowitz, Chairman of the Federal Trade Commission. "It's the law, it's the right thing to do, and, as today's settlement [with Disney's Playdom] demonstrates, violating COPPA will not come cheap" [57].

COPPA, however, does not address the issue that addiction to social networks at an early age can be detrimental to normal child development. A 2012 Stanford University study examined the children behaviors from a sample of nearly 3,500 girls aged 8–12. The researchers concluded that tween girls who spend much of their waking hours switching frantically between YouTube, Facebook, television, and text messaging are more likely to develop social problems [58]. Spending too many hours online takes away the time for face-to-face personal interactions that are essential for normal mental development.

At the 119th Annual Convention of the American Psychological Association held in August 2011, Professor Larry. Rosen at California State University, Dominguez Hills, gave a plenary talk entitled, "Poke Me: How Social Networks Can Both Help and Harm Our Kids." Rosen discussed the disturbing findings that "teens who use Facebook more often show more narcissistic tendencies while young adults who have a strong Facebook presence show more signs of other psychological disorders, including antisocial behaviors, mania and aggressive tendencies" [59].

2.5 Facebook and Peer Pressure

Facebook extends peer pressure from the physical world to the larger online world. Marlon Mundt from University of Wisconsin, Madison, studied the influence of peer social networks on adolescents. The findings suggest that adolescents are more likely to start drinking alcoholic beverages when they have large social networks of friends [60]. Soraya Mehdizadeh from York University, Toronto, published revealing research results that "individuals higher in narcissism and lower in self-esteem were related to greater online activity" and that women in particular used pictures that "include revealing, flashy and adorned photos of their physical appearance" [61].

In March 2012, CNN columnist Amanda Enayati reported on a story of a college student named Amanda Coleman who decided to quit Facebook. Being the president of her sorority, Coleman has counseled many young girls at her university. "They would call or come into see me for advice, crying that they were stressed out," Coleman said. "At some point I began noticing that Facebook was being mentioned in some way in just about every conversation. ... It's as if somewhere along the line, Facebook became the encyclopedia of beauty and status and comparisons. ... [The young girls, many of them college freshmen] were walking around saying, 'I'm not good enough. I'm not enough this or that" [62].

The story reminds us of Facemash, the predecessor to Facebook, which placed two photos next to each other at a time and asked users to choose the hotter person. In spite of Facebook's sophistication over Facemash, users can still compare themselves to their friends and their friends' friends in terms of looks, fashion, popularity, and so forth.

Children and young teens are particularly susceptible to messages and images coming from their friends on Facebook. How are they going to react to their "enemies" on Facebook? A new Facebook app "EnemyGraph," launched in March 2012, could exacerbate peer pressure by bonding like-minded haters online. EnemyGraph is "a Facebook application that allows you to list your enemies. Most social networks attempt to connect people based on affinities, but people are also connected and motivated by things they dislike, which joins them in ways not usually supported by social media platforms" [63]. So far the top trending enemies are teen pop Justin Bieber, GOP presidential hopeful Rick Santorum, and inter-estingly the Internet Explorer (IE) [64].

In his 2009 book *The Dumbest Generation: How the Digital Age Stupefies Young Americans and Jeopardizes Our Future,* Professor Mark Bauerlein at Emory University argues that the younger generation today is less informed, less literate, and more self-absorbed because the immediacy and intimacy of social-networking sites have focused young people's Internet use on themselves and their friends instead of on learning new knowledge and useful skills. He observed that the language of Internet communication, with its peculiar spelling, grammar, and punctuation, actually encourages illiteracy by making it socially acceptable [65].

In 2012, former U.S. Secretary of State Condoleezza Rice issued an alarming report in which she warned that "although the United States invests more in education than almost any other developed nation, its students rank in the middle of the pack in reading and toward the bottom in math and science. On average, U.S. students have fallen behind peers in Korea and China, Poland and Canada and New Zealand. This puts us on a trajectory toward massive failure" [66].

It is high time for a major overhaul of the U.S. educational system. Peter Thiel, co-founder of PayPal, argues that colleges and universities do a poor job pro-moting innovation. He predicts that higher education is the next bubble waiting to burst [67]. In a provocative move, Thiel awarded each of the 24 winners of the 2011 Thiel Fellowship $100,000 not to attend college for two years but to develop business ideas instead [68].

2.6 Reality TV and Social Media

Beginning in the year 2000, we have witnessed the exploding popularity of reality television shows such as *Big Brother, Survivor, American Idol, America's Next Top Model, Dancing With the Stars, The Apprentice*, and *Fear Factor*. A 2010 study showed that 15 of the top 20 highest-rated television programs among young adults 18–49 were reality shows [69].

Following the footsteps of Donald Trump's *The Apprentice*, other businesses are also taking a page from reality TV shows to discover new stars. The world's largest retailer Walmart launched its "Get on the Shelf" program on the same day *American Idol* began its eleventh season on January 18, 2012 [70]. The "Get on the Shelf" contest allows anyone in the U.S. to submit a video online pitching his or her invention. The public will vote on the products and three winners will have their products sold on Walmart.com, with the grand prizewinner also getting shelf space in select stores. Unlike *The Apprentice*, Walmart chose the Internet, instead of television, as the reality show medium.

While some reality shows have a certain amount of entertaining and educational values, others have little to no redeeming quality at all. *The Real Housewives of Beverly Hills*, for instance, is a prime example of legalized voyeurism and exhibitionism where the television viewers are the voyeurs and the participants in the reality show are the exhibitionists. Millions of people seem to enjoy access to private information that are really none of their business; and quite a large number of people want to expose their private lives to strangers in spite of potentially dangerous consequences including suicide [71] and murder [72]. In fact, a Brigham Young University study in 2010 reported that a reality show on average contains 52 acts of verbal, relational, or physical aggression per hour [73].

In addition to reality TV, popular television programs also have shown to increase online social activities on Twitter, Facebook, and other social networks [74]. Super Bowl XLVI on February 5, 2012 created an all-time record high of 17.46 million tweets, public Facebook posts, GetGlue check-ins, and Miso check-ins [75].

Analyst Nick Thomas at Informa wrote in a recent report on the future of TV worldwide, "Many [are] already using Facebook and Twitter and other tools to communicate via the handheld devices about the content they are simultaneously viewing on the TV" [76].

2.7 YouTube and Facebook Videos

While reality television may be losing steam [77] and the percentage of U.S. homes with a television set is declining [78], the Internet is flourishing with reality content and attentive audience. Mahir Çağrı, for instance, became an Internet celebrity in 1999 for his infamous homepage [79] and arguably was the main inspiration for British comedian Sacha Baron Cohen as the fictional Kazakhstan reporter "Borat" [80].

With the launch of the video-sharing website YouTube in February 2005, the Internet is becoming the new reality TV. Touted as "The Beast With A Billion Eyes" by the *Time Magazine* [81], YouTube reports in January 2012 that 4 billion online videos are viewed every day [82]. More than tripling the prime-time audiences of all three major U.S. broadcast networks combined, over 800 million unique users visit YouTube each month, and 30 % of whom are from the U.S. Users upload the equivalent of 240,000 full-length films every week. In fact, more video is uploaded to YouTube in one month than the 3 major U.S. networks created in 60 years [83].

In December 2011, more than 100 million Americans watch online video on an average day, representing a 43 % increase a year ago [84]. The numbers continue to skyrocket. In January 2012, some 181 million U.S. Internet users watched about 40 billion online videos [85]. Internet marketing research firm comScore's Video Metrix shows that YouTube has over 50 % share of content videos viewed, followed by the distant second Vevo, Hulu, Yahoo!, Microsoft, Viacom, AOL, Netflix, ESPN, Mevio, and others [86]. Thanks to Netflix, Amazon Prime, and Hulu, Americans watch more online movies than DVDs in 2012 [87].

Facebook took fifth place in the U.S. online video rankings in December 2011, with 238 million videos viewed in a month [88]. Together with Facebook, YouTube has ushered in the new era of exhibitionism and voyeurism. Not everyone can be on TV, but everyone can be on YouTube. The HTML title of youtube.com is "YouTube —Broadcast Yourself" and the description meta tag reads "Share your videos with friends, family, and the world".

Google video head Salar Kamangar said at News Corp.'s D: Dive Into Media 2012 conference, "We want YouTube to be the platform of these next generation of channels," [89] referring to bringing its audiences more high-quality content in partnership with Disney and other media companies in 2012 [90].

Nevertheless, the lion share of the YouTube videos have been and will continue to be created by amateurs [91]. Anyone can literally create a 15 min of fame on YouTube. Aspiring young singers hope to become the next pop star Justin Bieber who was discovered via his homemade YouTube videos [92]. Kate Upton's YouTube video of herself at a Los Angeles Clippers game "doing the Dougie" helped catapult her onto the cover of *Swimsuit Illustrated* [93].

In addition to individuals showcasing their talents, YouTube has also become an outlet for many teenagers seeking approval. Videos asking "Am I pretty or ugly" have popped up all over YouTube, some of them has accrued millions of views, rivaling blockbuster movie trailers and hit music videos. In the opening of one "Am I pretty or ugly" video, the YouTuber says: "Hey guys, this is my first video … but before I post any more videos making a fool of myself, and I know there's hundreds of videos like this. … I just wanna know, am I pretty or ugly? Cuz at school I get called ugly all the time" [94].

Indeed, many of those YouTubers are victims of bullying. Naomi Gibson's 13-year-old daughter Faye is constantly bullied by schoolmates who call her ugly. Faye went to YouTube to get a second opinion from strangers and received mixed reactions with nearly 3,000 comments [95]. Her mother appealed to YouTube to try to take down all those "Am I pretty or ugly" videos, but to no avail. Gibson told *ABC Good Morning America*, "I took away her Facebook and Twitter account because of bullying. She needs to stop putting herself out there. Now people are walking around asking her if she's pretty to her face. It's hurting her more in the long run, I think" [96].

Bullying victims are not limited to a young age group. On June 21, 2012, a 10 min YouTube video showed a 68-year-old bus monitor named Karen Klein being verbally bullied by a group of middle schoolers, on their way home from the Athena Middle School in Greece, New York [97]. The video was viewed one million times within a week. Klein received widespread support from sympathizers and nearly $650,000 in donations [98].

Another high-profile case is a graphic video uploaded to YouTube in October 2011 by 23-year-old Hillary Adams, showing Aransas County Court Judge William Adams viciously whipping her with a strap seven years earlier when she was 16 [99]. The video has been viewed almost seven million times as of January 2012 [100]. It is debatable whether the victim wanted to raise public awareness of child abuse or to retaliate against her father for withdrawing his financial support seven years after the incident [101].

YouTube has become the reality TV broadcast medium for the masses, and Facebook is the effective tool to disseminate the YouTube videos. Christopher Carpenter from Western Illinois University conducted research on the link between Facebook and narcissism. He concluded, "Facebook gives those with narcissistic tendencies the opportunity to exploit the site to get the feedback they need and become the center of attention" [102]. Self-promoters show signs of two narcissistic behaviors: grandiose exhibition (GE) and entitlement/exploitativeness (EE). GE refers to people who love to be the center of attention. EE indicates how far people will go to get the respect and attention that they think they deserve.

Although the GE and EE readings may be off the scale on many Facebook users and YouTubers, the situation is not necessarily as nefarious as some media have portrayed. Carol Hartsell, comedy editor of *The Huffington Post,* commented at the 2012 South by Southwest Interactive festival that social media has democratized comedy by giving everyone a platform to be funny. "People just naturally want to make other people laugh," said Hartsell. "It's hard to find an audience when you want to be funny. When you're a kid, it's your family. But when you're an adult, the Internet gives you a constant audience. It may just be 20 friends on Facebook, but it's an audience" [103].

A September 2010 survey by the Interactive Advertising Bureau (IAB) shows that one-third of the online population is on both YouTube and Facebook [104]. With over 955 million users on both social networks, the seamless integration of Facebook and YouTube videos offers a powerful communication tool for 100 of millions of people to disseminate and consume information, both private and public [105].

In February 2012, Apple is reportedly going to follow the footstep of YouTube in promoting its new iTV television product [106]. In addition to streaming content from iTunes, Apple's iTV may broadcast user-generated videos taken on iPads and iPhones. Without the need of a computer, mobile devices greatly simplify video taking, uploading, and sharing. In fact, an increasing number of users are accessing Facebook through mobile devices [107]. According to a December 2011 comScore report, 234 million Americans age 13 and older use mobile devices. 35.3 % of mobile subscribers access social networking sites or blogs [108].

2.8 Netflix and Social Apps on Facebook

In September 2011, Facebook began rolling out new "Read. Watch. Listen. Want." features that let "social apps" broadcast every interaction users have with them [109]. The apps are opt-in, but few users read the fine print or adjust the default settings [110]. Some users might be surprised to find applications like Spotify, Kobo eBooks, Hulu, Yahoo! News, and Nike + GPS broadcasting every song they stream, book they read, video they watch, news story they glance over, or place they visit [111].

Back in December 2007, Facebook launched Beacon, resulting in a class-action lawsuit against Facebook, Fandango, Blockbuster, Overstock, and Gamefly for violating the 1988 Video Privacy Protection Act (VPPA) that aims at preserving the confidentiality of people's movie-watching records. Facebook shut down Beacon in 2009 and agreed to pay $9.5 million to create a new foundation for promoting privacy and security [112].

Notwithstanding the fiasco of the defunct Facebook Beacon program, Netflix, with 26 million subscribers [113] and 1 billion hours of video views in June 2012 [114], allows Facebook users see what films or television content friends are watching and will let users watch as well via Facebook [115]. To clear the hurdle of the Video Privacy Protection Act (VPPA), Netflix has successfully lobbied the U.S. House of Representatives in passing a measure in December 2011 to amend the VPPA, allowing Netflix to integrate with Facebook more easily [116].

Earlier in 2011, Netflix was accused of violating VPPA that requires video rental services to destroy users' personal information "as soon as practicable, but no later than one year from the date the information is no longer necessary for the purpose for which it was collected." In February 2012, Netflix settled a class-action privacy lawsuit for $9 million; [117] and in May, Netflix announced that it would "decouple" former customers' movie rental history from their personal information within one year after they cancel their accounts [118].

With Netflix and social apps' integration with Facebook, we no longer need to call up our friends to ask what they were doing last weekend or what they are doing at the moment. Everything is on Facebook in real time. The "all-knowing" persuasive social network has diminished the necessity for real-life personal conversations. Other flourishing social apps such as the microblogging Twitter and the virtual pinboard Pinterest reinforce the popular trend of public sharing of information on the Internet [119].

2.9 Facebook Timeline

Not only does Facebook enable users to share current activities with one another, the social network has introduced the new Timeline feature in September 2011 for users to tell their life stories, share and highlight their most memorable posts, photos, and life events on their timelines [120]. "No activity is too big or too small to share," said Mark Zuckerberg. "You don't have to 'Like' a movie. You just watch a movie. … We think it's an important next step to help you tell the story of your life" [121].

Indeed, "to tell the story of your life" resonates with millions of Facebook addicts. But some critics have cautioned that Facebook may be invading too much into one's personal life, as the user will be asked to add date of birth, key events, memories, personal events and feelings that happen outside of the social network [122].

To help users tell the story of their life with minimal efforts, Facebook is launching more "frictionless sharing" features to allow users automatically publish information from other websites and apps to their Timeline profiles. By January 2012, 60 apps have launched with Facebook's auto-share; they include Hulu, Yahoo! News, *Wall Street Journal*, *USA Today*, *Washington Post*, Digg, Soundcloud, Turntable.fm, Rhapsody, and Spotify [123]. Apple's iTunes and Pandora, however, do not plan to participate in the Facebook Music auto-publish feature [124].

In March 2012, Facebook announced that nearly 3,000 Timeline apps have launched in the past two months [125]. The apps makers include foursquare, Nike, *The Onion*, Vevo, Fandango, Viddy, Endomondo, RootMusic, Foodspotting, Pose, and Votizen. Fandango, for instance, claims to have tens of millions online visitors and 1.4 million Facebook fans [126]. Launched on March 13, 2012, the Fandango Timeline app "Movies with Friends" allows Facebook fans to share:

- Movies they've rated and reviewed on Fandango, from "Must Go" to "Oh No!"
- Movies they want to see, indicated by the "I'm In!" button
- Movie trailers, clips and celebrity interviews they have just watched
- Articles they've read on Fandango's "Freshly Popped" blog

By using Facebook's Timeline and social apps, an average user is knowingly communicating with an average of 130 online friends. Unknowingly, however, many of the popular apps on Facebook have been transmitting user information such as names and their friends' names to dozens of advertising and Internet tracking companies. *The Wall Street Journal's* investigation in October 2010 uncovered that Rapleaf, a database marketing company in San Francisco, complied and sold profiles of Facebook users based in part on their online activities [127]. Facebook has since cracked down on apps that sold user data and banned Rapleaf from data scraping on Facebook [128].

2.10 Ambient Social Apps

Ambient social apps are the new generation of mobile apps that automatically share information about the user's whereabouts with nearby people in their social networks by broadcasting their locations at all times to friends.

Launched in March 2009, foursquare is a location-based social networking website and mobile app that allows users to check in at a venue, thereby posting their location based on the GPS hardware in the mobile device. As of June 2011, foursquare has 10 million users [129]. Within six month, by January 2012, it has grown to 15 million people worldwide with 1.5 billion check-ins [130]. President Barack Obama is one of its high-profile users. "The White House is now on foursquare, which is the latest way for you to engage with the administration," Kori Schulman, Deputy Director of Outreach for the Office of Digital Strategy, wrote in *The White House Blog,* "Now you'll be able to discover tips from the White House featuring the places President Obama has visited, what he did there, plus historical information and more" [131].

The growing popularity of foursquare has ignited a slew of new ambient social apps. Sonar, for instance, is a mobile app that analyzes Facebook, Twitter, and LinkedIn networks to see if any online friends are nearby physically. According to the Sonar website, they "bottle the 1000s of connections that you miss every day—friends, friends of friends, fellow alumni, likeminded strangers—and put them in the palm of your hand. Sonar helps you use the information you share about yourself online to connect with the person sitting next to you" [132]. A screenshot displayed on the Sonar homepage shows who, among friends and friends of friends, are currently in the Museum of Modern Art and how long they have been there.

Glancee is both a Facebook app and an iPhone/Android app that explores the Facebook profiles of people nearby and notify the user when someone nearby has common friends or mutual interests [133]. The Radar function on Glancee displays how close the friends are in the proximity, from steps away to hundreds of yards apart.

Banjo is another ambient social app that alerts its user about friends who are nearby and pinpoints their locations on a street map. Nine months after its launch, Banjo has registered 1 million users in April 2012 [134]. The Banjo website posted a story that inspired the creation of the app: "Banjo founder Damien Patton was in the Boston airport waiting for a flight to Vegas. A buddy he hadn't seen in years was waiting for a different flight just one gate over. Damien tweeted. His friend checked in. Both posted about their locations, yet they missed connecting simply because they were using different social networks" [135].

Highlight is a free iPhone app that enables its users to learn about each other when they are close by. Using Facebook's data, the users can see each other's names, photos, mutual friends, hobbies, interests, and anything they have chosen to share. Highlight states in its website: "When you meet someone, Highlight helps you see what you have in common with them. And when you forget their name at a party a week later, Highlight can help you remember it" [136]. Eric Eldon, Editor of *TechCrunch,* speculates that business cards will soon be replaced by Highlight [137].

2.11 Stalking Apps and Facebook for Sex

In May 2012, Facebook acquired Glancee and closed down its app [138]. On June 25, 2012, Facebook quietly tested a new mobile feature "Find Friends Nearby" (aka "Friendshake") that allowed users find other Facebook members nearby using the mobile web as well as iOS and Android apps [139]. Facebook engineer Ryan Patterson said, "I built Find Friends Nearby with another engineer for a hackathon project. ... For me, the ideal use case for this product is the one where when you're out with a group of people whom you've recently met and want to stay in contact with. Facebook search might be effective, or sharing your vanity addresses or business cards, but this tool provides a really easy way to exchange contact information with multiple people with minimal friction" [140].

However, Dave Copeland of *ReadWriteWeb* called Find Friends Nearby "Facebook's Newest Stalking App" [141]. Facebook quietly pulled the feature off its website and mobile apps after a few hours of testing. A Facebook spokesperson told *Wired,* "This wasn't a formal release—this was just something that a few engineers were testing. With all tests, some get released as full products, others don't. Nothing more to say on this for now, but we'll communicate to everyone when there is something to say" [142].

Ambient social apps on GPS-enabled devices can be useful and fun, but the tools inadvertently empower stalkers as well. "Girls Around Me" is an epitome of such controversial mobile apps in 2012. At the push of a button, the app would go into radar mode and fill the map with pictures of girls in the neighborhood: girls who have checked into the nearby locations using foursquare, and who have public pictures on their Facebook profiles.

After "Girls Around Me" had been downloaded 70,000 times, foursquare cut off access to the app, rendering the app useless. A foursquare spokeswoman said, "The application was in violation of our API policy, so we reached out to the developer and shut off their API access. foursquare has a policy against aggregating information across venues, to prevent situations like this where someone would present an inappropriate overview of a series of locations" [143].

"Girls Around Me" developer had no choice but to remove the app from the iTunes Store, but the developer defended itself in a public statement, "Girls Around Me does not provide any data that is unavailable to user when he uses his or her social network account, nor does it reveal any data that users did not share with others. The app was intended for facilitating discovering of great public venues nearby. The app was designed to make it easier for a user to step out of door and hang out in the city, find people with common interests and new places to go to" [144].

The demise of "Girls Around Me" only fueled the growing popularity of Badoo—the world's largest social network for "meeting new people" with 154 million members as of June 2012 [145]. Relatively unknown in the United States, Badoo has become a mass phenomenon in Brazil, Mexico, France, Spain, and Italy after the site launched in 2006. Inspired by the nightclub known as "Telephone Bar" in St. Petersburg, Badoo's founder Andrey Andreev created the social network to be like a nightclub on the phone [146].

The Badoo website and its mobile app enable users to meet people nearby. The app's "hook-up" feature accounts for an overwhelming 80 % of usage, and a third of a million U.K. users admitted to using Badoo to find sexual partners [147]. Around the world, Badoo has earned the notorious nickname "Facebook for Sex." [148].

Andreev defended his company amid controversy over heavy sexual overtones, "Badoo is not for sex, it's for adventure. If you go to a nightclub, of course you've got the opportunity to find a girl or a boy—but it's not necessarily for sex, it could be to enjoy five mojitos and nothing else. Badoo simply continues the offline lifestyle. Badoo is just a casual way to hook up with people, as you do in the street or nightclub. But we make the world work faster" [149].

As more people are broadcasting their real-time location and personal information, privacy and personal safety are becoming an issue. There have been reports of assaults and rapes of Skout and Grindr members while the majority of crimes tied to location-based apps may go unreported [150].

Pete Cashmore, founder and CEO of Mashable.com, questions whether ambient social networking is "the scariest tech trend of 2012" [151]. Paul Davison, CEO of Highlight, told *CNN* at the 2012 LeWeb London conference, "People freak out, they say it's creepy. And if they don't want to share, then that's fine, they don't have to. But the social benefits to this far outweigh any cost to privacy."

What can be creepier than a mobile app equipped with facial recognition?

2.12 Facial Recognition Apps

In October 2011, Alessandro Acquisti, professor of IT and public policy at Carnegie Mellon University's Heinz College, demonstrated a proof-of-concept iPhone application that can snap a photo of a person and within seconds display their name, date of birth and social security number [152]. "To match two photos of people in the United States in real time would take four hours," said Acquisti. "That's too long to do in real time. But assuming a steady improvement in cloud computing time, we can soon get much closer to that reality than many of us believed" [153].

In June 2012, Facebook acquired Face.com—a preeminent provider of facial recognition technology on the Internet [154]. Face.com wrote on its website, "Face.com builds facial recognition software that is not only highly accurate, but also works efficiently at web-scale. Our facial recognition analytics are able to identify faces well, despite difficult circumstances like poor lighting, poor focus, subjects wearing eyeglasses, facial hair, and even Halloween costumes. Face recognition isn't just for the government or in the movies—you can use it yourself in all kinds of ways, from tagging photos to social networking" [155].

Two years before Facebook's acquisition, face.com rolled out its free facial recognition API (application programming interface) in May 2010 to encourage developers to tap its facial recognition technology for use in their own websites and applications [156]. By November 2011, more than 35,000 developers have built apps to detect and recognize more than 37 billion photos [157].

Some of the popular applications include "Photo Finder," "Photo Tagger," and "Celebrityfindr." "Photo Finder" is a Facebook app that scans the public photos in the user's social network and suggests tags for the photos that are currently untagged or partially tagged [158]. The app recognizes people even if they are making odd facial expressions or are turned to the side. "Photo Tagger" searches through the user's photo albums or the albums of their friends, and tags people in batches. [159] And "Celebrityfindr" scans Twitter and looks for photos of celebrities and lookalikes that have been posted publicly [160].

Other facial recognition software applications in a prototype stage include "HoneyBadger," "Facialytics," and "Emotional Breakdown" [161]. Using face.com's technology, "HoneyBadger" sends an alert text message to the registered owner if the laptop is being used by someone else, "Facialytics" tracks a crowd's emotions over time, and "Emotional Breakdown" examines how happy or sad someone is in a photo.

2.13 Facial Recognition on Facebook, Google+, and iPhone

"We wouldn't exist without Facebook," said Gil Hirsch, CEO of face.com. "By far the biggest scale for face recognition is your friends on Facebook" [162].

Indeed, by April 2009, Facebook users had uploaded over 15 billion digital photographs to the social network, making Facebook the single largest repository of photographs in the world [163]. The growth rate is 220 million new photos per week. Every day, Facebook users are adding more than 100 million tags to photos on Facebook [164].

In December 2010, Facebook began to roll out its own facial recognition technology, Photo Tag Suggest, which scans users' and their friends' photos for recognizable faces, and suggests nametags for the faces by matching them with users' profile photos and other tagged photos on the social network [165]. Facebook automatically opts its users into the Photo Tag Suggest service, which prompted a security firm to issue a warning in June 2011 that Facebook is eroding the online privacy of its users by stealth [166]. Although Facebook users can disable "Suggest photos of me to friends" in the Facebook account's privacy settings, many people are unaware of this extra privacy setting.

When an *Engadget* published an article on Facebook's facial recognition in April 2011, a commenter beneath the story quipped, "Awesome! Now I can take pictures of cute girls at the grocery store or at the park, upload them and Facebook will tell me who they are!" [167].

Lee Tien, a senior staff attorney at the Electronic Frontier Foundation, wrote in his email to *PCWorld*, "Facial recognition is especially troubling because cameras are ubiquitous and we routinely show our faces. And of course, one can take pictures of crowds, so it scales a bit better than, say, fingerprints. ... If Facebook misidentifies someone, the consequences are not the same as when a police video-camera misidentifies you as a suspect" [168].

Facebook's acquisition of face.com in June 2012 solidifies the importance of facial recognition in social networking. The move can also be viewed as Facebook's preemptive tactic against Google and Apple.

Back in September 2008, Google deployed facial recognition technology to its online photo service Picasa [169]. Similarly, Apple released the "Faces" feature in iPhoto in January 2009 [170]. With a reasonable success rate, Picasa and iPhone helped users label their photos with the names of subjects. As facial recognition technology began to mature, Apple added the Faces feature to its professional photography software Aperture in 2010 [171].

In December 2011, Google followed the Facebook footstep and introduced "Find My Face" as a tagging suggestion tool for its Google+ social network [172]. The tool has the same functionality as Facebook's Photo Tag Suggest. Unlike Facebook, which activates its Photo Tag Suggest by default, Google prompts users to opt into the service before Find My Face is activated. Moreover, if the tagger is not in the tagee's circles of friends, Google requires the tagee to approve the name tagging before it goes public. Facebook, on the contrary, does not require pre-approval for tags. Facebook allows all tags to go live before notifying the tagees, who are then allowed to remove unwanted tags.

Amid concerns raised by privacy advocates and U.S. Federal Trade Commission, Benjamin Petrosky, product counsel for Google+, said, "Privacy has been baked right into this feature [Find My Face]. ... We've been researching vision technologies for many years, including pattern recognition, facial detection, and facial recognition, and our approach is to treat this very carefully. We don't want to deploy a technology until it's ready and the appropriate privacy tools are in place" [173]. Meanwhile, Erin Egan, Facebook's chief privacy policy officer, defended the company by claiming that it does enough to safeguard its members' privacy by notifying them when they have been tagged and allowing them to remove tags once they have been made [174].

While Prof. Alessandro Acquisti's 2011 proof-of-concept iPhone application is not yet a commercial product, face.com released a free iPhone app called Klik in March 2012 [175]. When Klik detects a face, it connects to the user's Facebook account and scans all the friends' photos in order to identify the person in view. Given the limited number of Facebook friends that a user may have, facial recognition can be done in real time.

As smartphones and iPads are connected to cloud computing services over the Internet, it is a matter of time for companies to introduce new mobile applications that can run millions of face comparisons in seconds, even without tapping into the power of the supercomputers at the National Security Agency or San Diego Supercomputing Center.

Privacy concerns with the growing adoption of facial recognition have prompted Adam Harvey at New York University to create *CV Dazzle*, a computer vision (CV) camouflage project that combines makeup and hair styling with face-detection thwarting designs [176]. Some of the camouflage techniques include wearing oversized sunglasses, avoiding enhancers such as eye shadow and lipstick, and partially obscuring the nose-bridge area and ocular region [177].

2.14 Virtual Passports: From Privacy to Data Use

When Spotify, a popular music streaming service, announced in September 2011 that all new Spotify accounts would require a Facebook login, the company justified by asking the users to think of it as a virtual "passport" [178]. The idea is reminiscent of Microsoft's Passport in 1999 to provide consumers a single login and wallet for communication and commerce on the Internet [179]. Privacy concerns, public distrust, and software security issues contributed to the failure of Microsoft's Passport in 2004 as an Internet-wide unified-login system [180].

With the rise of social networks, Facebook has become a large-scale consumer identity provider (IdP) that allows users to access multiple websites with a single login [181]. Unlike Microsoft, Facebook has succeeded in convincing media websites and users to adopt its unified-login system ("passport") such that personal information can be easily shared across the Internet. Even Microsoft's new social search network So.cl uses Facebook authentication [182].

As we know, countries issue passports. Facebook as a nation in 2012 would be the third largest country in the world with over 955 million citizens, after China and India [183]. Facebook even offers a memorialization feature for families and friends to leave posts on the deceased's profile Walls in remembrance [184]. Cybercitizens are becoming as real as citizens. Their Facebook pages are more revealing than their real passports.

In the Facebook nation, "power users" dominate the online space by excessively tagging photos, sending messages, "like"-ing things all the time, and obsessively "friend"-ing new people on Facebook. Power users make up between 20 and 30 % of the Facebook population [185].

Let me restate the staggering Facebook statistics: By June 2012, there are 955 million active Facebook users worldwide, including 160 million Americans—half of the United States population, and 7.5 million American children under the age of 13. Americans spend a total of 53.5 billion minutes every month on Facebook.

In the United States, Facebook ranks No. 1 in time spent and ad impressions, and No. 2 in total internet visits (behind Google) [186]. And the most popular free iPhone app of all time is Facebook [187].

Each Facebook user is sharing personal information among an average of 130 online friends, roughly 25 % of whom are strangers. 20–30 % of the Facebook populations are considered "power users" that have between 359 and 780 online friends. Without invoking complex mathematics, we can infer from the numbers that millions of people have access to information that is not really meant to be publicly shared.

Even if a Facebook user has zero online friends, they are still sharing all of their personal information with Facebook. In fact, Facebook has quietly renamed its "Privacy Policy" to "Data Use Policy" in September 2011 to reflect more accurately what Facebook does with the data collection [188].

At the January 2012 Digital Life Design (DLD) conference in Munich, Facebook's chief operating officer Sheryl Sandberg said, "We are our real identities online" [189]. Cybercitizens are becoming as real as citizens. Our online identities are more revealing than our own passports.

In light of Facebook's Timeline, social apps auto-share, facial recognition photo tagging, and violation of the Federal Trade Commission Act, a *Los Angeles Times* article in September 2011 declared, "Facebook has murdered privacy" [190].

Nevertheless, Facebook is not the only culprit.

2.15   Social Search: Google, Plus Your World and Microsoft's Bing

In December 2009, Google's then CEO Eric Schmidt told CNBC's Maria Bartiromo in an interview, "If you have something that you don't want anyone to know, maybe you shouldn't be doing it in the first place, but if you really need that kind of privacy, the reality is that search engines—including Google—do retain this information for some time, and it's important, for example that we are all subject in the United States to the Patriot Act. It is possible that that information could be made available to the authorities" [191].

On January 10, 2012, Google began to roll out its most radical transformation ever with "social search"—a new search engine that understands not only content, but also people and relationships [192]. Google search provides not only results from the public web, but also personal content or things shared on social networks such as Google+ and YouTube. Google Fellow Amit Singhal wrote in the Google Blog: "Search is pretty amazing at finding that one needle in a haystack of billions of webpages, images, videos, news and much more. But clearly, that isn't enough. You should also be able to find your own stuff on the web, the people you know and things they've shared with you, as well as the people you don't know but might want to … all from one search box" [193].

In January 2012, Google announced its new privacy policy, effective March 1, that replaces more than 60 different privacy polices across Google. They admitted that the company has been collecting and compiling data about its users based on their activities across Google products and services including search engine, Gmail, YouTube, and Android cell phones [194]. In regard to search particularly,

Google states in its policies and principles that "if you're signed into Google, we can do things like suggest search queries—or tailor your search results—based on the interests you've expressed in Google+, Gmail, and YouTube. We'll better understand which version of Pink or Jaguar you're searching for and get you those results faster" [195]. Some may argue that the new Google search is way too personal, as editor Brent Rose expressed in a January 2012 *Gizmodo* article: "The fact that you can't opt-out of shared search data, and that Google will know more about you than your wife? That's a little creepy" [196].

A letter signed by 36 state attorneys general was sent to Google co-founder and CEO Larry Page. The letter reads, "On a fundamental level, the policy appears to invade consumer privacy by automatically sharing personal information consumers input into one Google product with all Google products" [197]. In particular, questions were raised about whether users can opt-out of the new data sharing system either globally or on a product-by-product basis [198]. Google responded that by folding more than 60 product-specific privacy policies into one, the company is explaining its privacy commitments in a simpler and more understandable manner [199].

The Electronic Frontier Foundation explained, "Search data can reveal particularly sensitive information about you, including facts about your location, interests, age, sexual orientation, religion, health concerns, and more" [200]. Nick Mediati wrote in *PC World*, "This grand consolidation means that all of your Google account data will live in a single database that every Google service can access. Google Maps will have access to your Gmail data, which will have access to your YouTube history, and so on" [201]. Users who log on to Google, Gmail, and YouTube cannot opt out of the Google's new privacy policy [202].

Before Google plus Your World, Microsoft's search engine Bing has been collaborating with Twitter since 2009 and Facebook since 2010 to surface more personalized content in search results. Microsoft pays Twitter to obtain a real-time feed of tweets for its search engine Bing [203]. Bing users have the ability to see what their friends have liked across the web, including news articles, celebrities, movies, and music [204].

The idea behind the search integration is the "Friend Effect"—a decision made when someone obtains a friend's stamp of approval [205]. For example, critics may pan a movie that you are interested in, but if your friends say the movie is worth seeing anyway, you are more likely to watch that movie. A Nielsen report titled "Global Trust in Advertising and Brand Messages" has validated the "Friend Effect" by showing that an overwhelming 92 % of consumers around the world trust recommendations from friends and family above all other forms of advertising [206].

In 2011, Microsoft spruced up its mobile Bing site with Facebook integration [207] and deepened the ties between Bing and Facebook by displaying the social search results along with Facebook friends' pictures, cities of residence, education, employment details, travel locations, and even shopping lists [208].

In response to Google, plus Your World, Microsoft redesigned Bing in 2012 to feature the new "Sidebar," a social search function to scour user's social networks to surface information relevant to the search queries [209]. For instance, a search for "Los Angeles Chinese restaurants" will return existing posts from friends talking about a similar topic on Facebook, Twitter, and Google+.

In a 2012 interview with *The Guardian*, Google co-founder Sergey Brin complained, "all the information in [the Facebook and iPhone] apps—that data is not crawlable by web crawlers. You can't search it" [210]. Indeed, all search engines have the same mission of prying into every detail in every corner of the world in order to unearth as much information as possible. However, the walled garden of Facebook and social media have been increasingly driving more referral traffic than traditional search. Tanya Corduroy, digital development director for *The Guardian,* reported in March 2012 that Facebook made up more than 30 % of the newspaper's referrals compared to a mere 2 % 18 months ago [211].

Social search, Google, plus Your World & Microsoft's Bing, is shaping the future of search engines, making search results more personal, more comprehensive, and hopefully more useful. It is shifting the landscape of search engine optimization (SEO) to incorporate "Friend Effect" in addition to keywords, meta tags, cross-linking, and other traditional SEO techniques. Google co-founder Larry Page once said, "The ultimate search engine is something as smart as people—or smarter" [212].

2.16 Connected Cars: In-vehicle Social Networks

In January 2012, Mercedes-Benz publicized its efforts in bringing Facebook and Google to the automobile dashboard [213]. "We're working on a new generation of vehicles that truly serve as digital companions," said Dieter Zetsche, head of Mercedes-Benz Cars, in a keynote speech at CES 2012 in Las Vegas. "They learn your habits, adapt to your choices, predict you moves and interact with your social network" [214].

Meanwhile at CES 2012, Ford Motor Company introduced the new in-vehicle application called Roximity. The app provides real-time deals and specials relevant to a user's location, based on personal preferences and interests. A driver could easily get a customized verbal message for a special deal on food from a favorite nearby restaurant [215].

"Commonly referred to as a connected car, the prevailing trend is to integrate smartphone apps into the car's dashboard. This enables drivers and passengers to listen to online music, access news and other content, stream video and more," wrote *ReadWriteWeb* editor-in-chief Richard MacManus in February 2012. "The next big thing in computing isn't a new model smartphone or laptop. It's the Internet empowering everything else around us. Our cars, TVs and many other devices" [216].

Researchers at Virginia Tech Transportation Institute conducted several large-scale, naturalistic driving studies in 2009 to get a clear picture of driver distraction and cell phone use under real-world driving conditions [217]. The research shows that talking on a cell phone increases the risk of a crash or near-crash by 1.3 times over non-distracted driving, while physically dialing a number increased the risk 2.8 times. A person is more than 23 times more likely to be in a crash or near crash while text messaging.

"People are already distracted by their phones in their car, but we can make it safer for them to do what they are already doing," commented Ricardo Reyes, spokesman for the Tesla Model S electric car that features a 17-inch touch screen display with Internet access and four USB ports to attach devices in the electric car [218].

U.S. Transportation Secretary Ray LaHood issued the non-binding guidelines in February 2012 for automakers to design in-car social network devices such that they cannot be used while a car is in motion. LaHood also called for disabling manual texting, Internet browsing, 10-digit phone dialing, and the ability to enter addresses into a built-in navigation system for drivers unless the car is in park [219].

In-vehicle cell phone use remains debatable. In May 2012, Consumer Electronics Association sent a letter to the National Transportation Safety Board (NTSB): "CEA must disagree with the NTSB's broad recommendation calling for a ban on the nonemergency use of portable electronics devices (other than those designed to support the driving task) by all drivers. There is no real-world evidence to support such a blanket prohibition unless one would also ban other potential distractions, such as eating, drinking, applying make-up and engaging with children while in the vehicle" [220].

In July 2012, marketing research firm ABI Research estimated that in five years, 60 % of the world's cars would include built-in Internet and smart phone connectivity [221]. In-vehicle social networks will likely create more distractions for drivers.

References

1. Sprenger, Polly. (January 26, 1999). Sun on Privacy: 'Get Over It.' Wired. http://www.wired.com/politics/law/news/1999/01/17538
2. Newman, Jared. (December 11, 2009). Google's Schmidt Roasted for Privacy Comments. PCWorld. http://www.pcworld.com/article/184446/googles_schmidt_roasted_for_privacy_comments.html
3. Singel, Ryan. (April 24, 2012). The Internet gets a hall of fame (yes including Al Gore). CNN. http://www.cnn.com/2012/04/24/tech/web/internet-hall-of-fame/index.html
4. Ellis, Blake. (March 9, 2012). Craziest tax deductions: Carrier pigeons. http://money.cnn.com/galleries/2012/pf/taxes/1203/gallery.wacky-tax-deductions/
5. Wortham, Jenna. (December 15, 2011) Your Life on Facebook, in Total Recall. The New York Times. http://www.nytimes.com/2011/12/16/technology/facebook-brings-back-the-past-with-new-design.html
6. Consumer Reports magazine editors. (June 2012).Facebook & your privacy. Who sees the data you share on the biggest social network? Consumer Reports. http://www.consumerreports.org/cro/magazine/2012/06/facebook-your-privacy/index.htm
7. Facebook. (February 4, 2004). About Facebook. https://www.facebook.com/facebook/info
8. Facebook Company Timeline. (Retrieved January 25, 2012). http://www.facebook.com/press/info.php?timeline

9. Olivarez-Giles, Nathan. (September 22, 2011). Facebook F8: Redesigning and hitting 800 million users. Los Angeles Times. http://latimesblogs.latimes.com/technology/2011/09/facebook-f8-media-features.html

10. Tsukayama, Hayley. (February 1, 2012). Facebook's reach: 845 million and counting. The Washington Post. http://www.washingtonpost.com/business/technology/facebooks-reach-845-million-and-counting/2012/02/01/gIQAV0gwiQ_story.html

11. Sengupta, Somini. (February 26, 2012). Risk and Riches in User Data for Facebook. The New York Times. http://www.nytimes.com/2012/02/27/technology/for-facebook-risk-and-riches-in-user-data.html

12. Facebook. (Retrieved August 11, 2012). Facebook Newsroom. http://newsroom.fb.com/content/default.aspx?NewsAreaId=22

13. Facebook Statistics by country. (Retrieved August 11, 2012). http://www.socialbakers.com/facebook-statistics/

14. Nielsen. (2011). Nielsen Social Media Report: Q3 2011. http://blog.nielsen.com/nielsenwire/social/

15. NM Incite. (December 19, 2011). Friends & Frenemies: Why We Add and Remove Facebook Friends. NM Incite. http://www.nmincite.com/?p=6051

16. Bartz, Andrea and Ehrlich, Brenna. (December 20, 2011). Beware the Facebook 'friend collector'. CNN. http://www.cnn.com/2011/12/21/tech/social-media/netiquette-friend-collector/index.html

17. Gallaga, Omar L. (May 17, 2012). Why I won't be quitting Facebook. CNN. http://www.cnn.com/2012/05/17/tech/social-media/facebook-gallaga/index.html

18. Benoit, David. (February 1, 2012). Mark Zuckerberg's Letter From The Facebook Filing. The Wall Street Journal. http://blogs.wsj.com/deals/2012/02/01/mark-zuckerbergs-letter-from-the-facebook-filing/

19. Glenn, Devon. (February 3, 2012). AOL To Launch Huffington Post Streaming Network. Social Times. http://socialtimes.com/aol-to-launch-huffington-post-streaming-network_b89001

20. Khalid, Kiran. (December 28, 2011). A social-media addict tries to disconnect. CNN. http://www.cnn.com/2011/12/14/tech/social-media/khalid-social-media-unplug/index.html

21. Sutter, John D. (May 2, 2012). Prominent blogger: 'I'm leaving the Internet for a year'. CNN. http://www.cnn.com/2012/05/02/tech/web/paul-miller-quits-internet/index.html

22. Miller, Paul. (May 2, 2012). Offline: day one of life without internet. The Verge. http://www.theverge.com/2012/5/2/2994277/paul-miller-diary-offline-day-of-life-without-internet

23. Arrington, Michael. (September 7, 2005). 85 % of College Students use FaceBook. TechCrunch. http://techcrunch.com/2005/09/07/85-of-college-students-use-facebook/

24. Markoff, John and Sengupta, Somini. (November 21, 2011). Separating You and Me? 4.74 Degrees. New York Times. http://www.nytimes.com/2011/11/22/technology/between-you-and-me-4-74-degrees.html

25. Alves, David. (January 4, 2012). Facebook. https://www.facebook.com/notes/facebook-engineering/announcing-facebooks-2012-hacker-cup/10150468260528920

26. Segall, Laurie. (January 4, 2012) Announcing Facebook's 2012 Hacker Cup. CNN. http://money.cnn.com/2012/01/04/technology/facebook_hacker_cup/index.htm

27. Kaplan, Katharine A. (November 19, 2003). Facemash Creator Survives Ad Board. Harvard Crimson. http://www.thecrimson.com/article/2003/11/19/facemash-creator-survives-ad-board-the/

28. Milian, Mark. (May 8, 2012). Zuckerberg's Hoodie a 'Mark of Immaturity,' Analyst Says. Bloomberg. http://go.bloomberg.com/tech-deals/2012-05-08-zuckerbergs-hoodie-a-mark-of-immaturity-analyst-says-2/

29. Schaefer, Steve. (June 15, 2012). SEC Pressed Facebook On Zynga, Instagram And Zuckerberg's Control Pre-IPO. Forbes. http://www.forbes.com/sites/steveschaefer/2012/06/15/sec-pressed-facebook-on-zynga-instagram-pre-ipo/

30. Federal Trade Commission. (November 29, 2011). Facebook Settles FTC Charges That It Deceived Consumers By Failing To Keep Privacy Promises. http://www.ftc.gov/opa/2011/11/privacysettlement.shtm

31. Federal Trade Commission. (2011). FTC complaint against Facebook. http://www.ftc.gov/os/caselist/0923184/111129facebookcmpt.pdf

32. Pepitone, Julianne. (November 29, 2011). Facebook settles FTC charges over 2009 privacy breaches. CNN. http://money.cnn.com/2011/11/29/technology/facebook_settlement/index.htm

33. Federal Trade Commission. (2011). FTC proposed settlement. http://www.ftc.gov/os/caselist/0923184/111129facebookagree.pdf

34. Levine, Dan; McBride, Sarah. (June 16, 2012). Facebook to pay $10 million to settle suit. Reuters. http://www.reuters.com/article/2012/06/16/net-us-facebook-settlement-idUSBRE85F0N120120616

35. Madden, Mary; Smith, Aaron. (May 26, 2010). Reputation Management and Social Media. Pew Internet. http://pewinternet.org/Reports/2010/Reputation-Management/Part-2/Attitudes-and-Actions.aspx

36. Consumer Reports magazine editors. (June 2012).Facebook & your privacy. Who sees the data you share on the biggest social network? Consumer Reports. http://www.consumerreports.org/cro/magazine/2012/06/facebook-your-privacy/index.htm

37. Facebook Company Statistics. (Retrieved January 25, 2012). http://www.facebook.com/press/info.php?statistics

38. Pempek, Tiffany A.; Yermolayeva, Yevdokiya A.; Calvert, Sandra L. (Retrieved May 4, 2012). College Students' Social Networking Experiences on Facebook. http://cdmc.georgetown.edu/papers/College_Students'_Social_networking_Experiences_on_Facebook.pdf

39. Cohen, Jackie. (January 13, 2011). You Don't Know One-Fifth of Your Facebook Friends. All Facebook. http://www.allfacebook.com/you-dont-know-one-fifth-of-your-facebook-friends-2011-01

40. Podvey, Heather. (2009). Do you really KNOW your Facebook friends? Applywise. http://www.applywise.com/sep09_facebook.aspx

41. NM Incite. (December 19, 2011). Friends & Frenemies: Why We Add and Remove Facebook Friends. NM Incite. http://www.nmincite.com/?p=6051

42. Hampton, Keith. Goulet, Lauren Sessions. Marlow, Cameron. Rainie, Lee. (February 2, 2012). Why most Facebook users get more than they give. Pew Research Center. http://www.pewinternet.org/Press-Releases/2012/Facebook-users.aspx

43. Cheng, Jacqui. (February 7, 2012). Over 3 years later, "deleted" Facebook photos are still online. CNN. http://www.cnn.com/2012/02/06/tech/social-media/deleted-facebook-photos-online/index.html

44. The Internet Archive. (Retrieved February 17, 2012). About the Internet Archive. http://www.archive.org/about/about.php

45. Kang, Cecilia. (November 1, 2011). Parents help underage children lie to get on Facebook, survey finds. The Washington Post http://www.washingtonpost.com/blogs/post-tech/post/parents-help-underage-children-lie-to-get-on-facebook-survey-finds/2011/11/01/gIQAF6D1cM_blog.html

46. Fox, Jeffrey. (May 10, 2011). Five million Facebook users are 10 or younger. Consumer Reports. http://news.consumerreports.org/electronics/2011/05/five-million-facebook-users-are-10-or-younger.html

47. Boyd, Danah. (November 7, 2011) Why parents help their children lie to Facebook about age: Unintended consequences of the 'Children's Online Privacy Protection Act'. Journal of the Internet. http://www.uic.edu/htbin/cgiwrap/bin/ojs/index.php/fm/article/view/3850/3075

48. The Wall Street Journal. (September 17, 2010). What They Know - Kids. The Wall Street Journal Blogs. http://blogs.wsj.com/wtk-kids/

49. Stecklow, Steve. (September 17, 2010). On the Web, Children Face Intensive Tracking. The Wall Street Journal. http://online.wsj.com/article/SB10001424052748703904304575497903523187146.html

50. Federal Trade Commission. (Revised October 7, 2008). Frequently Asked Questions about the Children's Online Privacy Protection Rule. http://www.ftc.gov/privacy/coppafaqs.shtm
51. Mine, Mark R.; Shochet, Joe; Hughston, Roger. (October 2003). Building a massively multiplayer game for the million: Disney's Toontown Online. ACM Computers in Entertainment. http://dl.acm.org/citation.cfm?doid=950566.950589
52. Barnes, Brooks. (August 2, 2007). Disney Acquires Web Site for Children. The New York Times. http://www.nytimes.com/2007/08/02/business/02disney.html
53. Choney, Suzanne. (June 21, 2011). Disney lets Club Penguin domain lapse, site goes down. MSNBC. http://technolog.msnbc.msn.com/_news/2011/06/21/6907472-disney-lets-club-penguin-domain-lapse-site-goes-down
54. Sniderman, Zachary. (December 13, 2011). How Disney's Club Penguin Became the Biggest Social Network for Kids. Mashable. http://mashable.com/2011/12/13/club-penguin-disney/
55. McCarthy, Caroline. (July 27, 2010). Disney to acquire social-gaming company Playdom. CNET. http://news.cnet.com/8301-13577_3-20011844-36.html
56. Reisinger, Don. (May 13, 2011). FTC: Disney's Playdom violated child protection act. CNET. http://news.cnet.com/8301-13506_3-20062566-17.html
57. Federal Trade Commission. (May 12, 2011). Operators of Online "Virtual Worlds" to Pay $3 Million to Settle FTC Charges That They Illegally Collected and Disclosed Children's Personal Information. Federal Trade Commission News. http://www.ftc.gov/opa/2011/05/playdom.shtm
58. Milian, Mark. (January 25, 2012) Study: Multitasking hinders youth social skills. CNN. http://www.cnn.com/2012/01/25/tech/social-media/multitasking-kids/index.html
59. Rosen, Larry D. (August 6, 2011). Social Networking's Good and Bad Impacts on Kids. Psychologists explore myths, realities and offer guidance for parents. American Psychological Association Press Release. http://www.apa.org/news/press/releases/2011/08/social-kids.aspx
60. Mundt, Marlon P. (September/October 2011). The Impact of Peer Social Networks on Adolescent Alcohol Use Initiation. Academic Pediatrics. Volume 11, Number 5.
61. Mehdizadeh, Soraya. (August 2010). Self-Presentation 2.0: Narcissism and Self-Esteem on Facebook. Cyberpsychology, Behavior, and Social Networking. Volume 13, Number 4.
62. Enayati, Amanda. (March 16, 2012). Facebook: The encyclopedia of beauty? CNN. http://www.cnn.com/2012/03/16/living/beauty-social-networks/index.html
63. EnemyGraph. (Retrieved March 29, 2012). EnemyGraph Trends. http://www.enemygraph.com/
64. Guynn, Jessica. (March 27, 2012). Is Facebook too friendly? Plug-in EnemyGraph makes it less so. The Los Angeles Times. http://www.latimes.com/business/technology/la-fi-tn-facebook-enemygraph20120327,0,4664649.story
65. Bauerlein, Mark. (May 14, 2009). The Dumbest Generation: How the Digital Age Stupefies Young Americans and Jeopardizes Our Future(Or, Don't Trust Anyone Under 30). Tarcher.
66. Rice, Condoleezza; Klein, Joel. (March 20, 2012). Rice, Klein: Education keeps America safe. CNN. http://www.cnn.com/2012/03/20/opinion/rice-klein-education/index.html
67. Lacy, Sarah. (April 10, 2011). Peter Thiel: We're in a Bubble and It's Not the Internet. It's Higher Education. TechCrunch. http://techcrunch.com/2011/04/10/peter-thiel-were-in-a-bubble-and-its-not-the-internet-its-higher-education/
68. Wieder, Ben. (May 25, 2011). Thiel Fellowship Pays 24 Talented Students $100,000 Not to Attend College. The Chronicle of Higher Education. http://chronicle.com/article/Thiel-Fellowship-Pays-24/127622/
69. Carter, Bill. (September 13, 2010). Tired of Reality TV, but Still Tuning In. New York Times. http://www.nytimes.com/2010/09/13/business/media/13reality.html
70. Neff, Jack. (January 18, 2012). Move Over, 'American Idol': Walmart's the Next Reality Giant. Advertising Age. http://adage.com/article/news/move-american-idol-walmart-s-reality-giant/232178/

71. McNamara, Mary. (September 5, 2011). 'Real Housewives': Suicide should have scrapped Season 2. Los Angeles Times. http://latimesblogs.latimes.com/showtracker/2011/09/real-housewives-suicide-should-have-scrapped-season-2.html
72. Amedure, Scott. (March 12, 1995). Fatal Shooting Follows Surprise on TV Talk Show. New York Times. http://www.nytimes.com/1995/03/12/us/fatal-shooting-follows-surprise-on-tv-talk-show.html
73. Nelson, David. (May 20, 2010). Meaner than fiction: Reality TV high on aggression, study shows. Brigham Young University News Release. http://news.byu.edu/archive10-may-realitytv.aspx
74. Trendrr. (January 25, 2012). Social TV Has Talent. Trendrr Blog. http://blog.trendrr.com/2012/01/25/social-tv-has-talent/
75. Trendrr.TV. (Retrieved February 6, 2012). Trendrr.TV. http://trendrr.tv/
76. Smith, Steve. (March 30, 2012). Facebook A Quiet Second-Screen Giant In Social TV Space? Mobile Marketing Daily. http://www.mediapost.com/publications/article/171410/facebook-a-quiet-second-screen-giant-in-social-tv.html
77. Fitzgerald, Toni. (October 12, 2011). Is reality TV losing steam? Maybe so. Media Life Magazine. http://www.medialifemagazine.com/artman2/publish/Broadcastrecap_64/Is-reality-TV-losing-steam-Maybe-so-.asp
78. Nielsen. (May 3, 2011). Nielsen Estimates Number of U.S. Television Homes to be 114.7 Million. Nielsenwire. http://blog.nielsen.com/nielsenwire/media_entertainment/nielsen-estimates-number-of-u-s-television-homes-to-be-114-7-million/
79. Wood, Molly. (July 15, 2005). Top 10 Web fads. CNet. http://www.cnet.com/1990-11136_1-6268155-1.html
80. Gill, Steve. (November 3, 2006). Can Borat be Sued by the "I Kiss You!" Guy? Electronic News Network. http://electronicnewsnetwork.com/entertainment/borat-sued-by-mahir-cagri-201037/
81. Grossman, Lev. (January 30, 2012). The Beast With A Billion Eyes. Time Magazine. http://www.time.com/time/magazine/article/0,9171,2104815,00.html
82. Oreskovic, Alexei. (January 23, 2012). YouTube hits 4 billion daily video views. Reuters. http://www.reuters.com/article/2012/01/23/us-google-youtube-idUSTRE80M0TS20120123
83. YouTube press statistics. (Retrieved January 25, 2012). http://www.youtube.com/t/press_statistics
84. Constine, Josh. (February 9, 2012). 100 Million Americans Watch Online Video Per Day, Up 43 % Since 2010 -comScore. TechCrunch. http://techcrunch.com/2012/02/09/100-million-american-watch-video/
85. Broadcast Engineering. (February 22, 2012). 40 billion online videos viewed by U.S. Internet users in January, says comScore. Broadcast Engineering. http://broadcastengineering.com/ott/40-billion-online-videos-US-users-January-comScore-02222012/
86. comScore, Inc. (February 9, 2012). 2012 U.S. Digital Future in Focus. comScore. http://www.comscore.com/Press_Events/Presentations_Whitepapers/2012/2012_US_Digital_Future_in_Focus
87. Pepitone, Julianne. (March 22, 2012). Americans now watch more online movies than DVDs. CNN Money. http://money.cnn.com/2012/03/22/technology/streaming-movie-sales/index.htm
88. Protalinski, Emil. (January 17, 2012). Facebook fifth for online video in December 2011. ZDNet. http://www.zdnet.com/blog/facebook/facebook-fifth-for-online-video-in-december-2011/7503
89. Milian, Mark. (February 1, 2012). YouTube exec: We're heading for 'third wave' of TV. CNN. http://whatsnext.blogs.cnn.com/2012/02/01/youtube-third-wave/
90. Barnes, Brooks. (November 6, 2011). Disney and YouTube Make a Video Deal. The New York Times. http://www.nytimes.com/2011/11/07/business/media/disney-and-youtube-make-a-video-deal.html
91. Puopolo, Joseph. (January 29, 2012). The Emergence Of The Content Creation Class. TechCruch. http://techcrunch.com/2012/01/29/the-emergence-of-the-content-creation-class/

92. Adib, Desiree. (November 14, 2009). Pop Star Justin Bieber Is on the Brink of Superstardom. ABC Good Morning America. http://abcnews.go.com/GMA/Weekend/teen-pop-star-justin-bieber-discovered-youtube/story?id=9068403

93. Trebay, Guy. (February 13, 2012). Model Struts Path to Stardom Not on Runway, but on YouTube. The New York Times. http://www.nytimes.com/2012/02/14/us/kate-upton-uses-the-web-to-become-a-star-model.html

94. Zeidler, Sari. (March 3, 2012). CNN Blogs. http://inamerica.blogs.cnn.com/2012/03/03/on-youtube-teens-ask-the-world-am-i-ugly/

95. Gibson, Faye. (January 15, 2012). Am I Pretty or Ugly. YouTube. http://www.youtube.com/watch?v=WoyZPn6hKY4

96. Smith, Candace. (February 23, 2012). Teens Post 'Am I Pretty or Ugly?' Videos on YouTube. ABC News. http://abcnews.go.com/US/teens-post-insecurities-youtube-pretty-ugly-videos/story?id=15777830

97. John. (June 21, 2012). Bus Monitor Karen Klein bullied by vile school children. YouTube. http://www.youtube.com/watch?v=E12R9fMMtos

98. Schwartz, Alison. (June 25, 2012). Karen Klein, Bullied Bus Monitor, to Donate and Invest Her Nearly $650,000. People. http://www.people.com/people/article/0,,20606781,00.html

99. Sabo, Tracy and Hayes, Ashley. (November 2, 2011) Texas judge confirms video of him beating daughter, says 'I lost my temper'. CNN. http://articles.cnn.com/2011-11-02/justice/justice_texas-video-beating_1_texas-judge-disabled-daughter-video?_s=PM:JUSTICE

100. shoehedgie. (October 27, 2011). Judge William Adams beats daughter for using the internet. YouTube. http://www.youtube.com/watch?v=Wl9y3SIPt7o

101. Stump, Scott. (November 3, 2011). Daughter in beating video: Why I released it. MSNBC. http://today.msnbc.msn.com/id/45146961/ns/today-today_people/t/daughter-beating-video-why-i-released-it/

102. Carpenter, Christopher J. (March 2012). Narcissism on Facebook: Self-promotional and anti-social behavior. Personality and Individual Differences. Volume 52, Issue 4.

103. Griggs, Brandon. (March 10, 2012). Is political comedy inherently leftist? CNN. http://www.cnn.com/2012/03/10/tech/web/sxsw-internet-comedy/index.html

104. Interactive Advertising Bureau. (September 3, 2010). Social: A closer look at behaviour on YouTube & Facebook. iab. http://static.googleusercontent.com/external_content/untrusted_dlcp/www.google.com/en/us/googleblogs/pdfs/iab_research_youtube_and_facebook_oct_2010.pdf

105. theofficialfacebook. (Joined May 6, 2009). The Official Facebook Channel. YouTube. http://www.youtube.com/user/theofficialfacebook

106. Perlberg, Heather. (February 6, 2012). Apple May Introduce Television Called ITV, Jefferies Says. Bloomberg. http://www.bloomberg.com/news/2012-02-06/apple-may-introduce-television-called-itv-jefferies-says.html

107. Milian, Mark. (February 2, 2012). What scares Facebook: Privacy and phones. CNN. http://www.cnn.com/2012/02/01/tech/social-media/facebook-ipo-risks/index.html

108. comScore. (February 2, 2012). comScore Reports December 2011 U.S. Mobile Subscriber Market Share. comScore Press Release. http://www.comscore.com/Press_Events/Press_Releases/2012/2/comScore_Reports_December_2011_U.S._Mobile_Subscriber_Market_Share

109. Ho, Erica. (September 20, 2011). Report: Facebook Adding Read, Listened, Watched and Want Buttons. Time Magazine. http://techland.time.com/2011/09/20/report-facebook-to-launch-read-listened-watched-and-want-buttons/

110. MacManus, Richard. (September 22, 2011). "Read" in Facebook - It's Not a Button, So Be Careful What You Click! ReadWriteWeb. http://www.readwriteweb.com/archives/read_in_facebook_social_news_apps.php

111. Segall, Laurie. (September 29, 2011). Facebook's Ticker broadcasts everything you do. CNN. http://money.cnn.com/2011/09/29/technology/facebook_ticker_privacy/index.htm

112. Vascellaro, Jessica E. (September 18, 2009). Facebook Settles Class-Action Suit Over Beacon Service. The Wall Street Journal. http://online.wsj.com/article/SB12533 2446004624573.html

113. Netflix Company Facts. (Retrieved July 9, 2012). https://signup.netflix.com/MediaCenter/ Facts

114. Hastings, Reed. (July 3, 2012). Facebook. https://www.facebook.com/reed1960/posts/ 10150955446914584

115. NetFlix US & Canada Blog. (September 22, 2011). Watch this now: Netflix & Facebook. Netflix. http://blog.netflix.com/2011/09/watch-this-now-netflix-facebook.html

116. Davis, Wendy. (December 7, 2011). House Clears Way for Netflix Streams on Facebook. MediaPost News. http://www.mediapost.com/publications/article/163718/house-clears-way-for-netflix-streams-on-facebook.html

117. Davis, Wendy. (February 13, 2012). Netflix Settles Data Retention Suit For $9 M. MediaPost News. http://www.mediapost.com/publications/article/167755/netflix-settles-data-retention-suit-for-9m.html

118. Davis, Wendy. (May 30, 2012). Netflix To Revise Data Retention Practices. MediaPost News. http://www.mediapost.com/publications/article/175728/netflix-to-revise-data-retention-practices.html

119. Pidaparthy, Umika. (January 26, 2012). Interest, meet Pinterest: Site helps users catalog their passions. CNN. http://www.cnn.com/2012/01/26/tech/web/pinterest-website/ index.html

120. Facebook. (Retrieved January 25, 2012). Introducing Timeline: Tell your life story with a new kind of profile. http://www.facebook.com/about/timeline

121. Milian, Mark and Sutter, John D. (September 22, 2011). Facebook revamps site with 'Timeline' and real-time apps. CNN. http://www.cnn.com/2011/09/22/tech/social-media/ facebook-announcement-f8/index.html

122. Peters, Nikki. (November 21, 2011). Introducing the NEW Facebook Timeline. Social Media Today. http://socialmediatoday.com/marketmesuite-app/392011/introducing-new-facebook-timeline

123. Milian, Mark. (January 19, 2012). 60 apps launch with Facebook auto-share. CNN. http:// www.cnn.com/2012/01/18/tech/social-media/facebook-actions-apps/index.html

124. Milian, Mark. (January 18, 2012). Some apps steer clear of Facebook auto-publish tool. CNN. http://www.cnn.com/2012/01/18/tech/social-media/facebook-pandora/index.html

125. Baig, Edward C. (March 12, 2012). Fandango, Vevo, more launch Facebook apps. USA Today. http://content.usatoday.com/communities/livefrom/post/2012/03/facebook-3000-timeline-apps/1

126. Fandango. (March 13, 2012). Fandango Makes Moviegoing More Social than Ever with New Facebook Timeline App, "Movies with Friends." PRnewswire. http://www.prnewswire. com/news-releases/fandango-makes-moviegoing-more-social-than-ever-with-new-facebook-timeline-app-movies-with-friends-142449025.html

127. Steel, Emily and Fowler, Geoffrey A. (October 8, 2010). Facebook in Privacy Breach. The Wall Street Journal. http://online.wsj.com/article/SB1000142405270230477280457555 8484075236968.html

128. O'Neill, Nick. (October 29, 2010). Facebook Shuts Down Apps That Sold User Data, Bans Rapleaf. All Facebook. http://www.allfacebook.com/facebook-shuts-down-apps-that-sold-user-data-bans-rapleaf-2010-10

129. Tsotsis, Alexia. (June 20, 2011). foursquare Now Officially At 10 Million Users. TechCrunch. http://techcrunch.com/2011/06/20/foursquare-now-officially-at-10-million-users/

130. foursquare. (Retrieved March 9, 2012). About foursquare. https://foursquare.com/about/

131. Schulman, Kori. (August 15, 2011). Take a Tip from the White House on foursquare. The White House Blog. http://www.whitehouse.gov/blog/2011/08/15/take-tip-white-house-foursquare

132. Sonar. (Retrieved March 8, 2012). About Sonar. http://www.sonar.me/about

133. Glancee. (Retrieved March 8, 2012). Glancee. http://www.glancee.com/

134. Bryant, Martin. (April 18, 2012). Location-based social discovery app Banjo hits 1 million users in 9 months. The Next Web. http://thenextweb.com/insider/2012/04/18/location-based-social-discovery-app-banjo-hits-1-million-users-in-9-months/
135. Banjo. (Retrieved March 8, 2012). Banjo: Our Story. http://ban.jo/about/
136. Highlight. (Retrieved March 8, 2012). About Highlight. http://highlig.ht/about.html
137. Eldon, Eric. (March 3, 2012). foursquare And Glancee Are Cool, But Here's Why I'm So Excited About Using Highlight At SXSW. TechCrunch. http://techcrunch.com/2012/03/03/myhighlight/
138. Tsotsis, Alexia. (May 4, 2012). Facebook Buys Location-Based Discovery App Glancee. TechCrunch. http://techcrunch.com/2012/05/04/facebook-buys-location-based-discovery-app-glancee/
139. Chang, Alexandra. (June 25, 2012). Facebook Quietly Releases 'Find Friends Nearby,' Then Quietly Pulls It. Wired. http://www.wired.com/gadgetlab/2012/06/facebook-quietly-releases-find-friends-nearby-then-quietly-pulls-it/
140. Lunden, Ingrid. (June 24, 2012). 'Find Friends Nearby': Facebook's New Mobile Feature For Finding People Around You [Updated]. TechCrunch. http://techcrunch.com/2012/06/24/friendshake-facebooks-new-mobile-feature-for-finding-people-nearby-and-a-highlight-killer/
141. Copeland, Dave. (June 25, 2012). How To Use Facebook's Newest Stalking App. ReadWriteWeb. http://www.readwriteweb.com/archives/how-to-use-facebooks-newest-stalking-app.php
142. Chang, Alexandra. (June 25, 2012). Facebook Quietly Releases 'Find Friends Nearby,' Then Quietly Pulls It. Wired. http://www.wired.com/gadgetlab/2012/06/facebook-quietly-releases-find-friends-nearby-then-quietly-pulls-it/
143. Dowell, Andrew. (March 31, 2012). Tracking Women: Now There's Not An App For That. The Wall Street Journal. http://blogs.wsj.com/digits/2012/03/31/tracking-women-now-theres-not-an-app-for-that/
144. Austin, Scott; Dowell, Andrew. (March 31, 2012). 'Girls Around Me' Developer Defends App After foursquare Dismissal. The Wall Street Journal. http://blogs.wsj.com/digits/2012/03/31/girls-around-me-developer-defends-app-after-foursquare-dismissal/
145. Badoo. (Retrieved June 27, 2012). Badoo Corporate. The Company. http://corp.badoo.com/company/
146. Rooney, Ben. (January 24, 2012). A Very Social Network. The Wall Street Journal. http://blogs.wsj.com/tech-europe/2012/01/24/the-very-social-network/
147. Huffington Post Editors. (December 13, 2011). Badoo: Website 'Like Facebook But For Sex' Hits 130 Million Users. Huffington Post UK. http://www.huffingtonpost.co.uk/2011/12/13/badoo-facebook-sex-_n_1145909.html
148. Bloxham, Andy. (December 13, 2011). 'Sex social network' Badoo has 1 m users in Britain. The Telegraph. http://www.telegraph.co.uk/technology/news/8952240/Sex-social-network-Badoo-has-1m-users-in-Britain.html
149. Rowan, David. (April 25, 2011). How Badoo built a billion-pound social network... on sex. Wired UK. http://www.wired.co.uk/magazine/archive/2011/05/features/sexual-network
150. Segall, Laurie. (June 15, 2012). When location apps overshare, predators follow the signal. CNN Money. http://money.cnn.com/2012/06/15/technology/location-app-predators/index.htm
151. Cashmore, Pete. (March 6, 2012). The scariest tech trend of 2012? CNN. http://www.cnn.com/2012/03/01/tech/mobile/tech-trends-sxsw-cashmore/index.html
152. CNN. (October 7, 2011). CNN Money. Warning! 1 picture can hack your identity. http://money.cnn.com/video/technology/2011/10/05/t-ts-iphone-camera-id.cnnmoney/
153. Goldman, David. (January 13, 2012). CNN Money. http://money.cnn.com/2012/01/13/technology/face_recognition/index.htm
154. Peterson, Tim. (June 18, 2012). Facebook Gets a New Face(.com). Facial recognition startup follows Instagram buy. Adweek. http://www.adweek.com/news/technology/facebook-gets-new-facecom-141196

155. face.com (Retrieved March 11, 2012). About face.com and Face Recognition. face.com http://face.com/about.php
156. Casperson, Matthew. (May 4, 2010). Face.com Opens Free Facial Recognition API. ProgrammableWeb. http://blog.programmableweb.com/2010/05/04/face-com-opens-free-facial-recognition-api/
157. Goldman, David. (December 13, 2011). Your face is being tracked: Find My Facemate. CNN Money. http://money.cnn.com/galleries/2011/technology/1112/gallery.face-recognition-apps/6.html
158. Nicole, Kristen. (March 24, 2009). Photo Finder: 100 Invites to Auto Tag Facebook Photos. All Facebook. http://www.allfacebook.com/photo-finder-invite-2009-03
159. Nicole, Kristen. (July 21, 2009). Photo Tagger Automatically Tags Your Facebook Photos. All Facebook. http://www.allfacebook.com/photo-tagger-2009-07
160. CelebrityFindr. (Retrieved March 11, 2012). http://www.celebrityfindr.com/
161. Segall, Laurie. (September 7, 2011). Photo hackers explore the creepy zone. CNN Money. http://money.cnn.com/2011/09/07/technology/startups/photo_hack/index.htm
162. Goldman, David. (December 13, 2011). Your face is being tracked: Facebook. http://money.cnn.com/galleries/2011/technology/1112/gallery.face-recognition-apps/5.html
163. Vajgel, Peter. (April 30, 2009). Needle in a haystack: efficient storage of billions of photos. Facebook. http://www.facebook.com/note.php?note_id=76191543919
164. Mitchell, Justin. (December 15, 2010). Making Photo Tagging Easier. The Facebook Blog. http://www.facebook.com/blog/blog.php?post=467145887130
165. Ionescu, Daniel. (December 16, 2010). Facebook Adds Facial Recognition to Make Photo Tagging Easier. PCWorld. http://www.pcworld.com/article/213894/facebook_adds_facial_recognition_to_make_photo_tagging_easier.html
166. Cluley, Graham. (June 7, 2011). Facebook changes privacy settings for millions of users - facial recognition is enabled. Sophos naked security. http://nakedsecurity.sophos.com/2011/06/07/facebook-privacy-settings-facial-recognition-enabled/
167. Flatley, Joseph L. (April 5, 2011). Facebook planning facial recognition for picture uploads? (update: yes!) Engadget. http://www.engadget.com/2011/04/05/facebook-planning-facial-recognition-for-picture-uploads/#comments
168. Geuss, Megan. (April 26, 2011). Facebook Facial Recognition: Its Quiet Rise and Dangerous Future. PCWorld. http://www.pcworld.com/article/226228/facebook_facial_recognition_its_quiet_rise_and_dangerous_future.html
169. Shankland, Stephen. (September 2, 2008). Revamped Google Picasa site identifies photo faces. CNet. http://news.cnet.com/8301-13580_3-10026577-39.html
170. Lee, Nicole. (January 30, 2009). First taste of iLife '09: iPhoto's face recognition. CNet. http://news.cnet.com/8301-17938_105-10153818-1.html
171. Dalrymple, Jim. (February 9, 2010). Apple's Aperture 3 adds face recognition, GPS. CNet. http://news.cnet.com/8301-13579_3-10449880-37.html
172. Steiner, Matt. (December 8, 2011). Google + . https://plus.google.com/101560853443212199687/posts/VV45vivcFq4#101560853443212199687/posts/VV45vivcFq4
173. Goldman, David. (December 9, 2011). Your face is being tracked: Google. CNN Money. http://money.cnn.com/galleries/2011/technology/1112/gallery.face-recognition-apps/4.html
174. Goldman, David. (December 9, 2011). Google unveils 'Find My Face' tool. CNN Money. http://money.cnn.com/2011/12/09/technology/google_find_my_face/index.htm
175. Goldman, David. (March 12, 2012). Real-time face recognition comes to your iPhone camera. CNN Money. http://money.cnn.com/2012/03/12/technology/iPhone-face-recognition/index.htm
176. Harvey, Adam. (Retrieved May 29, 2012). Camouflage from Computer Vision. CV Dazzle. http://cvdazzle.com/
177. Cheshire, Tom. (January 4, 2012). How to use camouflage to thwart facial recognition. Wired. http://www.wired.co.uk/magazine/archive/2012/01/how-to/how-to-use-camouflage-to-thwart-facial-recognition

178. Van Buskirk, Eliot. (September 26, 2011). Spotify Defends Facebook Requirement as 'Good and Simple'. evolver.fm http://evolver.fm/2011/09/26/spotify-defends-facebook-log-in-requirement-as-good-and-simple/

179. Microsoft. (October 11, 1999). Microsoft Passport: Streamlining Commerce and Communication on the Web. Microsoft News Center. http://www.microsoft.com/presspass/features/1999/10-11passport.mspx

180. ZDNet UK. (January 4, 2005). Passport failure shows the folly of Microsoft's ways. ZDNet. http://www.zdnet.co.uk/news/it-at-work/2005/01/04/passport-failure-shows-the-folly-of-microsofts-ways-39183062/

181. Peterson, Robyn. (October 21, 2011). Who Owns Your Identity on the Social Web? Mashable. http://mashable.com/2011/10/21/web-identity/

182. Microsoft Research. (Retrieved May 21, 2012). About So.cl. Frequently Asked Questions. http://www.so.cl/about/faq

183. Baym, Nancy. (September 27, 2011). Introducing Facebook Nation. Social Media Collective Research Blog. http://socialmediacollective.org/2011/09/27/introducing-facebook-nation/

184. Kelly, Max. (October 26, 2009). Memories of Friends Departed Endure on Facebook. The Facebook Blog. http://www.facebook.com/blog.php?post=163091042130

185. Hampton, Keith. Goulet, Lauren Sessions. Marlow, Cameron. Rainie, Lee. (February 3, 2012). Why most Facebook users get more than they give. Pew Research Center. http://pewinternet.org/Reports/2012/Facebook-users/Summary/Power-Users.aspx

186. Delo, Cotton. (March 5, 2012). Facebook Warns Brands that Scale in Social Won't Come for Free. Advertising Age. http://adage.com/article/digital/facebook-warns-brands-scale-social-free/233105/

187. FORTUNE editors. (March 6, 2012). CNN Money. http://money.cnn.com/galleries/2012/technology/1203/gallery.most-popular-iPhone-apps.fortune/20.html

188. Facebook. (Retrieved April 22, 2012). Statement of Rights and Responsibilities Update. Facebook. http://www.facebook.com/fbsitegovernance/app_4949752878

189. Keen, Andrew. (January 25, 2012). Battle Lines Drawn as Data Becomes Oil of Digital Age. DLD (Digital Life Design). http://www.dld-conference.com/news/digital-business/battle-lines-drawn-as-data-becomes-oil-of-digital-age_aid_3097.html

190. Guynn, Jessica. (September 26, 2011). Is Facebook killing your privacy? Some say it already has. Los Angeles Time. http://latimesblogs.latimes.com/technology/2011/09/is-facebook-killing-your-privacy-.html

191. Newman, Jared. (December 11, 2009). Google's Schmidt Roasted for Privacy Comments. PCWorld. http://www.pcworld.com/article/184446/googles_schmidt_roasted_for_privacy_comments.html

192. Sutter, John D. (January 10, 2012). Google search undergoes 'most radical transformation ever'. CNN. http://www.cnn.com/2012/01/10/tech/web/google-search-plus/index.html

193. Singhal, Amit. (January 10, 2012). Search, plus Your World. The Official Google Blog. http://googleblog.blogspot.com/2012/01/search-plus-your-world.html

194. Gross, Doug. (January 27, 2012). Google seeks to clarify new privacy policy. CNN. http://www.cnn.com/2012/01/27/tech/web/google-privacy-clarified/index.html

195. Google Policies & Principles. (Retrieved January 27, 2012). One policy, one Google experience. http://www.google.com/policies/

196. Rose, Brent. (January 25, 2012). How Will Google's New Privacy Policy Affect You? Gizmodo. http://gizmodo.com/5879163/how-will-googles-new-privacy-policy-affect-you/

197. Gross, Doug. (February 22, 2012). Attorneys general have 'strong concerns' about Google privacy rules. CNN. http://www.cnn.com/2012/02/22/tech/web/google-privacy-attorneys-general/index.html

198. U.S. Congress. (January 26, 2012). Letter to Mr. Larry Page from Congress of the United States. http://markey.house.gov/sites/markey.house.gov/files/documents/2012_0126.Google%20Prviacy%20Letter.pdf

199. Chavez, Pablo. (January 31, 2012). Changing our privacy policies, not our privacy controls. Google Public Policy Blog. http://googlepublicpolicy.blogspot.com/2012/01/changing-our-privacy-policies-not-our.html

200. Galperin, Eva. (February 21, 2012). How to Remove Your Google Search History Before Google's New Privacy Policy Takes Effect. Electronic Frontier Foundation. https://www.eff.org/deeplinks/2012/02/how-remove-your-google-search-history-googles-new-privacy-policy-takes-effect

201. Mediati, Nick. (February 28, 2012). Google Privacy Checklist: What to Do Before Google's Privacy Policy Changes on March 1. PC World. http://www.pcworld.com/article/250950/google_privacy_checklist_what_to_do_before_googles_privacy_policy_changes_on_march_1.html

202. CNN Blogs. (March 1, 2012). Google's new privacy policy in effect today: 'Accept, or decline and be banished'. CNN. http://outfront.blogs.cnn.com/2012/03/01/googles-new-privacy-policy-accept-or-decline-and-be-banished

203. Yiu, Paul and the Bing Social Search Team. (October 21, 2009). Bing is Brining Twitter Search to You. Bing Community Search Blog. http://www.bing.com/community/site_blogs/b/search/archive/2009/10/21/bing-is-bringing-twitter-search-to-you.aspx

204. Ostrow, Adam. (October 13, 2010). Facebook and Bing's Plan to Make Search Social. Mashable. http://mashable.com/2010/10/13/facebook-bing-social-search/

205. Mehdi, Yusuf. (May 16, 2011). Facebook Friends Now Fueling Faster Decisions on Bing. Bing Community Search Blog. http://www.bing.com/community/site_blogs/b/search/archive/2011/05/16/news-announcement-may-17.aspx

206. The Nielsen Company. (April 10, 2012). Consumer Trust in Online, Social and Mobile Advertising Grows. Nielsen. http://blog.nielsen.com/nielsenwire/media_entertainment/consumer-trust-in-online-social-and-mobile-advertising-grows/ and http://www.nielsen.com/content/dam/corporate/us/en/reports-downloads/2012-Reports/global-trust-in-advertising-2012.pdf

207. Seifert, Dan. (September 12, 2011). Microsoft spruces up mobile Bing site with Facebook integration. MobileBurn.com. http://www.mobileburn.com/16588/news/microsoft-spruces-up-mobile-bing-site-with-facebook-integration

208. Slattery, Brennon. (May 17, 2011). Bing, Facebook Deepen Ties, Threaten Google +1. PC World. http://www.pcworld.com/article/228057/bing_facebook_deepen_ties_threaten_google_1.html

209. Goldman, David. (May 10, 2012). Bing fires at Google with new social search. CNN Money. http://money.cnn.com/2012/05/10/technology/bing-redesign/index.htm

210. Katz, Ian. (April 15, 2012). Web freedom faces greatest threat ever, warns Google's Sergey Brin. The Guardian. http://www.guardian.co.uk/technology/2012/apr/15/web-freedom-threat-google-brin

211. Keen, Andrew. (March 30, 2012). Opinion: Is the social web an asteroid for the Google dinosaur? CNN. http://articles.cnn.com/2012-03-30/opinion/opinion_keen-google-social-media_1_google-maps-google-products-larry-page?_s=PM:OPINION

212. Keay, Andra. (August 12, 2010). Google Search History. Presentation for ARIN 691ss http://www.slideshare.net/andragy/google-search-history

213. Albanesius, Chloe. (January 10, 2012). Mercedes-Benz Brings Facebook, Google to the Dashboard. PC Magazine. http://www.pcmag.com/article2/0,2817,2398685,00.asp

214. Griggs, Brandon. (January 13, 2012). 'Augmented-reality' windshields and the future of driving. CNN. http://www.cnn.com/2012/01/13/tech/innovation/ces-future-driving/index.html

215. Ford Motor Company. (January 6, 2012). Ford to Showcase Roximity at 2012 CES; Encourages Developers to Innovate New App Ideas for SYNC. Ford Motor Company Online. http://www.at.ford.com/news/cn/Pages/Ford%20to%20Showcase%20Roximity%20at%202012%20CES;%20Encourages%20Developers%20to%20Innovate%20New%20App%20Ideas%20for%20SYNC.aspx

216. MacManus, Richard. (February 3, 2012). Get Ready For a World of Connected Devices. ReadWriteWeb. http://www.readwriteweb.com/archives/get_ready_for_a_world_of_connected_devices.php

217. Virginia Tech Transportation Institute. (July 29, 2009). New data from Virginia Tech Transportation Institute provides insight into cell phone use and driving distraction. Virginia Tech News. http://www.vtnews.vt.edu/articles/2009/07/2009-571.html

218. Ramsey, Mike. (February 10, 2012). Don't Look Now: A Car That Tweets. As Distracted-Driving Push Fades, Auto Makers Will Let Drivers Check Facebook, Buy Movie Tickets. The Wall Street Journal. http://online.wsj.com/article/SB100014240529702038249045772130419440823700.html

219. Kohn, Bernard; Snyder, Andrea. (February 16, 2012). U.S. Calls for Ban on In-Car Facebook, Twitter While Driving. Bloomberg Businessweek. http://news.businessweek.com/article.asp?documentKey=1376-LZHQB31A1I4H01-68P3C92P2HL6F4L53B9P2100FB

220. Consumer Electronics Association. (May 8, 2012). CEA Responds to NTSB on Safe Driving Innovations. Yahoo! Finance. http://finance.yahoo.com/news/cea-responds-ntsb-safe-driving-190800191.html

221. Damsky, William. (July 5, 2012). 60% of Cars to Be Internet-Ready in 5 Years. CE Outlook. http://www.ceoutlook.com/2012/07/05/60-of-cars-to-be-internet-ready-in-5-years/

Chapter 3
Smartphones and Privacy

*We're as surprised as anybody to see all that information
flowing. It raises a lot of questions for the industry—and not
[only] for Carrier IQ.*
—Carrier IQ's Andrew Coward (December 2011)

*[Mobile World Congress] really should be held in Geneva,
close to where Mary Shelley created Frankenstein. With our
increasing addiction to our mobile phones, we are in danger of
creating a monster.*
—Social critic Andrew Keen (February 2012)

3.1 Smartphones

Smartphones are the most prevalent portable social networking devices. Worldwide smartphone sales soared to 491.4 million units in 2011 alone [1]. There are
1.2 billion active mobile web users in the world [2]. By September 2011,
82.2 million Americans own smartphones, 70 % of which are either iPhones or
Android phones [3]. 64.2 million U.S. smartphone users accessed social networking sites or blogs on their mobile devices at least once in December 2011 [4].
March 2012 marked the tipping point when a majority (50.4 %) of U.S. mobile
subscribers owned smartphones [5].

In June 2011, a Harris Interactive survey of 2,510 Americans aged 18 and older
showed that people are so addicted to their mobile devices that a majority of them
would "sneak-a-peek" at their smartphones even during work meetings by
employing tactics such as "hiding their mobile device under the table or in a
notebook" or "excusing themselves to go to the restroom" [6].

A U.K. study in 2012 revealed that two-thirds of people suffer from "nomophobia"—the fear of being without their phone [7]. Young adults, aged 18–24, are
more nomophobic (77 %) than average. 41 % of people, more men than women,
have two phones or more in an effort to stay connected.

The tremendous growth of cell phone usage in the United States has created
"spectrum crunch"—running out of the airwaves necessary to provide voice, text,
and Internet services [8]. To alleviate the problem, U.S. Congress authorized the
Federal Communications Commission (FCC) in 2012 to hold voluntary incentive
spectrum auctions for broadcast TV to turn into the FCC spectrum that they are not
using [9].

N. Lee, *Facebook Nation*, DOI: 10.1007/978-1-4614-5308-6_3,
© Springer Science+Business Media New York 2013

3.2 Location Tracking on iPhone and iPad

In April 2011, O'Reilly Radar reported that iPhones and 3G iPads are regularly recording the position of the device into a hidden file called "consolidated.db" [10]. The secret database file has been storing the locations (latitude-longitude coordinates) and time stamps, effectively tracking the history of movement of the iPhone and 3G iPad users for a year since iOS 4 was released in 2010. Although the data is unencrypted and unprotected on the mobile device, it is sent to Apple in an anonymous and encrypted form [11].

Apple has since learned to be more transparent and upfront with the customers. On the new iPad 2 setup procedure, user can enable or disable Location Services that allow Apple's Maps, Compass, Camera, Photos, Weather, Reminders, Safari, Find My iPad, and other apps to gather and use data indicating the user's approximate location. The user location is determined using GPS along with crowd-sourced Wi-Fi hotspot and cell tower locations. During the iPad 2 setup, Apple also asks the user for permission to automatically send diagnostics and usage data to Apple. Diagnostic data may include location information.

3.3 Carrier IQ

Not to be outdone by the iPhone location tracking software, the Carrier IQ software has been found on about 150 million cell phones including the iPhones, Android, BlackBerry, and Nokia phones [12]. On November 28, 2011, security researcher Trevor Eckhart posted a video on YouTube detailing hidden software installed on smartphones that secretly logs keypresses, SMS messages, and browser URLs [13]. Carrier IQ responded by saying "We're as surprised as anybody to see all that information flowing" [14] and went on to explain that the hidden software allows network operators to "better understand how mobile devices interact with and perform on their network" by uploads diagnostic data once per day, at a time when the device is not being used [15].

Amid the public outcry over the Carrier IQ tracking scandal, a lone columnist Matthew Miller at *ZDNet* concurred with Carrier IQ. He voiced his opinion: "A few years back I was asked if I could install software on my phone so that a company could track my usage patterns to improve services. I accepted and was paid something like $5 to $10 a month for each phone used and sending this data. … The media has made it more malicious than it really is and I am not concerned about my phone usage at all. … It sounds to me like the software is designed to BENEFIT consumers and is not being used to track and target you" [16].

Regardless of the real intention of Carrier IQ, the truth remains that no one wants some strangers or companies snooping around behind their backs. To know a person's location over time generates a great deal of information about the person. American Civil Liberties Union (ACLU) expounded on the severity of the issue,

"A person who knows all of another's travels can deduce whether he is a weekly church goer, a heavy drinker, a regular at the gym, an unfaithful husband, an out-patient receiving medical treatment, an associate of particular individuals or political groups—and not just one such fact about a person, but all such facts" [17].

Although AT&T, T-Mobile, Sprint, and Apple have said that they use the Carrier IQ software in line with their own privacy policies, the Federal Trade Commission and Federal Communications Commission have opened an investigation into the practices of Carrier IQ as possibly unfair or deceptive [18].

While secret location tracking and Carrier IQ are in the spotlight, they are just the tip of the iceberg that deserves scrutiny. As people are communicating via voice, photos, and videos on their cell phones, the phone companies are recording the metadata that travels with them, including locations, identify of the callers and receivers, amount of data transferred, and the costs of the transmissions [19]. Verizon keeps such data on their servers for 12 months, Sprint for 24 months, T-Mobile for 60 months, and AT&T for 84 months [20]. Most individuals have over 1 million pieces of personal information in the possession of cell phone companies over a 4 year span. This information is analyzed and sold to other companies that handle localized advertisements and offer personalized search results. According to *USA Today*, AT&T, Verizon, and BellSouth have also provided this information to the National Security Agency (NSA), which reportedly aims "to create a database of every call ever made within the nation's borders" [21].

3.4 Smartphone Data Collection Transparency

Under the increasing scrutiny from consumers to government officials, companies are learning to be more transparent with data collection practices, [22] and giving their customers the option to opt out of their data collection. For instance, Verizon Wireless sent their customers an email on November 17, 2011 about their new privacy programs—information the phone company collects and how the phone company uses the information:

1. Mobile Usage Information:

    a. Addresses of websites you visit when using our wireless service. These data strings (or URLs) may include search terms you have used.
    b. Location of your device ("Location Information").
    c. App and device feature usage.

2. Consumer Information:

    a. Information about your use of Verizon products and services (such as data and calling features, device type, and amount).
    b. Demographic and interest categories provided to us by other companies, such as gender, age range, sports fan, frequent diner, or pet owner ("Demographics").

The information is used by Verizon Wireless and shared with other companies to create business and marketing reports, as well as to make mobile ads more relevant for the consumers. As a consolation, Verizon Wireless assures their customers, "Under these new programs, we will not share outside of Verizon any information that identifies you personally." In addition, consumers are given a chance to opt out of the new privacy programs within 45 days of receiving the email notice.

We are witnessing more transparency in business practices today. In November 2011, two U.S. shopping malls (Promenade Temecula in California and Short Pump Town Center in Virginia) announced that they would track shoppers' movements throughout the premises by monitoring the signals from their cell phones [23]. The collected data monitored how the shopping crowds moved from store to store, and how long they lingered in any given shop. Consumers could opt out by turning off their cell phones. After an intervention from a U.S. Senator who raised privacy concerns, the shopping malls ceased their monitoring programs [24].

U.S. retailers including J.C. Penney and Home Depot are reportedly also considering using the same cell phone technology to track their customers [25]. Meanwhile, Neiman Marcus hosted its second in-store foursquare challenge in March 2012. For a chance to win a coffee table book, participating customers checked in using the location-based social site foursquare to a Neiman Marcus location on March 31 using their smartphones [26]. At Walgreens, customers checking into the drugstore via a foursquare or Facebook mobile app would receive e-flyers and e-coupons [27].

3.5 Always On

Some may say that smartphones are liberating and convenient anytime and anywhere, but others may vehemently disagree when "anytime and anywhere" becomes "all the time and everywhere." Social critic Andrew Keen declared in a February 2012 *CNN* article that our mobiles have become Frankenstein's monster: "As always, Mobile World Congress, the world's largest mobile telephone extravaganza, is being held in Barcelona this year. But it really should be held in Geneva, close to where Mary Shelley created Frankenstein. That's because, with our increasing addiction to our mobile phones, we are in danger of creating a monster that we are less and less able to control. … These hardware companies will articulate the benefits of their technology in terms of personal empowerment. But the real truth behind these increasingly intelligent devices is personal disempowerment" [28].

Keen's point of view is manifested in the mobile phone users' reactions to the April 2012 release of the photo-sharing Instagram app on Android devices. With 14 million users, Instagram was awarded the 2011 iPhone App of the Year [29]. A crossbreed between Facebook and Twitter, Instagram enables sharing and comments on friends' pictures as well as allows people to follow other users.

When the iPhone-exclusive app was made available for Android, an insidious tweet war broke out between iPhone and Android users. *CNET* associate editor Emily Dreyfuss remarked, "Which smartphone we own has begun to inform our identities. In our gadget-filled lives, our phones have become another way for us to organize ourselves into separate groups, to label each other as 'other' and 'apart.' Our tech has come to define us" [30].

Regardless of Android or iPhone, smartphone addiction can be a nuisance in public. In March 2012, a Philadelphia bus rider named Eric was so annoyed by loud phone calls on the bus that he decided to jam the cell phone signals using an electronic jammer [31]. "A lot of people are extremely loud, no sense of just privacy or anything. When it becomes a bother, that's when I screw on the antenna and flip the switch," said Eric before realizing that cell phone jamming is illegal in the United States. Apparently, many share Eric's sentiment. During the weekend after Eric appeared on NBC10 News, "cell phone jammer" became one of the top 10 searches on Google Trends [32]. Jokingly perhaps, controversial *CNN* contributor Bob Greene suggested bringing back the phone booths, or phoneless booths to be precise, in public places around the country for people to make their private cell phone calls [33]. No one believes that the idea would work. Stationary phone booths simply do not sit well with the consumer's need for mobility that makes cell phones so attractive in the first place.

3.6 Mobile Apps Privacy Invasion

Besides the carrier-installed apps on cell phones, there are plenty of utility and social media apps that users may download onto their cell phones. With an install base of over 1 million people, Path for iPhone and Android is one such free app that is "the smart journal that helps you share life with the ones you love" [34]. In February 2012, Arun Thampi in Singapore discovered that Path uploaded the entire iPhone address book (names, email addresses, phone numbers, etc.) to its servers without seeking permission from the user [35]. Within a couple of days, Path co-founder and CEO Dave Morin issued a public apology and released a new version of the app that asks the user for permission to upload the address book from iPhones and Android devices [36].

It turns out that Path is not alone. Twitter, a much bigger company with 140 million users as of March 2012 [37], also acknowledged in February that when a user taps the "Find friends" feature on its smartphone app, the company downloads the user's entire address book, including email addresses and phone numbers, and keeps the data on its severs for 18 months [38]. Unlike Path, Twitter did not apologize, and the company simplify clarified the language associated with Find Friends: Instead of "Scan your contacts," it would display "Upload your contacts" for iPhones and "Import your contacts" for Android devices in order to inform the users that the entire address book would be shared with Twitter.

Path and Twitter mobile apps have become emblematic of disrespect for individual privacy in the digital information age. It is conceivable that many more smartphone apps are collecting private information without the knowledge of the users. Facebook, Flickr, and other mobile apps have been accused of reading text messages and other personal information on their installed cell phones [39].

Security experts have demonstrated that Apple's iOS platform enables software developers to create mobile apps to upload all the photos, calendars, and record conversations on an iPhone [40]. Similarly, Google's Android platform also allows developers to build mobile apps to copy or steal photos and personal data from the Android phones of unwitting users [41].

3.7 Mobile Apps for Children

In September 2011, the Federal Trade Commission settled its first legal action against a mobile app developer in enforcement of the Children's Online Privacy Protection Act [42]. According to the consent decree, the iOS developer was fined $50,000 and ordered to start publishing information about the kinds of data collected via their apps and how that data is shared, to get parental consent before collecting any new data, and to delete all the data they had collected so far [43].

In February 2012, the Federal Trade Commission issued a staff report showing the results of a survey of mobile apps for children [44]. The survey reveals that neither the app stores nor the app developers provide adequate information for parents to determine what data is being collected from their children, how it is being shared, or who will have access to it. The report states, "[The FTC] staff was unable to determine from the promotion pages whether the apps collected any data at all—let alone the type of data collected, the purpose of the collection, and who collected or obtained access to the data. … Although the app store developer agreements require developers to disclose the information their apps collect, the app stores do not appear to enforce these requirements. This lack of enforcement provides little incentive to app developers to provide such disclosures and leaves parents without the information they need. … Ads running inside an app may incorporate various capabilities allowing the user to do things like directly call phone numbers or visit websites appearing in the ad" [45].

3.8 Android Market

As of October 2011, the Android Market has over 200,000 free and paid apps [46] available for 190 million activated Android devices around the world [47]. By December 2011, Google announced that 10 billion apps have been downloaded from the Android Market [48].

With the overwhelming number of new mobile apps, Google has fallen short of ensuring that the mobile apps are tested to be free of virus and suspicious behavior [49]. For example, DroidDream, a trojan rootkit exploit, was released in early March 2011 to the Android Market in the form of several free applications that ere, in many cases, pirated versions of existing priced apps [50]. This exploit allowed hackers to steal information such as IMEI and IMSI numbers, phone model, user ID, and service provider. Such information can be used in cloning a cell phone and using it illegally without the knowledge of the original owner. The exploit also installed a backdoor that allowed the hackers to download more code to the infected device.

In February 2012, Google revealed the use of "Bouncer" to automate the scanning of Android Market for potentially malicious software without requiring developers to go through an application approval process [51]. Google reported, "The [Bouncer] service has been looking for malicious apps in Market for a while now, and between the first and second halves of 2011, we saw a 40 % decrease in the number of potentially-malicious downloads from Android Market. This drop occurred at the same time that companies who market and sell anti-malware and security software have been reporting that malicious applications are on the rise" [52].

In the same report, Google also admitted, "no security approach is foolproof, and added scrutiny can often lead to important improvements." Indeed, while faking an SSL certificate enabled iOS developer Arun Thampi watch the transmitted data and expose the Path app, it would be more difficult if the data was encrypted without SSL.

3.9 Apple Store

Apple Store has over 500,000 free and paid apps [53] available for more than 100 million iPhone users worldwide [54]. As of July 2011, the Apple Store has reached 15 billion downloads [55]. In June 2012, Apple CEO Tim Cook announced at the annual Worldwide Developers Conference, "The App Store now has 400 million accounts—the largest number of accounts with credit cards anywhere on the Internet. Some 650,000 apps are now available. ... Customers have now downloaded an astounding 30 billion apps" [56].

Despite Apple's assertion of its tight quality control over its App Store, a scam Pokemon game reached number 2 on Apple's App Store charts in February 2012 and raked in $10,000 before it was pulled [57]. The 99-cent "Pokemon Yellow" game crashed as soon as it opened. The debacle called into question Apple's approval process, let alone ensuring that the mobile apps have a privacy policy in place. The consensus in the developer community believes that "overworked Apple reviewers, with thousands of apps waiting in the approval queue, likely don't test apps too thoroughly at first. But once they gain popularity, the Apple team gives them a closer look" [58].

On February 15, 2012, Apple announced that it will start requiring mobile apps to obtain explicit permission from iPhone to iPad users before the apps can collect and store information about user's personal contacts. "Apps that collect or transmit a user's contact data without their prior permission are in violation of our guidelines," Apple spokesman Tom Neumayr told *CNN* [59].

3.10 Facebook App Center

On May 9, 2012, Facebook unveiled Facebook App Center, a clearinghouse for social apps on the web and on smartphones. Facebook's Aaron Brady wrote in the Developer Blog, "For the over 900 million people that use Facebook, the App Center will become the new, central place to find great apps like Draw Something, Pinterest, Spotify, Battle Pirates, Viddy, and Bubble Witch Saga. ... The App Center is designed to grow mobile apps that use Facebook—whether they're on iOS, Android or the mobile web" [60].

The Facebook App Center opened in June 2012 with over 600 apps [61]. Featuring mobile and web apps, the App Center gives users personalized recommendations and lets them browse through the apps that their friends are using.

A Facebook app has access to plenty of user information on Facebook, which includes the user's name, profile pictures, username, user ID, networks, friend list, gender, age range, and locale as well as the user's email address and birthday on some occasions [62]. This makes a malicious Facebook app much more dangerous.

Back in January 2011, Facebook had disabled a feature that gave app developers access to user's address and phone number [63]. It remains to be seen whether the Facebook App Center will do a better job than the Google Android Market and Apple Store in screening their apps.

References

1. IDC. (February 6, 2012). Smartphone Market Hits All-Time Quarterly High Due To Seasonal Strength and Wider Variety of Offerings, According to IDC. IDC Press Release. http://www.idc.com/getdoc.jsp?containerId=prUS23299912
2. ITU Telecom World. (2011). International Telecommunication Union. The World in 2011. ICT Facts and Figures. http://www.itu.int/ITU-D/ict/facts/2011/material/ICTFactsFigures2011.pdf
3. Chansanchai, Athima. (August 31, 2011). MSNBC. 70 percent of US-owned smartphones are iPhones or Androids. http://technolog.msnbc.msn.com/_news/2011/08/31/7538973−70-percent-of-us-owned-smartphones-are-iphones-or-androids
4. comScore. (February 23, 2012). comScore Releases the "2012 Mobile Future in Focus" Report. comScore Press Release. http://www.comscore.com/Press_Events/Press_Releases/2012/2/comScore_Releases_the_2012_Mobile_Future_in_Focus_Report
5. Nielsen. (May 7, 2012). America's New Mobile Majority: a Look at Smartphone Owners in the U.S. Nielsen Wire. http://blog.nielsen.com/nielsenwire/online_mobile/who-owns-smartphones-in-the-us/

6. Qumu. (July 11, 2011). Harris Poll - Mobile Video in the Workplace. Qumu Press Release. http://www.qumu.com/news/news-releases/419-qumu-harris-survey.html

7. The Telegraph. (February 16, 2012). Rise in nomophobia: fear of being without a phone. The Telegraph. http://www.telegraph.co.uk/technology/news/9084075/Rise-in-nomophobia-fear-of-being-without-a-phone.html

8. Goldman, David. (February 21, 2012). Sorry, America: Your wireless airwaves are full. CNN Money. http://money.cnn.com/2012/02/21/technology/spectrum_crunch/

9. Shapiro, Gary. (February 22, 2012). Congress Gets It on Wireless Broadband. Forbes. http://www.forbes.com/sites/garyshapiro/2012/02/22/congress-gets-it-on-wireless-broadband/

10. Allan, Alasdair. (April 20, 2011). Got an iPhone or 3G iPad? Apple is recording your moves. O'Reilly Radar. http://radar.oreilly.com/2011/04/apple-location-tracking.html

11. Apple Inc. (April 27, 2011). Apple Q&A on Location Data. Apple Press Info. http://www.apple.com/pr/library/2011/04/27Apple-Q-A-on-Location-Data.html

12. Kravets, David. (November 29, 2011). Researcher's Video Shows Secret Software on Millions of Phones Logging Everything. Wired. http://www.wired.com/threatlevel/2011/11/secret-software-logging-video/

13. Eckhart, Trevor. (November 28, 2011). Carrier IQ Part #2. YouTube. http://www.youtube.com/watch?v=T17XQI_AYNo

14. Goldman, David. (December 2, 2011). Carrier IQ: 'We're as surprised as you'. CNN. http://money.cnn.com/2011/12/02/technology/carrier_iq/index.htm

15. Schroeder, Stan. (December 13, 2011). Understanding Carrier IQ: The Most Detailed Explanation So Far. Mashable. http://mashable.com/2011/12/13/understanding-carrier-iq/

16. Miller, Matthew. (December 2, 2011). Carrier IQ is good for you, so why get so spun up? ZDNet. http://www.zdnet.com/blog/cell-phones/carrier-iq-is-good-for-you-so-why-get-so-spun-up/6983

17. ACLU. (April 6, 2012). Cell Phone Location Tracking Public Records Request. American Civil Liberties Union. http://www.aclu.org/protecting-civil-liberties-digital-age/cell-phone-location-tracking-public-records-request

18. Horwitz, Sari. (December 14, 2011). Carrier IQ faces federal probe into allegations software tracks cellphone data. The Washington Post. http://www.washingtonpost.com/business/economy/feds-probing-carrier-iq/2011/12/14/gIQA9nCEuO_story.html

19. Popova, Maria. (January 10, 2012). Network: The Secret Life of Your Personal Data, Animated. Brain Pickings. http://www.brainpickings.org/index.php/2012/01/10/network-michael-rigley/

20. Rigley, Michael. (January 8, 2012). Network. Viemo. http://vimeo.com/34750078

21. Cauley, Leslie. (May 11, 2006). NSA has massive database of Americans' phone calls. USA Today. http://www.usatoday.com/news/washington/2006−05−10-nsa_x.htm

22. Knight, Kristina. (December 29, 2011). Expert Advice: Be more transparent with data collection practices. BizReport. http://www.bizreport.com/2011/12/expert-advice-be-more-transparent-with-data-collection-pract.html

23. Censky, Annalyn. (November 22, 2011). Malls track shoppers' cell phones on Black Friday. CNN. http://money.cnn.com/2011/11/22/technology/malls_track_cell_phones_black_friday/index.htm

24. Censky, Annalyn. (November 28, 2011). Malls stop tracking shoppers' cell phones. CNN. http://money.cnn.com/2011/11/28/news/economy/malls_track_shoppers_cell_phones/index.htm

25. U.S. Senator Charles E. Schumer. (November 28, 2011). Schumer Reveals: This Holiday Season, New Technology Could Be Tracking Shoppers' Movements In Shopping Centers Through Their Cell Phones; Calls For Mandatory Opt-In Before Retailers Are Allowed To Track Shoppers' Movements. U.S. Senate. http://schumer.senate.gov/Newsroom/record.cfm?id=334975

26. Dostal, Erin. (March 29, 2012). Neiman Marcus hosts bigger foursquare challenge. Direct Marketing News. http://www.dmnews.com/neiman-marcus-hosts-bigger-foursquare-challenge/article/234277/

27. Patel, Kunur. (February 8, 2012). At Walgreens, a Mobile Check-in Acts Like a Circular. Advertising Age. http://adage.com/article/digital/walgreens-a-mobile-check-acts-a-circular/232584/

28. Keen, Andrew. (February 28, 2012). How our mobiles became Frankenstein's monster. CNN. http://www.cnn.com/2012/02/28/opinion/mobile-frankenstein-keen/index.html

29. The Instagram Team. (December 8, 2011). Instagram. http://blog.instagram.com/post/13928169232/were-the-2011-app-store-iphone-app-of-the-year

30. Dreyfuss, Emily. (April 4, 2012). http://news.cnet.com/8301-1035_3-57409388-94/iphone-users-android-is-ruining-our-instagram-club/

31. Dress, Ed; Hairston, Harry. (March 5, 2012). Rider Jams Cell Phones on SEPTA Buses. NBC10 Philadelphia. http://www.nbcphiladelphia.com/news/local/Rider-Annoyed-by-Calls-Jams-Phones-on-Septa-Bus-140966733.html

32. Gross, Doug. (March 6, 2012). Why the interest in illegal cell-phone jammers? CNN. http://www.cnn.com/2012/03/05/tech/mobile/cell-phone-jammer/index.html

33. Greene, Bob. (March 24, 2012). Time for a new kind of phone booth. CNN. http://www.cnn.com/2012/03/24/opinion/greene-phone-booths/index.html

34. Path. (Retrieved February 14, 2012). About Path. https://path.com/about

35. Thampi, Arun. (February 8, 2012). Path uploads your entire iPhone address book to its servers. McLovin. http://mclov.in/2012/02/08/path-uploads-your-entire-address-book-to-their-servers.html

36. Morin, Dave. (February 8, 2012). We are sory. Path Blog. http://blog.path.com/post/17274932484/we-are-sorry

37. Whittaker, Zack. (March 21, 2012). Twitter turns six: 140 million users, 340 million tweets daily. ZDNet. http://www.zdnet.com/blog/btl/twitter-turns-six-140-million-users-340-million-tweets-daily/72123

38. Sarno, David. (February 14, 2012). Twitter stores full iPhone contact list for 18 months, after scan. Los Angeles Times. http://www.latimes.com/business/technology/la-fi-tn-twitter-contacts-20120214,0,5579919.story

39. Whittaker, Zack. (February 26, 2012). Facebook, Flickr, others accused of reading text messages. ZDNet. http://www.zdnet.com/blog/btl/facebook-flickr-others-accused-of-reading-text-messages/70237

40. Weintraub, Seth. (February 15, 2012). Apple's iOS problem: Contacts uploading is just the tip of the iceberg. Apps can upload all your photos, calendars or record conversations. 9to5Mac: Apple Intelligence. http://9to5mac.com/2012/02/15/apples-ios-problem-contacts-uploading-is-just-the-tip-of-the-iceberg-apps-can-upload-all-your-photos-calendars-or-record-conversations/

41. Chen, Brian X.; Bilton, Nick. (March 1, 2012). Et Tu, Google? Android Apps Can Also Secretly Copy Photos. The New York Times. http://bits.blogs.nytimes.com/2012/03/01/android-photos/?pagewanted=all

42. Gahran, Amy. (February 21, 2012). Parents need more privacy info about kids' apps, feds say. CNN. http://www.cnn.com/2012/02/21/tech/mobile/privacy-info-kids-apps/index.html

43. Federal Trade Commission. (August 15, 2011). Mobile Apps Developer Settles FTC Charges It Violated Children's Privacy Rule. Federal Trade Commission News. http://ftc.gov/opa/2011/08/w3mobileapps.shtm

44. Federal Trade Commission. (February 16, 2012). FTC Report Raises Privacy Questions About Mobile Applications for Children. Federal Trade Commission News. http://ftc.gov/opa/2012/02/mobileapps_kids.shtm

45. Federal Trade Commission. (February 2012). Mobile Apps for Kids: Current Privacy Disclosures are Disappointing. Federal Trade Commission Staff Report. http://www.ftc.gov/os/2012/02/120216mobile_apps_kids.pdf

46. Barra, Hugo. (May 10, 2011). Google Blog. http://googleblog.blogspot.com/2011/05/android-momentum-mobile-and-more-at.html

47. Melanson, Donald. (October 13, 2011). Engadget. Google announces Q3 earnings: $9.72 billion in revenue, $2.73 billion net income, 40 million Google+ users. http://www.engadget.com/2011/10/13/google-announces-q3-earnings−9−72-billion-revenue/
48. Panzarino, Matthew (December 6, 2011). Android Market hits 10B apps downloaded, now at 53 apps per device, 10c app sale to celebrate. The Next Web. http://thenextweb.com/google/2011/12/06/android-market-hits−10b-apps-downloaded-now-at−1b-a-month−10c-app-sale-to-celebrate/
49. Vaughan-Nichols, Steven J. (July 12, 2011). Google needs to clean up its Android Market malware mess. ZDNet. http://www.zdnet.com/blog/open-source/google-needs-to-clean-up-its-android-market-malware-mess/9219
50. Gingrich, Aaron. (March 6, 2011). The Mother Of All Android Malware Has Arrived: Stolen Apps Released To The Market That Root Your Phone, Steal Your Data, And Open Backdoor. Android Police. http://www.androidpolice.com/2011/03/01/the-mother-of-all-android-malware-has-arrived-stolen-apps-released-to-the-market-that-root-your-phone-steal-your-data-and-open-backdoor/
51. Chen, Brian X. (February 3, 2012). Google's 'Bouncer' Service Aims to Toughen Android Security. The New York Times. http://bits.blogs.nytimes.com/2012/02/03/google-bouncer-android/
52. Lockheimer, Hiroshi. (February 2, 2012). Android and Security. Google Mobile Blog. http://googlemobile.blogspot.com/2012/02/android-and-security.html
53. Apple. (Retrieved February 20, 2012). Apple App Store. http://www.apple.com/ipodtouch/from-the-app-store/
54. Warren, Christina. (March 2, 2011). Apple: 100 Million iPhones Sold. Mashable. http://mashable.com/2011/03/02/100-million-iphones/
55. Elmer-DeWitt, Philip (July 11, 2011). Apple users buying 61 % more apps, paying 14 % more per app. CNN. http://tech.fortune.cnn.com/2011/07/11/apple-users-buying−61-more-apps-paying−14-more-per-app/
56. Griggs, Brandon; Gross, Doug. (June 11, 2012). Apple announces high-res laptops, a smarter Siri. CNN. http://www.cnn.com/2012/06/11/tech/innovation/apple-wwdc-keynote/index.html
57. Pepitone, Julianne. (February 21, 2012). Fake Pokemon app becomes Apple App Store bestseller. CNN. http://money.cnn.com/2012/02/21/technology/pokemon_yellow/index.htm
58. Goldman, David. (April 27, 2012). A look behind Apple's App Store curtain. CNN Money. http://money.cnn.com/2012/04/27/technology/carriercompare-apple/index.htm
59. Gross, Doug. (February 15, 2012). Apple: Apps need 'explicit approval' before collecting user contacts. CNN. http://www.cnn.com/2012/02/15/tech/mobile/apple-user-contacts/index.html
60. Brady, Aaron. (May 9, 2012). Introducing the App Center. Facebook Developers. https://developers.facebook.com/blog/post/2012/05/09/introducing-the-app-center/
61. Wyndowe, Matt. (June 7, 2012). App Center: A New Place to Find Social Apps. Facebook Newsroom. http://newsroom.fb.com/News/App-Center-A-New-Place-to-Find-Social-Apps−175.aspx
62. Facebook. (Retrieved May 10, 2012). What does an app do with my information? Facebook Help Center. http://www.facebook.com/help/?faq=187333441316612
63. Segall, Laurie. (January 18, 2011). Facebook halts phone number sharing feature. CNN Money. http://money.cnn.com/2011/01/18/technology/facebook_privacy/index.htm

Chapter 4
Consumer Privacy in the Age of Big Data

America needs a robust privacy framework that preserves consumer trust in the evolving Internet economy while ensuring the Web remains a platform for innovation, jobs, and economic growth.
—U.S. Commerce Secretary Gary Locke (December 2010)

I will include easier access to one's own data in the new rules. People must be able to easily take their data to another provider or have it deleted if they no longer want it to be used.
—E.U. Justice Commissioner Viviane Reding (January 2012)

4.1 Oil of the Digital Age–Personal Information for Sale

No matter how we safeguard our privacy by turning off our cell phones, avoiding the use of in-vehicle apps, deactivating Facebook accounts, opting out on all data collections, and evading Google and Bing's social searches, there are still plenty of public records that are obtainable by anyone who is willing to pay. Websites such as Intelius (whose trademark is "Live in the know") displays the age, past cities of residence, and names of the relatives on any person whom we search for. This and several other websites also sell public records including full name, date of birth, phone, address history, marriage/divorce records, property ownership, lawsuits, convictions, and other public information for a nominal fee [1].

The need-to-know maxim and the respect for personal privacy have largely been abandoned in the Internet era and commercial age. Journalists from *News of the World*, for example, paid police for information and hacked into the phone messages of celebrities, a missing 13-year-old murder victim, and the grieving families of dead soldiers [2]. The illegal and immoral tactics brought down the 168 year-old tabloid *News of the World* in July 2011.

In late 2011, security software company Symantec commissioned Scott Wright of Security Perspectives Inc. to conduct an experiment codenamed The Symantec Smartphone Honey Stick Project [3]. In the experiment, they intentionally lost 50 smartphones in high-traffic public places in five major cities: New York City, Washington D.C., Los Angeles, San Francisco, and Ottawa, Canada. Only 50 % of the people who found one of the "lost" smartphones made an attempt to return it. That statistics alone may not be too startling, but the following key findings are more disturbing [4]:

N. Lee, *Facebook Nation*, DOI: 10.1007/978-1-4614-5308-6_4,
© Springer Science+Business Media New York 2013

- 96 % of lost smartphones were accessed by the finders of the devices.
- 89 % attempted to access personal mobile apps or data.
- 72 % attempted to access a private photos app.
- 60 % attempted to access social networking accounts and personal email.
- 53 % accessed a "HR Salaries" file.
- 57 % accessed a "Saved Passwords" file.

  And the scariest of them all:
- 43 % attempted to access an online banking app on the lost smartphone.

Andrew Grove, co-founder and former CEO of Intel Corporation, offered his thoughts on Internet privacy in an *Esquire* magazine interview reported on May 1, 2000: "Privacy is one of the biggest problems in this new electronic age. At the heart of the Internet culture is a force that wants to find out everything about you. And once it has found out everything about you and two hundred million others, that's a very valuable asset, and people will be tempted to trade and do commerce with that asset. This wasn't the information that people were thinking of when they called this the information age" [5].

A February 12, 2012 article on *The New York Times* reads, "Facebook's pending initial public offering gives credence to the argument that personal data is the oil of the digital age. The company was built on a formula common to the technology industry: offer people a service, collect information about them as they use that service and use that information to sell advertising" [6].

Data mining in the age of big data is a lucrative business. Using applied statistics and artificial intelligence to analyze complex datasets, companies repackage our private information for their own use as well as selling it to make a profit.

In a February 2012 report on data services for U.S. insurance companies, Martina Conlon and Thuy Nguyen wrote, "In addition to claims, credit, consumer and cost information, we can now collect information on buying behaviors, geospatial and location information, social media and internet usage, and more. Our electronic trails have been digitized, formatted, standardized, analyzed and modeled, and are up for sale. As intimidating as this may sound to the individual, it is a great opportunity for insurers to use this data and insight to make more informed and better business decisions" [7].

While Facebook, Google, and other online businesses collect information about us and make billions of dollars from selling our data, some startup companies believe that we can better organize our own information online in a secure "data vault" and we may even be compensated for sharing that information [8]. However, given the plentiful information from public records and data scraping on the web, much of our information is already available to big businesses.

4.2 Consumer Privacy Bill of Rights

American Civil Liberties Union (ACLU) is a strong advocate for privacy: "Americans shouldn't have to choose between new technology and keeping their personal information private. Protections for online privacy are justified and necessary, and the government must help draw boundaries to ensure that Americans' privacy stays intact in the Digital Age" [9].

Since 2010, the Obama administration has been pushing for an online privacy bill of rights. Commerce Secretary Gary Locke said in a prepared statement, "America needs a robust privacy framework that preserves consumer trust in the evolving Internet economy while ensuring the Web remains a platform for innovation, jobs, and economic growth. Self-regulation without stronger enforcement is not enough. Consumers must trust the Internet in order for businesses to succeed online" [10].

In February 2012, the White House unveiled its proposed "Consumer Privacy Bill of Rights," a voluntary set of guidelines for Internet companies to provide transparency, security, and user control of their data. The Consumer Privacy Bill of Rights calls for [11]:

1. Individual Control: Consumers have a right to exercise control over what personal data companies collect from them and how they use it.
2. Transparency: Consumers have a right to easily understandable and accessible information about privacy and security practices.
3. Respect for Context: Consumers have a right to expect that companies will collect, use, and disclose personal data in ways that are consistent with the context in which consumers provide the data.
4. Security: Consumers have a right to secure and responsible handling of personal data.
5. Access and Accuracy: Consumers have a right to access and correct personal data in usable formats, in a manner that is appropriate to the sensitivity of the data and the risk of adverse consequences to consumers if the data is inaccurate.
6. Focused Collection: Consumers have a right to reasonably limit the amount of personal data that companies collect and retain.
7. Accountability: Consumers have a right to have personal data handled by companies with appropriate measures in place to assure they adhere to the Consumer Privacy Bill of Rights.

Although the White House fell short of making the Consumer Privacy Bill of Rights mandatory, Jon Leibowitz, Chairman of the Federal Trade Commission, acknowledged that, "it's not the end, it may not be the beginning of the end, but it's a very important step forward" [12].

On April 2, 2012, John M. Simpson, Privacy Project Director at Consumer Watchdog, called on the U.S. Department of Commerce to offer legislation to implement the Consumer Privacy Bill of Rights. Simpson said, "Calls for action in policy papers are easy. The test of commitment is to translate high-minded principles like the Consumer Privacy Bill of Rights into real legislative language" [13].

4.3 California's Online Privacy Protection Act

On February 22, 2012, California's Office of the Attorney General has gotten agreements from Apple, Google, Microsoft, Amazon, Hewlett-Packard, and Research In Motion to improve privacy protections on mobile apps. California's Online Privacy Protection Act, one of the strongest consumer privacy laws in the country, will now be applied to mobile apps.

"This will give more information to the consumers so they understand how their personal and private information can be used and potentially manipulated," said California Attorney General Kamala Harris. "Most mobile apps make no effort to inform users. ... Consumers should be informed what they're giving up before they download the app" [14].

4.4 European Union's "Right to be Forgotten" Law

In January 2012, the European Commission proposed a comprehensive reform of the EU's 1995 Data Protection Directive in order to strengthen online privacy rights and to unify the implementation of privacy law in the 27 EU Member States [15]. European Union Justice Commissioner Viviane Reding unveiled details of the proposed "Right to be Forgotten" law at the January 2012 Digital Life Design (DLD) conference in Munich. Reding outlined her proposal:

"First, people need to be informed about the processing of their data in simple and clear language. Internet users must be told which data is collected, for what purposes and how long it will be stored. They need to know how it might be used by third parties. They must know their rights and which authority to address if those rights are violated.

"Second, whenever users give their agreement to the processing of their data, it has to be meaningful. In short, people's consent needs to be specific and given explicitly.

"Thirdly, the reform will give individuals better control over their own data. I will include easier access to one's own data in the new rules. People must be able to easily take their data to another provider or have it deleted if they no longer want it to be used" [16].

Professor Jeffrey Rosen at The George Washington University wrote in *Stanford Law Review* of how the EU law could affect Facebook and Google: "The right to be forgotten could make Facebook and Google, for example, liable for up to two percent of their global income if they fail to remove photos that people post about themselves and later regret, even if the photos have been widely distributed already" [17].

4.5 A Response to Zero Privacy

In response to Scott McNealy's statement, "You have zero privacy anyway. Get over it" [18], *PC World* columnist Stephen Manes wrote, "He's right on the facts, wrong on the attitude. It's undeniable that the existence of enormous databases on everything from our medical histories to whether we like beef jerky may make our lives an open book, thanks to the ability of computers to manipulate that information in every conceivable way. But I suspect even McNealy might have problems with somebody publishing his family's medical records on the Web, announcing his whereabouts to the world, or disseminating misinformation about his credit history. Instead of 'getting over it,' citizens need to demand clear rules on privacy, security, and confidentiality" [19].

References

1. Intelius. (Retrieved January 25, 2012). Intelius Facts. *Intelius.* http://www.intelius.com/corp/intelius-facts
2. The Associated Press. (July 8, 2011). U.K. phone hacking leads to arrest of ex-Cameron aide. *The Associated Press.* http://www.cbc.ca/news/world/story/2011/07/08/phone-hacking-cameron.html
3. Haley, Kevin. (March 9, 2012). Introducing the Symantec Smartphone Honey Stick Project. *Symantec Official Blog.* http://www.symantec.com/connect/blogs/introducing-symantec-smartphone-honey-stick-project
4. Symantec Corporation. (2012). The Symantec Smartphone Honey Stick Project. http://www.symantec.com/content/en/us/about/presskits/b-symantec-smartphone-honey-stick-project.en-us.pdf
5. Sager, Mike. (May 1, 2000). What I've Learned: Andy Grove. *Esquire Magazine.* http://www.esquire.com/features/what-ive-learned/learned-andy-grove-0500
6. Brustein, Joshua. (February 12, 2012). Start-Ups Seek to Help Users Put a Price on Their Personal Data. *The New York Times.* http://www.nytimes.com/2012/02/13/technology/start-ups-aim-to-help-users-put-a-price-on-their-personal-data.html
7. Conlon, Martina; Nguyen, Thuy. (February 2012). Data Services for US Insurers 2012 (Q1). *Novarica.* http://www.novarica.com/data_services_nmn2012/
8. Gross, Doug. (February 27, 2012). Manage (and make cash with?) your data online. *CNN.* http://www.cnn.com/2012/02/24/tech/web/owning-your-data-online/index.html
9. ACLU. (Retrieved May 29, 2012). Internet Privacy. *American Civil Liberties Union.* http://www.aclu.org/technology-and-liberty/internet-privacy
10. U.S. Department of Commerce Office of Public Affairs. (December 16, 2010). Commerce Department Unveils Policy Framework for Protecting Consumer Privacy Online While Supporting Innovation. *United States Department of Commerce.* http://www.commerce.gov/

news/press-releases/2010/12/16/commerce-department-unveils-policy-framework-protecting-consumer-priv

11. CNNMoneyTech. (February 23, 2012). Consumer Privacy Bill of Rights. *CNN Money.* http://money.cnn.com/2012/02/22/technology/bill_of_rights_privacy/index.htm

12. Goldman, David. (February 23, 2012). White House pushes online privacy bill of rights. *CNN Money.* http://money.cnn.com/2012/02/23/technology/privacy_bill_of_rights/index.htm

13. Consumer Watchdog. (April 2, 2012). Consumer Watchdog Calls on Commerce Department to Offer Privacy Legislation; Says Proposed "Multi-Stakeholder Process" Must Be Fair, Transparent and Credible. *MarketWatch.* http://www.marketwatch.com/story/consumer-watchdog-calls-on-commerce-department-to-offer-privacy-legislation-says-proposed-multi-stakeholder-process-must-be-fair-transparent-and-credible-2012-04-02

14. Mills, Elinor. (February 22, 2012). Tech firms agree to privacy protections for mobile apps. *CNET.* http://news.cnet.com/8301-1009_3-57382965-83/tech-firms-agree-to-privacy-protections-for-mobile-apps/

15. European Commission. (January 25, 2012). Commission proposes a comprehensive reform of the data protection rules. *European Commission Newsroom.* http://ec.europa.eu/justice/newsroom/data-protection/news/120125_en.htm

16. Rooney, Ben. (January 23, 2012). Reding Details Sweeping Changes to EU Data Laws. *The Wall Street Journal.* http://blogs.wsj.com/tech-europe/2012/01/23/reding-details-sweeping-changes-to-e-u-data-laws/

17. Rosen, Jeffrey. (February 13, 2012). The Right to Be Forgotten. *Stanford Law Review.* http://www.stanfordlawreview.org/online/privacy-paradox/right-to-be-forgotten

18. Sprenger, Polly. (January 26, 1999). Sun on Privacy: 'Get Over It.' *Wired.* http://www.wired.com/politics/law/news/1999/01/17538

19. Manes, Stephen. (April 18, 2000). Private Lives? Not Ours! *PC World.* http://www.pcworld.com/article/16331/private_lives_not_ours.html

Part III
The Rise of Facebook Nation

Chapter 5
Twitter: A World of Immediacy

The pen is mightier than the sword.
—Edward Bulwer-Lytton (1839)

Say all you know and say it without reserve.
Blame not the speaker but be warned by his words.
—Chinese Maxims

Freedom of expression is essential.
—Twitter's @biz and @amac (January 2011)

5.1 The Pen is Mightier Than the Sword

Edward Bulwer-Lytton coined the metonymic adage "the pen is mightier than the sword" in 1839 [1]. In the ancient historical past, however, the sword had exerted considerable influences on the pen. Qin Shi Huang (秦始皇), the first emperor of the unified China in 221 B.C., outlawed and burned many books in order to enforce the uniformity of the Chinese language [2]. His censorship succeeded in imposing one basic written language throughout China, even though there still exists today hundreds of spoken Chinese dialects that sound like entirely different languages [3].

For some periods of time in the Catholic history, Lay Catholics were discouraged from directly reading the Bible for fear that they would misinterpret the Scripture. The printing press and Protestant Reformation in the 16th century resulted in the proliferation of the Bible and the freedom of new Bible translations.

In George Orwell's novel *Nineteen Eighty-Four*, the totalitarian regime deliberately promotes Newspeak, an impoverished language without any words or possible constructs that describe the ideas of freedom and rebellion. "We're cutting the language down to the bone", said philologist Syme. "It's a beautiful thing, the destruction of words" [4].

When I was in college, a saleswoman tried her best to sell me a set of Encyclopedia Britannica that contains all of the above historical events and literary commentaries. After 244 years, Encyclopedia Britannica decided to cease production of its iconic multi-volume print book sets, making the 2010 version its final edition. The company would instead focus on digital encyclopedia and educational tools. "The print set is an icon", said Britannica president Jorge Cauz. "But it's an icon that doesn't do justice to how much we've changed over the years. Updating dozens of books every two years now seems so pedestrian. The younger generation consumes data differently now, and we want to be there" [5].

N. Lee, *Facebook Nation*, DOI: 10.1007/978-1-4614-5308-6_5,

For the same reason of the behavioral change in consumers' data consumption, AT&T in April 2012 ditched the Yellow Pages directories that used to go out to about 150 million homes and businesses in 22 states [6]. It was inevitable, since major cities such as Seattle and San Francisco were moving to ban the unsolicited delivery of Yellow Pages in order to reduce waste [7].

In the digital age, information is abundant with immediacy and is easily accessible anytime and anywhere. In June 2012, Google.org launched the Endangered Language Project in attempt to save 3,054 dying languages around the world [8]. Project managers Clara Rivera Rodriguez and Jason Rissman said, "Documenting the 3,000+ languages that are on the verge of extinction is an important step in preserving cultural diversity, honoring the knowledge of our elders, and empowering our youth" [9].

Thanks to the Internet, words can travel at the speed of light, and no amount of censorship can stop the flow of information. Although the online social networking site Twitter said in January 2012 that it would delete users' tweets in countries that require it, Twitter would still keep those deleted tweets visible to the rest of the world [10].

5.2 Citizen Journalists

On May 1, 2011, Sohaib Athar was coding some software after midnight in Pakistan when he heard the annoying noise outside his apartment. Athar tweeted [11]:

"Helicopter hovering above Abbottabad at 1AM (is a rare event)"
"Go away helicopter—before I take out my giant swatter"
"A huge window shaking bang here in Abbottabad. I hope its [sic] not the start of something nasty".

Little did Athar know that he was live tweeting the secret U.S. military raid by the SEAL Team Six that killed Osama bin Laden at a hideout compound in Abbottabad, Pakistan. He went on to photograph bin Laden's compound a mile away from his home, and interviewed neighbors living in that area. Athar was soon hailed as the accidental "citizen journalist," the man who live-tweeted Osama's death. His 750 or so Twitter followers on May 1, 2011 have swelled to over 73,000 in March 2012 [12].

Steve Myers, managing editor of Poynter.org, said at the 2012 South by Southwest Interactive festival, "In an era when mobile-phone owners walk around with a video camera in their pocket at all times and tools like Twitter, Facebook and YouTube make broadcasting the results quick and simple, people like Athar can turn into journalists without even knowing it" [13].

CNN's sports columnist Terence Moore agreed, "New media have created a slew of investigative reporters among average citizens through personal blogs, Twitter, YouTube, talk-show radio, cellphone cameras and recorders, Facebook and fan websites" [14].

#	Name (Screen Name)	Location	URL	Followers	Following	Updates	Joined
1.	Lady Gaga (ladygaga)	New York, NY	http://www.ladygaga.com	26007375	139740	1472	51 months ago
2.	Justin Bieber (justinbieber)	The World	http://www.youtube.com/justin	22633320	122673	15885	39 months ago
3.	Katy Perry (katyperry)	Cloud 9	http://www.katyperry.com	20439970	96	3954	40 months ago
4.	Rihanna (rihanna)	LA BABY!	http://www.rihannanow.com	19755165	768	5297	
5.	Britney Spears (britneyspears)	Los Angeles, CA	http://facebook.com/britneyspe...	17251919	416624	1445	45 months ago
6.	Shakira (shakira)	Barranquilla	http://www.shakira.com	16264760	44	1402	35 months ago
7.	Barack Obama (BarackObama)	Washington, DC	http://www.barackobama.com	16021092	677643	4104	64 months ago
8.	Kim Kardashian (KimKardashian)	where I'm meant to be...	http://kimkardashian.celebuzz...	14611925	167	11514	39 months ago
9.	Taylor Swift (taylorswift13)		http://twitter.com/taylorswift13	14530645	75	1516	42 months ago
10.	YouTube (YouTube)	San Bruno, CA	http://youtube.com	13148607	412	5410	66 months ago

Fig. 5.1 Top 10 Twitterholics based on followers (as of May 31, 2012)—courtesy of Twitaholic.com

5.3 A World of Immediacy

Twitter, in particular, has created a world of immediacy. Twitter's mission is "to instantly connect people everywhere to what is most meaningful to them". For this to happen, Twitter expresses in its official blog, "freedom of expression is essential. Some Tweets may facilitate positive change in a repressed country, some make us laugh, some make us think, some downright anger a vast majority of users. We don't always agree with the things people choose to tweet, but we keep the information flowing irrespective of any view we may have about the content" [15].

In 2011, Apple integrated Twitter into its iOS 5, making Twitter the default social graph and social network on iPhone, iPod Touch, and iPad [16]. As a direct result of the iOS integration, Twitter has enjoyed a 25 % increase in monthly signups [17]. In October 2011, Twitter CEO Dick Costolo announced at the Web 2.0 Summit that there were 250 million tweets every day [18].

The Super Bowl XLVI on February 5, 2012 set a new record for simultaneous tweeting in the United States, with 12,233 tweets a second at its peak during the final three minutes of the game [19]. Super Bowl XLVI host city Indianapolis built the first-ever "social media command center" for a team of strategists, analysts, and techies to monitor the fan conversation via Facebook and Twitter from a 2,800-square-foot space downtown [20].

The U.S. record, though impressive as is, was dwarfed by the world record of 25,088 tweets per second during the December 9, 2011 television screening in Japan of the animated film *Castle in the Sky* directed by Hayao Miyazaki [21]. The Japanese viewers were challenged to use social networks to say the spell "balse" together with the two characters at the climax of the film. It was a resounding success in audience engagement.

Not only does Twitter provide up-to-the-minute personal news to keep us informed of the people and events that we are following, it also helps spread information among would-be followers. NASCAR driver Brad Keselowski, for example, tweeted about the explosion and fire caused by a crash during the Daytona 500 in February 2012. Some of his fans re-tweeted the accident. Within two hours, Keselowski gained more than 100,000 new followers on Twitter [22].

5.4 Prevalence of Twitter

Twitter is so prevalent that even President Barack Obama, First Lady Michele Obama, Dalai Lama, and Pope Benedict XVI are tweeting [23]. Since Obama joined Twitter on March 5, 2007, his popularity has grown to 16 million followers on May 31, 2012 as Obama was ranked #7 on twitaholic.com in terms of number of followers, behind Shakira (#6) and above Kim Kardashian (#8) [24] (See Fig. 5.1).

Twitter is not off-limits to dead celebrities whose legends live on. Among the verified authentic accounts on Twitter are Marilyn Monroe, Elvis Presley, and Michael Jackson [25]. Behind Twitter's Marilyn Monroe, for instance, is a marketing firm who purchased the rights to all things Marilyn Monroe.

In June 2009, Twitter began to institute the verification of accounts in order to establish authenticity of identities on Twitter and to reduce user confusion [26]. Verified accounts display a blue "Verified Badge" on their Twitter bio. However, this program is currently closed to the public as of March 2012. Twitter only verifies some trusted sources from their advertisers, partners, and high-profile personalities [27].

Twitter's concoction of the hashtag as a short and handy identifier is becoming as important as Tim Berners-Lee's creation of web URLs for companies and politicians alike. For example, during the 2012 Super Bowl XLVI, eight out of 42 TV advertisers included a Twitter hashtag in their commercials [28]. And shortly after Clint Eastwood's Super Bowl commercial was shown to more than 111 million Americans watching the game, White House communications director Dan Pfeiffer sent a tweet: "Saving the America Auto Industry: Something Eminem and Clint Eastwood can agree on" [29].

Twitter has become the most prevalent tool for spreading news and getting feedback in real-time. Immediately following President Obama's State of the Union address on January 24, 2012, an online panel from the White House answered questions submitted by citizens via Twitter (#WHChat and #SOTU), Google+, Facebook, and the in-person audience of "tweetup" participants [30]. A "tweetup" is an event where people who tweet come together to meet in person. On March 24, 2012, a piece of a debris from a Russian Cosmos satellite passed dangerously close to the International Space Station hosting the Expedition 30 crew [31]. NASA tweeted at 11:29 PM on March 23 as the event was unfolding: "The six crew members are in their Soyuz spacecraft and will close the hatches to isolate themselves from #ISS until the debris passes" [32]. Such was the quintessential real-life, real-time drama via Twitter.

5.5 Advertisements on Twitter

Advertisers seem to have caught Twitter fever as well. Twitter CEO Dick Costolo said in October 2010, "We feel like we've cracked the code on a new form of advertising" [33]. Businesses pay a fee to have their "promoted tweets" appear near the top of a user's feed. Some brands are using the hashtag to engage consumers in constant conversation and to spread the news through retweeting by the more proactive customers to their friends. Politicians pay Twitter to help shape opinions. Social media consultant Vincent Harris said, "The beauty of Twitter's ad unit is that it's the best rapid-response tool that exists in politics right now" [34]. In February 2012, Twitter announced that it would also start sending promoted tweets to mobile phones [35].

Nevertheless, freedom of speech on Twitter carries its own risk for advertisers. In January 2012, McDonald's launched a marketing campaign with the innocuous hashtag #McDStories as part of a larger campaign to share stories about the farmers who grow McDonald's food and their commitment to fresh produce and meats. Within two hours after the launch, however, McDonald's pulled down #McDStories due to the critics of McDonald's tweeting stories of food poisoning, weight gain, and poor employee hygiene. In defense of the Twitter campaign fiasco, McDonald's social media director Rick Wion wrote, "McDonald's is mentioned on Twitter more than 250,000 times each week, it is very easy to cherry pick negative (or positive) tweets that are not representative of the overall picture. Bottom line—the negative chatter wasn't as much as today's headlines have lead [*sic*] people to believe. This happened almost a week ago and the hashtag is only living on because many media outlets are using the chance to push a provocative and tweetable headline" [36].

5.6 Creative Uses of Twitter

Given the skyrocketing volume of public tweets, analytical tools are being developed to comb through the tweets to gauge public opinions. Developed by the *Los Angeles Times*, IBM, and the USC Annenberg Innovation Lab, the Oscar Senti-Meter uses language recognition technology to analyze the positive, negative, and neutral opinions about the 2012 Academy Awards race [37]. When the Academy announced the best actor nominations, Jean Dujardin of *The Artist* scored the highest in positive sentiment while George Clooney of *The Descendants* had the highest volume of tweets. The Oscar Senti-Meter analysis seemed to concur that Dujardin beat Clooney and won the best actor in a leading role. MIT Professor Erik Brynjolfsson explained, "Data measurement is the modern equivalent of the microscope. Google searches, Facebook posts and Twitter messages, for example, make it possible to measure behavior and sentiment in fine detail and as it happens" [38].

With more than 250 million tweets per day as of October 2011, people around the world are co-authoring the equivalent of a 12.5 million-page book every day (assuming that an average tweet has 100 characters and an average book page contains roughly 2,000 characters). That is a gigantic book, to say the least.

Speaking of books, author Neil Gaiman and BBC Audiobooks America in 2009 used Twitter for interactive storytelling [39]. In May 2012, Pulitzer Prize winner Jennifer Egan released her new novel *Black Box* on Twitter in a series of 140-character bursts every minute for the hour between 8 and 9 p.m. daily from May 24 to June 2 [40]. This is just the beginning of brave new possibilities empowered by Twitter in specific and social media in general.

References

1. Bulwer-Lytton, Edward. (1839). *Richelieu; Or the Conspiracy: A Play in Five Acts.* (second ed.). London.
2. Ren, Changhong; Wu, Jingyu. (2000). *Rise and Fall of the Qin Dynasty.* Asiapac Books Pte Ltd.
3. Wikipedia. (Retrieved March 15, 2012). List of varieties of Chinese. *Wikipedia.* http://en.wikipedia.org/wiki/List_of_varieties_of_Chinese
4. Orwell, George. (1949). *1984.* Part 1, Chapter 5. http://www.george-orwell.org/1984/4.html
5. Pepitone, Julianne. (March 13, 2012). Encyclopedia Britannica to stop printing books. *CNN.* http://money.cnn.com/2012/03/13/technology/encyclopedia-britannica-books/index.htm
6. Segall, Laurie. (April 9, 2012). AT&T ditches the Yellow Pages. *CNN Money.* http://money.cnn.com/2012/04/09/technology/ATT-sells-yellow-pages/index.htm
7. Gonzales, Richard. (May 16, 2011). San Francisco Moves To Ban Yellow Pages. *NPR.* http://www.npr.org/2011/05/16/136368752/san-francisco-moves-to-ban-yellow-pages
8. Google.org. (Retrieved June 28, 2012). The Endangered Languages. A project to support language preservation and documentation around the world. http://www.endangeredlanguages.com/
9. Hopkins, Curt. (June 21, 2012). Google launches Endangered Language Project. *Ars technica.* http://arstechnica.com/science/2012/06/google-launches-endangered-language-project/
10. CNN Wire Staff. (January 28, 2012). Twitter to delete posts if countries request it. *CNN.* http://www.cnn.com/2012/01/27/tech/twitter-deleting-posts/index.html
11. Gross, Doug. (May 2, 2011). Twitter user unknowingly reported bin Laden attack. *CNN.* http://www.cnn.com/2011/TECH/social.media/05/02/osama.twitter.reports/index.html
12. Sohaib Athar twitter stats. (Retrieved March 15, 2012). *Twitter Counter.* http://twittercounter.com/reallyvirtual
13. Gross, Doug. (March 12, 2012). Tweeting Osama's death: The accidental citizen journalist. *CNN.* http://www.cnn.com/2012/03/10/tech/social-media/twitter-osama-death/index.html
14. Moore, Terence. (April 13, 2012). Bobby Petrino and social media prove a bad mix. *CNN.* http://www.cnn.com/2012/04/13/us/petrino-social-media/index.html
15. @biz; @amac. (January 28, 2011). The Tweets Must Flow. *Twitter Blog.* http://blog.twitter.com/2011/01/tweets-must-flow.html
16. Warren, Christina. (October 12, 2011). How Twitter Integrates With iOS 5. *Mashable.* http://mashable.com/2011/10/12/twitter-ios-5-integration/
17. Rao, Leena. (December 8, 2011). Twitter's Monthly Signups By 25 Percent. *TechCrunch.* http://techcrunch.com/2011/12/08/apple-ios-5-integration-boosted-twitter-signups-by-25-percent/

18. Sloan, Paul. (October 17, 2011). Twitter CEO: 250 million tweets a day – now what? *CNet*. http://news.cnet.com/8301-1023_3-20121714-93/twitter-ceo-250-million-tweets-a-day-now-what/

19. Twitter. (Retrieved February 6, 2012). Twitter Tweets. https://twitter.com/twitter

20. Laird, Sam. (January 23, 2012). Super Bowl gets social-media command center. *CNN*. http://www.cnn.com/2012/01/23/tech/social-media/super-bowl-social-media-center/index.html

21. Evangelista, Benny. (December 14, 2011). Social spelling during "Castle in the Sky" rerun smashes Twitter record. *San Francisco Chronicle*. http://blog.sfgate.com/techchron/2011/12/14/mass-spelling-during-castle-in-the-sky-rerun-smashes-twitter-record/

22. Laird, Sam. (February 28, 2012). NASCAR driver tweets from car, gains 100,000 followers. *CNN*. http://www.cnn.com/2012/02/28/tech/social-media/nascar-driver-tweetsrace/-index.html

23. Gross, Doug. (February 2, 2012). The pope's on Twitter? 10 unlikely tweeters. *CNN*. http://www.cnn.com/2012/02/02/tech/social-media/unlikely-twitter-users/index.html

24. Twitaholic. (Retrieved June 1, 2012). Stats & Rankings for Barack Obama. *Twitaholic*. http://twitaholic.com/barackobama/

25. Farrell, Maureen. (February 8, 2012). Marilyn Monroe 'officially' joins Twitter. *CNN*. http://money.cnn.com/2012/02/08/markets/marilyn_monroe_twitter/index.htm

26. Cashmore, Pete. (June 11, 2009). Twitter Launches Verified Accounts. *Mashable*. http://mashable.com/2009/06/11/twitter-verified-accounts-2/

27. Twitter. (Retrieved March 20, 2012). *Twitter FAQs about Verified Accounts*. http://support.twitter.com/groups/31-twitter-basics/topics/111-features/articles/119135-about-verified-accounts

28. Stone, Brad. (March 1, 2012). Twitter, the Startup That Wouldn't Die. *Bloomberg Businessweek*. http://www.businessweek.com/articles/2012-03-01/twitter-the-startup-that-wouldnt-die

29. Monroe, Bryan. (February 7, 2012). Were politics buried inside Eastwood's 'Halftime' commercial? *CNN*. http://www.cnn.com/2012/02/06/politics/eastwood-ad-politics/index.html

30. Curtis, Colleen. (January 20, 2012). State of the Union 2012: We Want to Hear From You. *The White House Blog*. http://www.whitehouse.gov/blog/2012/01/20/state-union-2012-we-want-hear-you

31. CNN Wire Staff. (March 24, 2012). Space junk forces astronauts into escape capsules on International Space Station. *CNN*. http://www.cnn.com/2012/03/24/tech/tech-space-station-debris/index.html

32. NASA. (March 23, 2012). *Twitter*. http://twitter.com/#!/NASA/status/183440480854491136

33. Miller, Claire Cain; Vega, Tanzina. (October 10, 2010). After Building an Audience, Twitter Turns to Ads. *The New York Times*. http://www.nytimes.com/2010/10/11/business/media/11twitter.html

34. Stone, Brad. (March 1, 2012). Twitter, the Startup That Wouldn't Die. *Bloomberg Businessweek*. http://www.businessweek.com/articles/2012-03-01/twitter-the-startup-that-wouldnt-die#p4

35. Greenfield, Rebecca. (March 2, 2012). Twitter Is Growing Up! (No It's Not). *The Atlantic Wire*. http://www.theatlanticwire.com/technology/2012/03/twitter-growing-no-its-not/49416/

36. Hsu, Tiffany. (January 23, 2012). McDonald's #McDStories Twitter marketing effort goes awry. *Los Angeles Times*. http://www.latimes.com/business/money/la-fi-mo-mcdonalds-twitter-fail-20120123,0,7220567.story

37. Gettell, Oliver. (February 26, 2012). Oscars 2012: Streep and Clooney top the Twitter charts, volume-wise. *Los Angeles Times*. http://latimesblogs.latimes.com/movies/2012/02/oscars-2012-streep-and-sentimeter-clooney-top-the-twitter-charts-volume-wise.html

38. Lohr, Steve. (February 11, 2012). The Age of Big Data. *The New York Times*. http://www.nytimes.com/2012/02/12/sunday-review/big-datas-impact-in-the-world.html

39. Dybwad, Barb. (October 13, 2009). Neil Gaiman + Twitter = Interactive Storytelling. *Mashable*. http://mashable.com/2009/10/13/neil-gaiman-twitter-audiobook/

40. Gross, Doug. (May 24, 2012). Pulitzer winner to publish new story, one tweet at a time. *CNN*. http://www.cnn.com/2012/05/24/tech/social-media/new-yorker-story-twitter/index.html

Chapter 6
Generation C in the Age of Big Data

*Digital omnivores consume content everywhere they go across
every device whether it's their PC, tablet or smartphone.*
—ComScore's communications analyst Sarah Radwanick
(February 2012)

*No activity is too big or too small to share. You don't have to
'Like' a movie. You just watch a movie.*
—Facebook co-founder and CEO Mark Zuckerberg
(September 2011)

6.1 Digital Omnivores and Generation C

In October 2011, Internet marketing research company comScore coined the term
"digital omnivores" to describe the new generation of digital media consumers,
especially those living in the United States, the United Kingdom, Singapore,
Japan, and Australia [1].

"Today's digital media environment is rapidly evolving, driven by the proliferation of devices people use to consume content both at home, at work and on the
go," the comScore report affirmed. "With smartphones, tablets and other connected devices, consumers have become digital omnivores—not just because of
the media they consume, but also in *how* they consume it. Cross-platform consumption has created a vastly different digital landscape, and it is one that requires
insight into both the individual usage of devices as well as the nature of their
complementary use" [2]. For example, comScore's study shows that during the
day, a higher share of digital content is consumed over computers and mobile
phones due to workplace and daily activity; whereas during the nighttime hours,
tablets have the highest usage as the consumers are winding down at home on the
couch or bed.

"Digital omnivores consume content everywhere they go across every device
whether it's their PC, tablet or smartphone", said ComScore communications
analyst Sarah Radwanick. "We will see a spotlight on these consumers during
multimedia extravaganzas like the Summer Olympics and the presidential election
where (they) need to stay plugged into the latest news and events" [3].

Nielsen and NM Incite issued a report in 2012 titled "State of the Media: U.S.
Digital Consumer Report, Q3-Q4 2011." The report says, "Born sometime
between the launch of the VCR and the commercialization of the Internet,
Americans 18–34 are redefining media consumption with their unique embrace of

N. Lee, *Facebook Nation*, DOI: 10.1007/978-1-4614-5308-6_6,
© Springer Science+Business Media New York 2013

all things digital. … This group—dubbed 'Generation C' by Nielsen—is taking their personal connection—with each other and content—to new levels, new devices and new experiences like no other age group [4].

In the world overflowing with digital information, the digital omnivores devour both nutritious information as well as empty information calories. Clay Johnson, author of *The Information Diet,* warns that "just as we have grown morbidly obese on sugar, fat, and flour—so, too, have we become gluttons for texts, instant messages, emails, RSS feeds, downloads, videos, status updates, and tweets" [5].

Indeed, some people are starting to feel overwhelmed and reacting to information overload. A recent survey commissioned by Citi Investment analyst Mark Mahaney in 2012 indicated that 71 % of Netflix subscribers are "not at all interested" in "seeing what [their] Facebook friends have watched on Netflix" [6]. If this sentiment prevails among Facebook users, it will eventually undermine the idea of "frictionless sharing" on Facebook. For the time being, nonetheless, more and more data is being generated and consumed every second in the modern age of big data.

6.2 Big Data Research and Development Initiative

Global market intelligence firm IDC estimates that the amount of data is growing at 50 % a year, or more than doubling every two years [7]. Much of the data are online in the form of text, images, and videos on the Internet, from personal data to public records and everything in between.

At the World Economic Forum in January 2012, a report titled *Big Data, Big Impact* declared data a new class of economic asset, like currency or gold. It reads, "The amount of data in the world is exploding—large portion of this comes from the interactions over mobile devices being used by people in the developing world—people whose needs and habits have been poorly understood until now" [8].

In an email dated March 27, 2012, the Office of Science and Technology Policy stated, "Researchers in a growing number of fields are generating extremely large and complicated data sets, commonly referred to as big data. A wealth of information may be found within these sets, with enormous potential to shed light on some of the toughest and most pressing challenges facing the Nation. To capitalize on this unprecedented opportunity to extract insights and make new connections across disciplines, we need better tools and programs to access, store, search, visualize, and analyze these data. To maximize this historic opportunity—and in support of recommendations from the President's Council of Advisors on Science and Technology—the Obama Administration is launching a Big Data Research and Development Initiative, coordinated by the White House Office of Science and Technology Policy and supported by several Federal departments and agencies".

On March 29, 2012, the Obama administration announced more than $200 million in funding for "Big Data Research and Development Initiative" [9]. The first wave of agency commitments includes National Science Foundation,

National Institutes of Health, Department of Energy, U.S. Geological Survey, and Department of Defense (including DARPA) [10].

Not to imply that DARPA intends to resurrect the Total Information Awareness program, the DARPA-proposed Anomaly Detection at Multiple Scales (ADAMS) program is one of several key technologies that are directly applicable to Total Information Awareness. And Information Innovation Office has replaced the Information Awareness Office [11]. According to the White House document, ADAMS "addresses the problem of anomaly detection and characterization in massive data sets. In this context, anomalies in data are intended to cue collection of additional, actionable information in a wide variety of real-world contexts. The initial ADAMS application domain is insider threat detection, in which anomalous actions by an individual are detected against a background of routine network activity" [12].

6.3 Big Data in Public Health and Economics

Centers for Disease Control and Prevention (CDC) is also a beneficiary of the Big Data Research and Development Initiative. CDC's BioSense program "tracks health problems as they evolve and provides public health officials with the data, information and tools they need to better prepare for and coordinate responses to safeguard and improve the health of the American people" [13].

The predictive power of big data has shown great promise in public health forecasting. For example, Google Flu Trends uses aggregated Google search data to estimate current flu activity around the world in near real-time [14]. A spike in Google search requests for terms like "flu symptoms" and "flu treatments" often predicts quickly and correctly an increase of flu patients in a monitored region. In comparison, emergency room reports usually lag behind patient visits by two weeks or more.

In economic development and forecasting, *Forbes* has been advising CEOs and IT people to take an inventory of all the data that their business produces, and turn the data into new revenue streams [15]. For instance, MasterCard has built an advisory business using its core credit card purchasing data to help merchants analyze consumer-buying trends [16].

6.4 Big Data in Facebook and Google

Facebook and Google are experts in harnessing big data with Internet advertising. According to the Facebook IPO S-1 filing statement, Facebook's 2011 advertising revenues were $3.15 billion [17]. Meanwhile, Google's 2011 advertising revenues were a striking $36.53 billion according to Google's Income Statement Information [18].

Since Facebook renamed its "Privacy Policy" to "Data Use Policy" in September 2011, Sarah A. Downey, an analyst at the online privacy company Abine, said, "This is a significant acknowledgement that Facebook is focused on data collection, data storage and data sales, because that's where they make their money" [19].

In promoting "frictionless sharing," Mark Zuckerberg suggested that people would benefit from publishing more data and letting computer algorithms sort out what is important. "No activity is too big or too small to share", Zuckerberg said. "You don't have to 'Like' a movie. You just watch a movie" [20].

How does Facebook determine what is important to the users? Facebook CTO Bret Taylor disclosed, "Facebook programmers have created a mathematical algorithm that will examine the types of posts a person has chosen to give prominent placement to on his or her profile. ... Whether food, movies or exercises logged into Facebook, the site will try to predict what you're most passionate about based on past choices, similar to how the system determines its news feed based partly on the people you contact most often" [21]. The official Facebook site also describes, "Just like the search engines we all know and love, Facebook utilise a number of algorithms as part of their system for sharing information. EdgeRank is the algorithm which determines who sees what, basically—it determines what social objects (i.e. updates, posts, photos, actions etc.) you will see in your Facebook news feed" [22].

Google also uses mathematical algorithms such as PageRank to determine the relevance of the search results it gives back to the users [23]. In addition, artificial intelligence techniques are being used to construct a giant "knowledge graph" to better understand the context of search terms and to return more in-depth search results to the questions posted by the users. Google Fellow and Senior Vice President Amit Singhal revealed in 2012, "Google is building a huge, in-house understanding of what an entity is and a repository of what entities are in the world and what should you know about those entities. ... The huge knowledge graph of interconnected entities and their attributes now has north of 200 million entities. ... Google is building the infrastructure for the more algorithmically complex search of tomorrow" [24].

Google began rolling out knowledge graph in May 2012 to users in the U.S [25]. While knowledge graph is helpful in optimizing search for everyone, Google also personalizes its search results based on the user's preferences determined by cookies, IP addresses, and signing in with a Google account. Google explains, "When the web first started, it was a set of static pages that looked the same for everybody. Nowadays, the web has become even more useful because websites can know something about you that helps them guess what you would like to view. For example, they can remember whether you want them in English or French, can suggest books or movies you might enjoy based on what you've viewed in the past, and can store your delivery address ready for your next purchase" [26].

Using computer algorithms and our past online activities, Facebook and Google are guessing what we want to find, to see, and to like. The results can be helpful but at the same time can be limiting the possibilities of us discovering new ideas and new interests on the Internet. Michael Rigley made an interesting argument in his video titled *Network:* "Ad servers assign an individual a demographic, based on their digital histories. Once assigned, individualized information is deployed to the user. Location data is filtered into intrusive localized advertising. Facebook 'Likes' transform into custom Walmart ads, and search engine results are narrowed to a limited scope. The global Internet becomes the personal Internet. And information ceases to be information at all" [27].

Google's mission is to "organize the world's information and make it universally accessible and useful" [28]. The phrase "Google it!" has become a universal slang. In searching for information in the modern world of big data, it would be a great disservice to users if Google were to filter its search results through colored glasses. University of Virginia professor Siva Vaidhyanathan considered Google insidious and questioned the search giant's influence on our society: "What is the nature of the transaction between Google's computer algorithms and its millions of human users? Are we heading down a path toward a more enlightened age, or are we approaching a dystopia of social control and surveillance?" [29].

References

1. Donovan, Mark. (November 15, 2011). The Rise of Digital Omnivores. *comScore.* http://blog.comscore.com/mdonovan.html
2. comScore. (October 2011). Digital Omnivores: How Tablets, Smartphones and Connected Devices are Changing U.S. Digital Media Consumption Habits. *comScore.* http://www.comscore.com/Press_Events/Presentations_Whitepapers/2011/Digital_Omnivores
3. Snider, Mike. (February 24, 2012). Analysis details digital lives in USA. *USA Today.* http://www.usatoday.com/tech/news/story/2012-02-23/nielsen-digital-consumers/53228194/1
4. The Nielsen Company. (February 2012). State of the Media: U.S. Digital Consumer Report, Q3-Q4 2011. *The Nielsen Company.* http://www.nielsen.com/content/dam/corporate/us/en/reports-downloads/2012%20Reports/Digital-Consumer-Report-Q4-2012.pdf
5. Johnson, Clay A. (January 2012). *The Information Diet: A Case for Conscious Consumption.* O'Reilly Media, California.
6. Kafka, Peter. (March 13, 2012). Please Don't Tell Me What You're Watching on Netflix. *AllThingsD.* http://allthingsd.com/20120313/please-dont-tell-me-what-youre-watching-on-netflix/
7. Lohr, Steve. (February 11, 2012). The Age of Big Data. *The New York Times.* http://www.nytimes.com/2012/02/12/sunday-review/big-datas-impact-in-the-world.html
8. The World Economic Forum. (2012). Big Data, Big Impact: New Possibilities for International Development. *WEF.* http://www.weforum.org/reports/big-data-big-impact-new-possibilities-international-development
9. Kalil, Tom. (March 29, 2012). Big Data is a Big Deal. *The White House.* http://www.whitehouse.gov/blog/2012/03/29/big-data-big-deal
10. Office of Science and Technology Policy. Executive Office of the President. (March 29, 2012). Obama Administration Unveils "Big Data" Initiative: Announces $200 Million In New R&D Investments. *The White House.* http://www.whitehouse.gov/sites/default/files/microsites/ostp/big_data_press_release.pdf
11. Information Innovation Office. (Retrieved April 3, 2012). *DARPA.* http://www.darpa.mil/Our_Work/I2O/

12. Executive Office of the President. (March 29, 2012). Big Data Across the Federal Government. *The White House.* http://www.whitehouse.gov/sites/default/files/microsites/ostp/big_data_fact_sheet_final_1.pdf

13. CDC BioSense Program. (February 8, 2012). *Centers for Disease Control and Prevention.* CDC BioSense Program. (February 8, 2012). *Centers for Disease Control and Prevention.* http://www.cdc.gov/biosense/

14. Google.org. (Retrieved March 25, 2012). Explore flu trends around the world. *google.org Flu Trends.* http://www.google.org/flutrends/

15. Upbin, Bruce. (April 18, 2011). The Data Explosion and the Networked Enterprise. *Forbes.* http://www.forbes.com/sites/bruceupbin/2011/04/18/the-data-explosion-and-the-networked-enterprise/2/

16. Bughin, Jacques; Chui, Michael; Manyika, James. (September 22, 2010). McKinsey Column: Clouds, big data, and smart. *Financial Times.* http://www.ft.com/cms/s/0/97701346-c273-11df-956e-00144feab49a.html

17. Facebook, Inc. (February 1, 2012). Form S-1. Registration Statement. *United States Securities and Exchange Commission.* http://www.sec.gov/Archives/edgar/data/1326801/000119312512034517/d287954ds1.htm

18. Google. (Retrieved March 23, 2012). Google's Income Statement Information. *Google Investor Relations.* http://investor.google.com/financial/tables.html

19. Segall, Laurie. (March 23, 2012). Facebook strips 'privacy' from new 'data use' policy explainer. *CNN Money.* http://money.cnn.com/2012/03/22/technology/facebook-privacy-changes/index.htm

20. Milian, Mark. (January 18, 2012). Some apps steer clear of Facebook auto-publish tool. *CNN.* http://www.cnn.com/2012/01/18/tech/social-media/facebook-pandora/index.html

21. Milian, Mark. (January 19, 2012). 60 apps launch with Facebook auto-share. *CNN.* http://www.cnn.com/2012/01/18/tech/social-media/facebook-actions-apps/index.html

22. Tamar. (November 1, 2011). Facebook's EdgeRank, in a nutshell. *Facebook.* http://www.facebook.com/notes/tamar/facebooks-edgerank-in-a-nutshell/284652911558091

23. Google. (Retrieved March 25, 2012). Technology overview. *Google.* http://www.google.com/about/company/tech.html

24. Ulanoff, Lance. (February 13, 2012). Google Knowledge Graph Could Change Search Forever. *Mashable.* http://mashable.com/2012/02/13/google-knowledge-graph-change-search/

25. Gross, Doug. (May 16, 2012). Google revamps search, tries to think more like a person. *CNN.* http://www.cnn.com/2012/05/16/tech/web/google-search-knowledge-graph/index.html

26. Google. (Retrieved March 25, 2012). Your data on the web. *Google Privacy Center.* https://www.google.com/goodtoknow/data-on-the-web/

27. Rigley, Michael. (January 8, 2012). Network. *Vimeo.* http://vimeo.com/34750078

28. Google. (Retrieved March 25, 2011). *Google Company Mission.* http://www.google.com/about/company/

29. Vaidhyanathan, Siva. (March 8, 2011). *The Googlization of Everything: (And Why We Should Worry).* University of California Press.

Chapter 7
Privacy Breaches

Quite simply, it was a mistake.
—Google's Senior VP Alan Eustace (May 2010)

This is a bug, which we plan to fix shortly.
—Apple Press Info (April 2011)

We are sorry. We made a mistake.
—Path co-founder and CEO Dave Morin (February 2012)

7.1 Google Street View

Google Street View is a great service in conjunction with online maps and driving directions [1]. It allows Google Map users explore places through 360 ° panoramic street-level imagery. It is handy for planning a trip to a new restaurant or an unfamiliar neighborhood. Since 2007, Google has employed Street View cars, trikes, snowmobiles, and trolleys to take pictures in the streets, national parks, university campuses, sports stadiums, and museums around the world [2]. (See Fig. 7.1).

Many of the pictures taken contain unsuspecting individuals and private vehicles who happened to be at the right place and the right time. It would be impractical for a moving Google Street View car to issue a privacy warning such as: "By your presence in this area, you acknowledge that you have been informed that you may be photographed as part of the Google Street View. Further, by your presence here, you grant your irrevocable permission for your likeness and mannerisms to be included in the Google Street View without compensation and/or credit, and for such data to be exploited in any and all media worldwide in all perpetuity. If you do not wish to be photographed or appear in the Google Street View, please leave this immediate area. Thank you for your cooperation."

Since Google intentionally blurs the individual faces and license plates, no one has raised serious objections. The useful information for the millions outweighs the privacy of the few. That was the case, until April 2010 when the Data Protection Authority (DPA) in Hamburg, Germany raised concerns about exactly what information Google Street View cars collected as they drove the streets.

At first, Google confirmed taking photos, WiFi network information, and 3-D building imagery, but denied collecting any payload data sent over the WiFi networks [3]. However, in May 2010, Google made a stunning admission that for over three years, its camera-toting Street View cars have inadvertently collected snippets of private information that people send over unencrypted WiFi networks [4].

N. Lee, *Facebook Nation*, DOI: 10.1007/978-1-4614-5308-6_7,
© Springer Science+Business Media New York 2013

Fig. 7.1 A Google street view car—Courtesy of Enrique Bosquet http://bosquetphotography.com/

In October 2010, Google admitted to accidentally collecting and storing entire e-mails, URLs, and passwords from unsecured WiFi networks with its Street View cars in more than 30 countries, including the United States, Canada, Mexico, some of Europe, and parts of Asia [5]. Alan Eustace, Google's senior vice president of engineering and research, wrote in the Google Public Policy Blog, "It's clear from those inspections that while most of the data is fragmentary, in some instances entire emails and URLs were captured, as well as passwords. We want to delete this data as soon as possible, and I would like to apologize again for the fact that we collected it in the first place [6]."

In 2011, Apple and Carrier IQ joined Google in their privacy blunders. Apple, Carrier IQ, and Google all blamed their mistakes on software bugs. Were they really bugs or were they company-sanctioned Easter eggs?

7.2 Google Easter Eggs in Disguise

Software based Easter eggs are intentionally hidden messages or unusual program behaviors that occur in response to some user inputs or external factors. Easter eggs are normally harmless and humorous. *The Easter Egg Archive*, www.eeggs.com, uncovers many instances of Easter eggs [7].

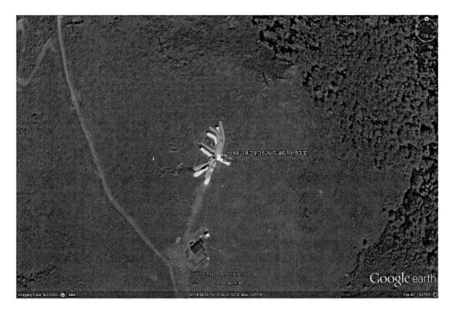

Fig. 7.2   An easter egg on Google earth. Courtesy of Google and Tele Atlas

Google is well known for Easter eggs. If we search for the words "zerg rush" in Google, an army of O's would descend on the page, devour each search result one by one, and form the red/golden letters "GG" (Good Game) no matter how hard we manage to click on some O's to eradicate them [8]. In Google Earth, for another example, flying to the coordinates 44°14'39.35"N 7°46'11.53"E surprisingly reveals a pink bunny rabbit overlaid on the Satellite map. (See Fig. 7.2).

However, some software Easter eggs are more like a variant of Trojan horse, worms, adware, or spyware. Anti-virus software is useless against them because they are not malware per se, but they hide secret functionalities from their users. Indeed, uncovered Easter eggs are often disguised as software bugs by their makers.

Let us examine Google's Street View privacy blunder. Google wrote in its official blog on May 14, 2010:

> … It's now clear that we have been mistakenly collecting samples of payload data from open (i.e. non-password-protected) WiFi networks, even though we never used that data in any Google products. However, we will typically have collected only fragments of payload data because: our cars are on the move; someone would need to be using the network as a car passed by; and our in-car WiFi equipment automatically changes channels roughly five times a second. … So how did this happen? *Quite simply, it was a mistake.* In 2006 an engineer working on an experimental WiFi project wrote a piece of code that sampled all categories of publicly broadcast WiFi data. A year later, when our mobile team started a project to collect basic WiFi network data like SSID information and MAC addresses using Google's Street View cars, *they included that code in their software—although the project leaders did not want, and had no intention of using, payload data* [9].

It is a common software engineering practice to reuse pieces of software code from other projects in order to expedite the development of the current project. Repurposing well-written and thoroughly tested codes generally improves system performance and reduces software bugs. Nevertheless, no trained engineer would blindly reuse a piece of software code without reading its functional specification, examining its inline documentation, and performing unit testing. Google engineers are some of the world's brightest and most experienced software developers who pride themselves in writing efficient and clean code. It is mind-blogging to imagine that the Google engineers would leave extra and unnecessary code in the software by mistake, and the software ends up consuming more CPU cycles and taking up more data storage.

To read between the lines of the Google blog, "although the project leaders did not want" does not necessarily mean that "the upper management at Google did not want." Moreover, "quite simply, it was a mistake" might have meant, "quite simply, it was a mistake to get caught."

Five months later after the initial discovery, Google wrote in its official blog on October 22, 2010:

> … Finally, I would like to take this opportunity to update one point in my May blog post. When I wrote it, *no one inside Google had analyzed in detail the data we had mistakenly collected,* so we did not know for sure what the disks contained. Since then a number of external regulators have inspected the data as part of their investigations (seven of which have now been concluded). It's clear from those inspections that while most of the data is fragmentary, in some instances entire emails and URLs were captured, as well as passwords. *We want to delete this data as soon as possible, and I would like to apologize again for the fact that we collected it in the first place.* We are mortified by what happened, but confident that these changes to our processes and structure will significantly improve our internal privacy and security practices for the benefit of all our users [10].

Google admitted, "no one inside Google had analyzed in detail the data we had mistakenly collected" and yet they knew with certainty that "an engineer working on an experimental WiFi project wrote a piece of code that sampled all categories of publicly broadcast WiFi data." It is unfathomable that no one inside Google cared to examine the code or at least talk to the engineer who wrote the code in order to determine what type of data could have been collected.

In April 2012, the Federal Communications Commission delivered a subpoena to the Google software engineer who developed the code for downloading information from the WiFi routers. However, Engineer Doe invoked his Fifth Amendment right to avoid self-incrimination. As a result, the FCC conceded that "significant factual questions … cannot be answered" [11].

Google released the FCC order document after Consumer Watchdog filed a Freedom of Information Act request for an uncensored version with the FCC. The document reveals, "As early as 2007 or 2008, Street View team members had wide access to Engineer Doe's design document and code in which the plan to intercept 'payload data' was spelled out. One engineer reviewed the code line by line, five engineers pushed the code into Street View cars and Engineer Doe specifically told two engineers working on the project, including a senior manager about collecting 'payload data' [12]."

Google's code of conduct is "Don't be evil [13]." It only makes sense to expect Google to practice what it preaches, and to come clean about its engineers and managers.

7.3 Apple Software Bugs

Back in 2008, some users had noticed Apple's Trojan app installer that sneaked in the Safari app installation during iTunes and QuickTime software upgrade [14]. It did not create much attention, unlike the 2011 discovery of the Apple iPhone location tracking app that secretly stores up to a year's worth of location data on the users' iPhones.

Apple addressed the location data issue on its company website on April 27, 2011: [15]

> **Question:** People have identified up to a year's worth of location data being stored on the iPhone. Why does my iPhone need so much data in order to assist it in finding my location today?
> **Answer:** This data is not the iPhone's location data—it is a subset (cache) of the crowd-sourced Wi-Fi hotspot and cell tower database which is downloaded from Apple into the iPhone to assist the iPhone in rapidly and accurately calculating location. *The reason the iPhone stores so much data is a bug we uncovered and plan to fix shortly* (see Software Update section below). *We don't think the iPhone needs to store more than seven days of this data.*
> **Question:** When I turn off Location Services, why does my iPhone sometimes continue updating its Wi-Fi and cell tower data from Apple's crowd-sourced database?
> **Answer:** *It shouldn't. This is a bug, which we plan to fix shortly* (see Software Update section below).

Dissecting Apple's official answers unveils the following suspicions about Apple's real intentions:

1. The iPhone location tracking app was to store at least seven days of location data. But the more the better.
2. Even with Location Services turned off, the tracking app was to continue to perform its function at least sporadically.
3. The twice-repeated statement "this is a bug which we plan to fix shortly" does not connote the same urgency as something along the line "this is a bug which we are working on fixing."

Apple is a company renowned for combining art and science in the creation of innovative products. Apple's zealous engineers and rigorous quality assurance would have easily discovered such an obvious "bug."

Simon Davies, director of Privacy International, said about the iPhone location tracking app:

This is a worrying discovery. Location is one of the most sensitive elements in anyone's life ... The existence of that data creates a real threat to privacy. The absence of notice to users or any control option can only stem from an ignorance about privacy at the design stage [16].

7.4 Carrier IQ and Other Privacy Blunders

Joining Google and Apple's privacy blunders, Carrier IQ released a report on 12 Dec 2011: [17]

... Over the course of the past week, as Carrier IQ conducted extensive reviews with the Network Operators, *Carrier IQ has discovered an unintended bug in a diagnostic profile to measure radio-network-to-mobile device signaling.* This diagnostic profile is used to gather network conditions during voice calls to determine why they fail. Using these profiles, the IQ Agent collects 'layer 3' signaling traffic between the mobile device and radio tower, to help the Network Operator determine, for example, why a call might be dropped or which radio towers are communicating with a device during a voice call. Carrier IQ has discovered that, due to this bug, in some unique circumstances, such as when a user receives an SMS during a call, or during a simultaneous data session, SMS messages may have unintentionally been included in the layer 3 signaling traffic that is collected by the IQ Agent. ... Our investigation of Trevor Eckhart's video indicates that location, key presses, SMS and other information appears in log files as a result of debug messages from pre-production handset manufacturer software. Specifically it appears that the handset manufacturer software's debug capabilities remained 'switched on' in devices sold to consumers.

The high-profile privacy blunders have not stopped other companies from repeating the same mistakes. Path co-founder and CEO Dave Morin issued the statement on 8 Feb 2012: "We are sorry. We made a mistake. Over the last couple of days users brought to light an issue concerning how we handle your personal information on Path, specifically the transmission and storage of your phone contacts [18]." Path did not blame on software bugs but took full responsibility of its action.

It is too easy for a company to disguise questionable software behavior as Easter eggs, and use software bugs as scapegoats when they are caught. Agile software development and quality assurance testing do not allow these kinds of bugs to slip pass production into consumer's hand. More often than not, many companies intentionally inserted secret codes into their software.

In February 2012, Jonathan Mayer, a graduate student at Stanford University, demonstrated that four advertising companies, Google's DoubleClick, Vibrant Media, Media Innovation Group, and PointRoll, has been deliberately circumventing Apple Safari's privacy feature by installing temporary cookies on the user devices in order to track user's behavior [19]. Safari is the primary web browser on the iPhone, iPad, and Macintosh computers. The Stanford findings contradicted Google's own instructions to Safari users on how to avoid tracking.

According to a *Wall Street Journal* Research conducted by Ashkan Soltani, Google placed the tracking code within ads displayed on 29 of the top 100 most-visited U.S. websites [20]. Among them are household names YouTube, AOL, *People Magazine*, *New York Times*, WebMD, Merriam-Webster Dictionary, Fandango.com, Match.com, TMZ, and Yellow Pages. After *The Wall Street Journal* contacted Google about these findings, Google disabled its tracking code on Safari and removed the Safari's privacy settings language from its website.

Consumer Watchdog wrote a letter to the U.S. Federal Trade Commission about Google's unfair and deceptive violation of Safari users' privacy and the company's apparent violation of the "Buzz" Consent Decree [21]. "Google has clearly engaged in 'unfair and deceptive' practices," said John M. Simpson, Consumer Watchdog's privacy project director. "They have been lying about how people can protect their privacy in their instructions about how to opt out of receiving targeted advertising [22]."

Companies, big and small, have gone to great lengths and are taking chances to collect user data in order to facilitate business intelligence.

References

1. Google Maps. (Retrieved January 1, 2012). Street View: Explore the world at street level. http://maps.google.com/intl/en/help/maps/streetview/
2. Google Maps. (Retrieved January 1, 2012). Google Cars, Trikes, & More http://maps.google.com/help/maps/streetview/technology/cars-trikes.html
3. Fleischer, Peter. (April 27, 2010). Data collected by Google cars. *Google's European Public Policy Blog.* http://googlepolicyeurope.blogspot.com/2010/04/data-collected-by-google-cars.html
4. Stone, Brad. (May 14, 2010). Google Says It Inadvertently Collected Personal Data. *The New York Times.* http://bits.blogs.nytimes.com/2010/05/14/google-admits-to-snooping-on-personal-data/
5. Landis, Marina. (October 22, 2010). Google admits to accidentally collecting e-mails, URLs, passwords. *CNN.* http://articles.cnn.com/2010-10-22/tech/google.privacy.controls_1_wifi-data-alan-eustace-google-s-street-view?_s=PM:TECH
6. Eustace, Alan. (October 22, 2010). Creating stronger privacy controls inside Google. *Google Public Policy Blog.* http://googlepublicpolicy.blogspot.com/2010/10/creating-stronger-privacy-controls.html
7. The Easter Egg Archive. (Retrieved March 26, 2012). http://www.eeggs.com/
8. Netburn, Deborah. (April 27, 2012). Zerg Rush Easter egg and other great time wasters from Google. *Los Angeles Times.* http://www.latimes.com/business/technology/la-fi-tn-zerg-rush-easter-egg-google-20120427,0,5134704.story
9. Eustace, Alan. (May 14, 2010). WiFi data collection: An update. *The Official Google Blog.* http://googleblog.blogspot.com/2010/05/wifi-data-collection-update.html
10. Eustace, Alan. (October 22, 2010). Creating stronger privacy controls inside Google. *The Official Google Blog.* http://googleblog.blogspot.com/2010/10/creating-stronger-privacy-controls.html
11. Goldman, David. (April 16, 2012). Google fined $25,000 for 'willfully' stonewalling FCC. *CNN.* http://money.cnn.com/2012/04/16/technology/google-fcc/index.htm
12. Simpson, John M. (April 30, 2012). Letter to Senator Al Franken on Google Wi-Spy. *Consumer Watchdog.* http://www.consumerwatchdog.org/resources/ltrfranken043012.pdf

13. Google. (Updated April 25, 2012). Google's Code of Conduct. *Google Investor Relations.* http://investor.google.com/corporate/code-of-conduct.html
14. Ashley, Mitchell. (March 25, 2008). Apple's Trojan Easter Egg - Apple Safari. *Network World.* http://www.networkworld.com/community/node/26291
15. Apple Inc. (April 27, 2011). Apple Q&A on Location Data. *Apple Press Info.* http://www.apple.com/pr/library/2011/04/27Apple-Q-A-on-Location-Data.html
16. Arthur, Charles. (April 20, 2011). iPhone keeps record of everywhere you go. *The Guardian.* http://www.guardian.co.uk/technology/2011/apr/20/iphone-tracking-prompts-privacy-fears
17. Fisher, Dennis. (December 13, 2011). Carrier IQ Says Bug Can Cause Some SMS to Be Recorded in Coded Form. *Threat Post.* http://threatpost.com/en_us/blogs/carrier-iq-says-bug-can-cause-some-sms-be-recorded-coded-form-121311
18. Morin, Dave. (February 8, 2012). *Path Blog.* http://blog.path.com/post/17274932484/we-are-sorry
19. Mayer, Jonathan. (February 17, 2012). Web Policy. Safari Trackers. *Web Policy Blog.* http://webpolicy.org/2012/02/17/safari-trackers/
20. Angwin, Julia; Valentino-Devries, Jennifer. (February 17, 2012). Google's iPhone Tracking. Web Giant, Others Bypassed Apple Browser Settings for Guarding Privacy. *The Wall Street Journal.*   http://online.wsj.com/article_email/SB10001424052970204880404577225380456599176-lMyQjAxMTAyMDEwNjExNDYyWj.html
21. Simpson, John M. (February 17, 2012). Google's unfair and deceptive violation of Safari users' privacy and the company's apparent violation of the "Buzz" Consent Decree. *Consumer Watchdog.* http://www.consumerwatchdog.org/resources/ltrleibowitz021712.pdf
22. Consumer Watchdog. (February 17, 2012). Stanford Study Finds Google Violated Privacy Choices, iPhone and iPads Targeted; Consumer Watchdog Says Internet Giant Lied to Users, Calls for FTC Action. *The Business Journals.* http://www.bizjournals.com/prnewswire/press_releases/2012/02/17/DC5544

Chapter 8
Business Intelligence

> We're pretty opposed to advertising. It really turns our stomachs.
>> —Tumblr founder and CEO David Karp (April 2010)

> I was probably being an idiot then.
>> —David Karp said of his earlier renunciation of all advertising (April 2012)

8.1 Intelligent Digital Billboards

In Steven Spielberg's futuristic movie *Minority Report* (2002), computers scan human faces and display targeted advertisements to individuals as they walk down the street.

In July 2010, some billboards in Tokyo subway stations employed cameras and face recognition software to determine the gender and age of passersby [1]. The goal was to collect data on what sorts of people look at certain ads at what times of day. "The camera can distinguish a person's sex and approximate age, even if the person only walks by in front of the display, at least if he or she looks at the screen for a second," said a spokesman for the Digital Signage Promotion Project. "Companies can provide interactive advertisements which meet the interest of people who use the station at a certain time" [2].

In February 2012, a billboard in a London bus stop used facial recognition technology to determine whether a viewer was male or female, and it displayed a different advertisement depending on the gender [3]. With about 90 % accuracy, the Oxford Street billboard had a built-in camera that measured a viewer's facial features in order to determine the gender. Women were shown a commercial for the "Because I Am a Girl" campaign, whereas men only saw the campaign website [4].

Meanwhile in New York City, Tic Tac's new interactive Times Square billboard used augmented reality to enable passerby to view the ad through the Tic Tac Times Square app on their smartphones, and the app would insert their Facebook pictures in various ads. A manager for Tic Tac explained, "The big thing we learned from our research is that this audience is not willing to see an ad, go home and log onto their computer to learn more—they are not interested in engaging with a brand in that way. Mobile is the new medium that this group likes to engage in but it has to be fun, fresh and entertaining" [5].

N. Lee, *Facebook Nation*, DOI: 10.1007/978-1-4614-5308-6_8,

These are a few of the latest hi-tech examples of businesses collecting data, engaging the audience, and selling their products in an innovative way. The billboards might save anonymous data, but not images that are personally identifiable information. If Twitter or foursquare data indicate that there is a sports game going on in the area, the billboards might show a Nike ad instead of a FedEx ad. In response to privacy concerns about billboards collecting data of passersby, Immersive Labs CEO Jason Sosa said, "If you use a service like Amazon, have a Facebook Page, or even carry a cellphone, there is data being collected about you that is a lot more personal than anything we're collecting" [6].

8.2 Tumblr and Gmail: Yes to Advertisements

No matter where we are, in private or in public, advertisers seem to follow us. Companies that were known for their anti-ad stance have succumbed to offering their customers advertisements. David Karp, founder and CEO of the microblogging platform Tumblr, uttered his famous statement in an interview with *The Los Angeles Times* in April 2010: "We're pretty opposed to advertising. It really turns our stomachs" [7]. By February 2012, the self-described "accidental social network" [8] Tumblr has over 500 million page views a day, 50 + million posts a day, 40,000 requests per second, and hundreds to millions of followers for an average post with text, images, and videos [9]. In April 2012, exactly two years after the famous anti-advertisement quote, Karp announced at the Ad Age Digital conference that Tumblr would start displaying ads on the users' dashboard, and that he had probably been an "idiot" to say no to advertising [10].

In addition, saying no to email spam does not necessarily mean no advertisement. In October 2007, Microsoft CEO Steve Ballmer publicly jabbed Google for "reading your emails" [11]. Google defended and clarified its practice: "Ads that appear in Gmail are similar to the ads that appear next to Google search results and on content pages throughout the web. In Gmail, ads are related to the content of your messages. Our goal is to provide Gmail users with ads that are useful and relevant to their interests. ... Ad targeting in Gmail is fully automated, and no humans read your email in order to target advertisements or related information. This type of automated scanning is how many email services, not just Gmail, provide features like spam filtering and spell checking" [12]. Figure 8.1 shows an ad based on an email in my mailbox.

8.3 Social Ads on Facebook

Andrew Lewis, a commenter on MetaFilter, expressed his wise opinion in August 2010, "If you're not paying for something, you're not the customer; you're the product being sold" [13]. Indeed, when users sign up for free accounts on

Fig. 8.1 Gmail displays an ad in my mailbox based on the content of the email that I just sent

Facebook, they volunteer their personal information such as their gender, birthday, education, workplace, city of residence, interests, hobbies, photos, and even private matters like relationship status.

User activities such as clicking the "like" button can appear as part of an advertisement on the Facebook pages of their friends. Social apps' auto-share feature simplifies activity sharing without the need to click on "like."

"Facebook already has more data than they are leveraging," said Rebecca Lieb, an online advertising analyst at the research firm Altimeter Group. "There are so many infinite ways to slice and dice the data Facebook currently has, that it's rather daunting. Slicing and dicing the data for the purposes of serving up advertisements is a tricky business. It can't freak people out; it has to be cost-effective; it has to be relatively easy to do at scale" [14].

A game-changing advertising platform, Facebook has done an effective job in delivering "social ads" to the consumers. Social ads are "those served to users who have friends that are fans of or have interacted with the advertised brand and prominently call the relationship out" [15]. Advertisers tailor messages on Facebook based on demographics like age and gender, on the preferences and affinities of its users as well as those of their friends on Facebook.

Financial analyst Martin Pyykkonen at Wedge Partners said, "Facebook is highly appealing to advertisers because about two-thirds of its users fall into the coveted age demographic of 18–49. The 'Like' button option is a basic example of targeting. [It's] likely that advertisers will be able to even better target their audiences as Facebook goes deeper with integrating apps, games, movies, music" [16].

A 2011 study from the Consumer Electronics Association (CEA) indicated that 81 % of social media users are using social networks to help them make purchasing decisions about consumer electronics, and 84 % of them are influenced by reviews on the social media sites [17].

According to the April 2012 Nielsen report, "Global Trust in Advertising and Brand Messages," an overwhelming 92 % of consumers around the world trust recommendations from friends to family above all other forms of advertising, and 70 % of them believe in consumer opinions posted online [18].

The CEA and Nielsen reports have validated the growing trend that more businesses are using Facebook, Twitter, or other social networks to communicate with and advertise to consumers. "Social media now is not an option, it's a necessity," opined Anthony DeRosa, social-media editor at Reuters. "A couple of years ago that wasn't the case, but I think now people have to be a part of it, whether it's one social network or a couple of them" [19].

On the contrary, a 2011 report from Forrester Research analyst Sucharita Mulpuru painted a not-so-rosy picture. It showed that 68 % of U.S. retailers said if Facebook went away, it would not hurt their online sales. While 77 % said the top benefits of Facebook are brand building, only 1 % said it helped them get new customers. In fact, Gamestop, Gap, Penney, and Nordstrom have all opened and closed their storefronts on Facebook. The report stated, "In the history of retail, there has probably been nothing that has been so widely anticipated yet underwhelming as the 'era of social commerce" [20]. And Mulpuru said in a follow-up interview, "There was a lot of anticipation that Facebook would turn into a new destination, a store, a place where people would shop, but it was like trying to sell stuff to people while they're hanging out with their friends at the bar" [21].

The LIM College National Retail Federation Student Association released in January 2012 the result of a poll of shopping trends among 18–25 years olds [22]. The poll indicated that shoppers in this age group will "like" a brand on Facebook but would not go any further. In fact, more than 88 % said they do not want to shop through Facebook or Twitter.

In May 2012, General Motors announced that it would stop paid advertising on Facebook after having already spent $10 million, because the social media paid ads were not delivering the hoped-for buyers [23]. On the contrary, spokeswoman Kelli Felker from GM's rival Ford Motor Company said, "We've found Facebook ads to be very effective when strategically combined with engagement, great content and innovative ways of storytelling" [24].

The conflicting reports point to the significance of social ads on one hand and downplay the effectiveness of social ads on the other hand, which can be nerve-racking for Facebook. Advertising accounted for an overwhelming 85 % of Facebook's 2011 revenue of $3.7 billion [25], which amounted to nearly $3.2 billion [26]. Globally, marketers spent $84.8 billion on web advertisements in 2011, and the U.S. digital advertising expenditures amounted to $32.2 billion [27]. Facebook raked in a respectable 10 % of the total U.S. online advertisement revenue in 2011. To continue the momentum, Facebook has to do something more than just leveraging the "like" button and social app auto-share.

8.4 Sponsored Stories and Facebook Exchange

In March 2012, Facebook suggested that its ads would no longer be "ads" but "sponsored stories" [28]. Using Facebook's new tool Reach Generator, the user-engaging stories created by advertisers would show up on the fans' Facebook homepage or in their news feed on desktop or mobile. Reach Generator guarantees that advertisers can reach 75 % of their fans each month and an estimated 50 % of fans each week in a simple, always-on way [29]. In other words, Reach Generator effectively overrides Facebook's EdgeRank algorithm designed to enhance users' experience by putting only the most relevant content in their news feeds. It appears to have confirmed some analysts' forewarning that the Facebook IPO would only make the company even more financially driven in using personal data for marketing purposes.

Back in November 2007, Facebook launched Facebook Beacon, which was an ultimately failed attempt to advertise to friends of Facebook users based on the knowledge of what purchases the users had made online. After the initial fiasco, Facebook has successfully revamped its social ads. Facebook's "like," social app auto-share, and Reach Generator are just the beginning of "targeted social advertising."

Since 2009, Facebook's measurement research team headed by Sean Bruich has been helping agencies and brands make better ads. "Ads that were rewarding tended to be pretty clear—there wasn't an overload of information," said Bruich, who conducted a 2012 study with measurement researcher Adrienne Polich on best practices for brand-page postings. "But [the] rewarding ads also seemed to connect. The information seemed meaningful" [30].

Furthermore, Facebook can capitalize on the power of "Friend Effect" by publicizing users' "likes" of advertisers on "sponsored stories." Researchers have shown that an overwhelming 92 % of consumers around the world trust recommendations from friends to family above all other forms of advertising [31]. Facebook CEO Mark Zuckerberg was quoted as saying that a trusted referral was the "Holy Grail" of advertising; and Facebook's chief operating officer Sheryl Sandberg commented that the value of a "Sponsored Story" advertisement was at least twice and up to three times the value of a standard Facebook ad without a friend endorsement [32].

In June 2012, Facebook took another giant leap forward by introducing real-time ad bidding Facebook Exchange [33]. With standard Facebook ads, users were targeted based on their Facebook profiles and what pages they "liked." The Exchange enables advertisers to reach users based on their Internet browsing history. For example, a travel website can drop a cookie on a user who looks at vacation packages without making a purchase. When the user enters Facebook, advertisers can show the user travel deals on flights, hotels, car rentals, and cruises.

Facebook Exchange offers real-time advertising auctions similar to Google Adwords. An auction determines what ads will appear after a user does a search, the ad's position on the page, and the Cost Per Click (CPC) to the advertiser, among others. Marketers manage their bids and optimize performance using a demand-side platform (DSP). The DSPs with the highest bids get their ads shown to the targeted user.

In 2011, real-time bids generated $1.07 billion in display ad sales. According to global market intelligence firm IDC's projection, real-time bidding will account for about $5.08 billion to be spent on U.S. online display ads in 2015 [34].

8.5 Mobile Market and Instagram

In April 2012, Facebook took another major step towards strengthening its mobile market and growing its advertising revenue by acquiring the popular photo-sharing application Instagram for a whopping $1 billion dollars [35].

Instagram has 40 million users as of April 2012 [36] and over 200 million photos as of September 2011 [37]. These numbers are small compared to Facebook's 900 million users as of April 2012 and 140 billion photos as of September 2011 [38]. Nonetheless, some businesses are early Instagram adopters. Josh Karpf, PepsiCo's digital head, told *ClickZ* in an interview, "We use Instagram to humanize the brand and take people behind the curtains. You can let them see things they wouldn't normally see, whether its photos of Drew Brees at the Super Bowl, Pepsi Max at the MLB Fan Cave, or [Nascar star] Jeff Gordon during a photo shoot. Clearly, photo-sharing is something people are into. For brands, it's a lightweight way to connect with consumers" [39].

After its acquisition by Facebook, Instagram released an update for iOS devices in June 2012 to enhance user search and Facebook integration [40]. Instagram also announced its plan to improve the software to go beyond the "10 h" window of viewable photos. "We are trying really hard to take all the data that you've put into Instagram and let you see into the past," said co-founder Kevin Systrom. "I think we need to do a better job of creating these channels and silos that allow people to learn new things about the world" [41].

An April 2012 report by the research firm Strategy Analytics revealed that in-app spending by advertisers in the U.S. and Europe is set to overtake spending on display ads on smartphones [42]. A May 2012 report by comScore showed that Facebook had achieved an impressive 80.4 % reach or 78 million visitors on smartphones in the month of March [43]. Acquiring Instagram will also help Facebook in seeking a much-needed breakthrough in the mobile ad market [44].

Facebook is reportedly looking to release its own smartphone by 2013. "Mark is worried that if he doesn't create a mobile phone in the near future that Facebook will simply become an app on other mobile platforms," a Facebook employee said anonymously [45].

8.6 Location-Based Mobile Advertisements

In the wake of the Facebook IPO, Professor Catherine Tucker at MIT Sloan School of Management said, "Facebook is probably going to face some difficult balancing issues, in terms of meeting its new shareholders' expressed desire to exploit the data they have with the fact that if they exploit the data too much it can drag down the effectiveness of advertising" [46].

After the rocky IPO in May 2012, Facebook has been hard at work on a location-based mobile-advertising product that will enable advertisers to target users based on their whereabouts in real time. "The holy grail of advertising is finding people when they are at their closest point to making a purchase," said Colin Sebastian, an analyst with Robert W. Baird & Co. in San Francisco [47].

In June 2012, Snapette, a 500 Startups accelerator program alum, launched the first location-based shopping application Snapette 2.0 on iPhone and iPod Touch. Snapette lets shoppers share photos and comments with friends, and see what products are trending both around the corner and around the world. Fashion brands can send real-time notifications to potential customers already shopping nearby with special discounts and inside scoops on exclusive items.

"E-commerce is growing but offline is still 90 % of sales," Snapette co-founder Sarah Paiji told *Women's Wear Daily* (*WWD*). "For the stores, we really hope that this is a great mechanism to actively drive foot traffic" [48]. Snapette co-founder Jinhee Kim added, "With Snapette, retailers can reach consumers in real time and based on location. It's a unique and immediate way to showcase new merchandise and attract fashion-conscious customers shopping nearby" [49].

8.7 Disney and Other Businesses on Facebook

In addition to paid advertisements, businesses are increasingly using Facebook to communicate with their customers directly. The Walt Disney Company, one of the most recognizable brands worldwide, has almost 35 million "likes" on its corporate Facebook page as of April 2012 [50]. Disney's *Toy Story* has more than 28 million "likes," *Pirates of the Caribbean* has over 15 million "likes," and the list goes on and on. Andy Mooney, former Chairman of Disney Consumer Products, told a reporter from *Mashable*, "Social media is fundamental to the nature of how we communicate with the fans. The tone and the content is [*sic*] more causal and insight-based and insider-based, especially for the most ardent fans of the franchises" [51].

It is an understatement to say that Disney has mastered the skill of successful social media campaigns. There are annual Disney Social Media Moms Celebrations at the Walt Disney World Resort in Orlando [52]. In January 2012, Track Social awarded Disney the "Facebook Audience Growth Award" for a remarkable 17,716 new fans per day, and the "Facebook Likes Per Post Award" with a phenomenal 30,291 likes per post [53].

Nevertheless, Disney has its own share of missteps. In February 2011, Disney made public its social media ambition by acquiring Togetherville, a Facebook-like social network for children under 10 years old [54]. "Togetherville is very focused on trying to really reflect what the adult community has been doing on the Web and build a real online experience that adults enjoy for kids, but do it in a safe, COPPA-compliant way," said Togetherville founder and CEO Mandeep S. Dhillon. However, a year later in March 2012, Disney shut down Togetherville social network.

Like Disney, any business on Facebook can reach their audiences directly and in a timely manner without relying on third-party reporters. In March 2012, for example, some advertisers decided to withdraw their ads from the popular Rush Limbaugh radio talk show [55]. AOL explained their decision via a post on their corporate Facebook page: "At AOL one of our core values is that we act with integrity. We have monitored the unfolding events and have determined that Mr. Limbaugh's comments are not in line with our values. As a result we have made the decision to suspend advertising on The Rush Limbaugh Radio show" [56].

Nonetheless, Facebook businesses are not like Facebook friends. A majority of the time, social media business-consumer communication seems to be a one-way street. According to a STELLAService survey of 20 top online retailers on Facebook, their level of responsiveness to customers is less than desirable: one out of four companies ignored customer questions posted on Facebook, and five companies took more than two days to respond to a wall post. "Retailers need to realize that two days in Facebook time is like two years in real time," said Jordy Leiser, STELLAService's co-founder. "Customer questions on Facebook should be granted the same urgency as a phone call. ... Brands are doing an enthusiastic job of bringing people to their [Facebook] pages, [but] I don't think they're also necessarily bringing with them a desire to be social. It's just turning into a marketing message for many companies" [57].

The lack of two-way communication online can provoke consumer's distrust and dissatisfaction towards businesses. Commerce Secretary Gary Locke once said, "Consumers must trust the Internet in order for businesses to succeed online."

But can the Internet be truly trusted?

References

1. Katz, Leslie. (July 19, 2010). Japan tests billboards that know your gender, age. CNet. http://news.cnet.com/8301-17938_105-20010963-1.html
2. AFP. (July 15, 2010). Tokyo trials digital billboards that scan passers-by. Agence France-Presse. http://www.google.com/hostednews/afp/article/ALeqM5iDd1xzYx7CaahlxkLnvo4Xtcksug
3. Sutter, John D. (February 22, 2012). This London advertisement knows your gender. CNN. http://whatsnext.blogs.cnn.com/2012/02/22/this-london-advertisement-knows-your-gender/
4. Garber, Megan. (February 21, 2012). The Bus Stop That Knows You're a Lady. The Atlantic. http://www.theatlantic.com/technology/archive/12/02/the-bus-stop-that-knows-youre-a-lady/253365/
5. Tode, Chantal. (February 17, 2012). Tic Tac enlists augmented reality for interactive Times Square billboard. Mobile Marketer. http://www.mobilemarketer.com/cms/news/software-technology/12140.html
6. Kessler, Sarah. (April 15, 2011). Startup Aims To Build Billboards That Target You, Personally. Mashable. http://mashable.com/2011/04/16/smart-billboard/
7. Milian, Mark. (April 17, 2010). Tumblr: 'We're pretty opposed to advertising'. Los Angeles Times. http://latimesblogs.latimes.com/technology/2010/04/tumblr-ads.html
8. Gannes, Liz. (January 23, 2012). Tumblr's Inflection Point Came When Curators Joined Creators. All Things D. http://allthingsd.com/20120123/tumblrs-inflection-point-came-when-curators-joined-creators/

9. Higginbotham, Stacey. (February 13, 2012). GigaOM. How Tumblr went from wee to webscale. http://gigaom.com/cloud/how-tumblr-went-from-wee-to-webscale/.
10. Delo, Cotton. (April 18, 2012). Tumblr Announces First Foray Into Paid Advertising. Ad Age. http://adage.com/article/special-report-digital-conference/social-media-tumblr-announces-foray-paid-ads/234214/
11. Nicole, Kristen. (October 8, 2007). Steve Ballmer Attacks Google's Gmail Ads. http://mashable.com/2007/10/08/ballmer-google-email-ads/
12. Google. (Retrieved April 29, 2012). Ads in Gmail and your personal data. Google Gmail. http://support.google.com/mail/bin/answer.py?hl=en&answer=6603
13. Lewis, Andrew. (August 26, 2010). User-driven discontent. MetaFilter. http://www.metafilter.com/95152/Userdriven-discontent#3256046
14. Sengupta, Somini. (February 26, 2012). Risk and Riches in User Data for Facebook. The New York Times. http://www.nytimes.com/2012/02/27/technology/for-facebook-risk-and-riches-in-user-data.html
15. Nielsen. (March 6, 2012). Ads with Friends: Analyzing the Benefits of Social Ads. Nielsenwire. http://blog.nielsen.com/nielsenwire/online_mobile/ads-with-friends-analyzing-the-benefits-of-social-ads/
16. Pepitone, Julianne. (January 30, 2012). Is Facebook worth $100 billion? CNN Money. http://money.cnn.com/2012/01/30/technology/facebook_valuation/index.htm
17. Consumer Electronics Association (CEA). (February 22, 2012). CEA Study Examines Social Media Influence on CE Purchase Decisions. Yahoo! Finance. http://finance.yahoo.com/news/cea-study-examines-social-media-150200002.html
18. The Nielsen Company. (April 10, 2012). Consumer Trust in Online, Social and Mobile Advertising Grows. Nielsen. http://blog.nielsen.com/nielsenwire/media_entertainment/consumer-trust-in-online-social-and-mobile-advertising-grows/ and http://www.nielsen.com/content/dam/corporate/us/en/reports-downloads/2012-Reports/global-trust-in-advertising-2012.pdf
19. Gross, Doug. (February 7, 2012). Employers, workers navigate pitfalls of social media. CNN. http://www.cnn.com/2012/02/07/tech/social-media/companies-social-media/index.html
20. Tsuruoka, Doug. (February 7, 2012). Social Media Impact On E-Commerce Called Overrated. Investor's Business Daily. http://news.investors.com/Article/600351/201202071711/social-media-disappoints-as-ecommerce-driver.html
21. Lutz, Ashley. (February 28, 2012). Gamestop to J.C. Penney Shut Facebook Stores: Retail. Bloomberg Businessweek. http://www.businessweek.com/news/2012-02-28/gamestop-to-j-c-penney-shut-facebook-stores-retail.html
22. LIM College. (January 17, 2012). New Study "Shopping Trends Among 18-25 Year Olds" Reveals Technology Use Overrated. PRNewswire. http://www.prnewswire.com/news-releases/new-study-shopping-trends-among-18-25-year-olds-reveals-technology-use-overrated-137504888.html
23. Terlep, Sharon; Vranica, Suzanne; Raice, Shayndi. (May 16, 2012). GM Says Facebook Ads Don't Pay Off. The Wall Street Journal. http://online.wsj.com/article/SB10001424052702304192704577406394017764460.html
24. Valdes-Dapena, Peter. (May 15, 2012). GM to stop advertising on Facebook. CNN Money. http://money.cnn.com/2012/05/15/autos/gm_facebook/index.htm
25. Schonfeld, Erick. (February 1, 2012). Facebook's Profits: $1 Billion, On $3.7 Billion In Revenues. TechCrunch. http://techcrunch.com/2012/02/01/facebook-1-billion-profit/
26. Pepitone, Julianne. (February 2, 2012). Facebook files for $5 billion IPO. CNN Money. http://money.cnn.com/2012/02/01/technology/facebook_ipo/index.htm
27. O'Leary, Noreen. (April 9, 2012). GroupM: Global Web Ad Spend Up 16 Percent in 2011. New research says marketers spent $84.8 billion. Adweek. http://www.adweek.com/news/advertising-branding/groupm-global-web-ad-spend-16-percent-2011-139483
28. Delo, Cotton. (March 5, 2012). Facebook Warns Brands that Scale in Social Won't Come For Free. Advertising Age. http://adage.com/article/digital/facebook-warns-brands-scale-social-free/233105/
29. Facebook. (Retrieved March 31, 2012). Reach Generator. Facebook. http://ads.ak.facebook.com/ads/FacebookAds/Reach_Generator_Guide_2.28.12.pdf

30. Creamer, Matt. (May 14, 2012). Facebook Ads: What Works, What Doesn't. Advertising Age. http://adage.com/article/digital/facebook-ads-works/234731/
31. The Nielsen Company. (April 10, 2012). Consumer Trust in Online, Social and Mobile Advertising Grows. Nielsen. http://blog.nielsen.com/nielsenwire/media_entertainment/consumer-trust-in-online-social-and-mobile-advertising-grows/ and http://www.nielsen.com/content/dam/corporate/us/en/reports-downloads/2012-Reports/global-trust-in-advertising-2012.pdf
32. Levine, Dan; McBride, Sarah. (June 16, 2012). Facebook to pay $10 million to settle suit. Reuters. http://www.reuters.com/article/2012/06/16/net-us-facebook-settlement-idUSBRE85F0N120120616
33. Constine, Josh. (June 13, 2012). Facebook Exchange: A New Way For Advertisers To Target Specific Users With Real-Time Bid Ads. TechCrunch. http://techcrunch.com/2012/06/13/facebook-exchange/
34. MacMillan, Douglas; Erlichman, Jonathan. (June 14, 2012). Facebook to Debut Real-Time Bidding on Advertising Prices. Bloomberg Businessweek. http://www.businessweek.com/news/2012-06-13/facebook-to-debut-real-time-bidding-for-advertising
35. Mayer, Andrew. (April 11, 2012). What Facebook will do with Instagram. CNN. http://www.cnn.com/2012/04/11/opinion/mayer-instagram-facebook/index.html
36. Burns, Matt. (April 13, 2012). Instagram's User Count Now At 40 Million, Saw 10 Million New Users In Last 10 Days. TechCrunch. http://techcrunch.com/2012/04/13/instagrams-user-count-now-at-40-million-saw-10-million-new-users-in-last-10-days/
37. Perez, Sarah. (September 2, 2011). Instagram Adds 50 Million Photos In August, Now Over 200 Million Total. TechCrunch. http://techcrunch.com/2011/09/02/instagram-adds-50-million-photos-in-august-now-over-200-million-total/
38. Diaz, Jesus. (September 19, 2011).Facebook Photo Library Dwarfs Everything Else on the Planet. Gizmodo. http://gizmodo.com/5841667/facebook-photo-library-dwarfs-everything-else-in-the-planet
39. Heine, Christopher. (April 17, 2012). Pepsi and Red Bull Talk Instagram Activations. ClickZ. http://www.clickz.com/clickz/news/2168388/pepsi-red-bull-talk-instagram-activations
40. Saunders, Krystal. (June 26, 2012). Instagram App Gets Update for iOS. Market News. http://www.marketnews.ca//LatestNewsHeadlines/InstagramAppGetsUpdateforiOS.html
41. Neild, Barry. (June 20, 2012). Instagram wants photos to be seen beyond '10-hour' window. CNN. http://www.cnn.com/2012/06/19/tech/mobile/instagram-le-web/index.html
42. Prodhan, Georgina. (April 21, 2012). Apps become key to mobile advertising - report. Reuters. http://in.reuters.com/article/2012/04/21/mobile-advertising-apps-idINDEE83J0GJ20120421
43. comScore. (May 7, 2012). comScore Introduces Mobile Metrix 2.0, Revealing that Social Media Brands Experience Heavy Engagement on Smartphones. comScore Press Release. http://www.comscore.com/Press_Events/Press_Releases/2012/5/Introducing_Mobile_Metrix_2_Insight_into_Mobile_Behavior
44. Prodhan, Georgina. (March 2, 2012). Analysis: Facebook seeks breakthrough in mobile ad market. Reuters. http://www.reuters.com/article/2012/03/02/us-facebook-mobile-advertising-idUSTRE8210PH20120302
45. Bilton, Nick. (May 27, 2012). Facebook Tries, Tries Again on a Smartphone. The New York Times. http://bits.blogs.nytimes.com/2012/05/27/facebook-tries-tries-again-on-a-smartphone/
46. Rushe, Dominic; Chaudhuri, Saabira. (January 31, 2012). Facebook IPO: six things you need to know. The Guardian. http://www.guardian.co.uk/technology/2012/jan/31/facebook-ipo-six-things
47. Frier, Sarah. (June 18, 2012). Facebook Working on Location-Based Mobile-Ad Product. Bloomberg. http://www.bloomberg.com/news/2012-06-18/facebook-readying-location-based-mobile-ad-product.html
48. Strugatz, Rachel. (June 27, 2012). Digital World Now Coaxing Shoppers Back to Stores. Women's Wear Daily. http://www.wwd.com/retail-news/direct-internet-catalogue/digital-world-now-coaxing-shoppers-back-to-stores-6002645?full=true

49. Snapette. (June 28, 2012). Snapette Redefines The Shopping Experience Again With Major Update To Popular Location-Based App For iPhone And iPod Touch. The Sacramento Bee. http://www.sacbee.com/2012/06/28/4595490/snapette-redefines-the-shopping.html
50. Disney. (Retrieve April 2, 2012). Disney. Facebook. http://www.facebook.com/Disney
51. Warren, Christina. (August 3, 2011). Disney Marketing: The Happiest Social Media Strategy on Earth. Mashable. http://mashable.com/2011/08/03/disney-social-media/
52. Ford, Kristin. (March 17, 2011). Orlando Sentinel to deliver latest from Disney Social Media Moms Celebration. Orlando Sentinel. http://blogs.orlandosentinel.com/disney-a-mom-and-the-mouse/2011/03/orlando-sentinel-to-deliver-latest-from-disney-social-media-moms-celebration/
53. Track Social. (January 5, 2012). The Track Social Awards: Best of 2011. PRWeb. http://www.prweb.com/releases/2012/1/prweb9079817.htm
54. Chmielewski, Dawn C. (February 25, 2011). Disney buys social networking site Togetherville. The Los Angeles Times. http://articles.latimes.com/2011/feb/25/business/la-fi-ct-disney-togetherville-20110225
55. CNN Political Unit. (March 6, 2012). Stations, advertisers drop Limbaugh. CNN. http://politicalticker.blogs.cnn.com/2012/03/06/more-limbaugh-stations-advertisers-jump-ship/
56. AOL. (March 5, 2012). AOL. Facebook. http://www.facebook.com/aol/posts/356690557687629
57. Gross, Doug. (March 27, 2012). Which companies respond quickest (or not at all) on Facebook? CNN. http://www.cnn.com/2012/03/27/tech/social-media/retailers-facebook-ques

Chapter 9
Misinformation and Disinformation

Information is power. Disinformation is abuse of power.
—Newton Lee (2012)

There's an old economic principle, that bad money drives out good. One thing that worries me is that bad information is driving out good.
—Professor Frank Farley (2012)

The loudest voices should be particularly careful not to rush to conclusions.
—Former U.S. Secretary of Education William J. Bennett (March 2012)

9.1 The War of the Worlds

On Sunday, October 30, 1938, millions of radio listeners were stunned by the CBS radio "news" on the Martian invasion of Earth:

Good heavens! Something's wriggling out of the shadow like a gray snake. Now it's another, and another. They look like tentacles to me. There, I can see the thing's body. It's large as a bear and it glistens like wet leather. But that face. It … It's indescribable. I can hardly force myself to keep looking at it. The eyes are black and gleam like a serpent. The mouth is V-shaped with saliva dripping from its rimless lips that seem to quiver and pulsate…. The thing is raising up. The crowd falls back. They've seen enough. This is the most extraordinary experience. I can't find words…. I'll have to stop the description until I've taken a new position. Hold on, will you please. I'll be back in a minute [1].

Orson Welles' radio adaption of H.G. Wells' novel *The War of the Worlds* (1898) caused widespread panic in America. Thousands of people called the police about the Martian landing in central New Jersey. Some residents loaded up their cars and fled their homes as the radio broadcasted a statement from the U.S. Secretary of the Interior voiced by an actor who sounded like President Franklin D. Roosevelt:

Citizens of the nation: I shall not try to conceal the gravity of the situation that confronts the country, nor the concern of your government in protecting the lives and property of its people. However, I wish to impress upon you—private citizens and public officials, all of you—the urgent need of calm and resourceful action. Fortunately, this formidable enemy is still confined to a comparatively small area, and we may place our faith in the military forces to keep them there. In the meantime placing our faith in God we must continue the

N. Lee, *Facebook Nation*, DOI: 10.1007/978-1-4614-5308-6_9,
© Springer Science+Business Media New York 2013

performance of our duties each and every one of us, so that we may confront this destructive adversary with a nation united, courageous, and consecrated to the preservation of human supremacy on this earth. I thank you [2].

Surprisingly, the Federal Communications Commission decided not to fine CBS Radio or Orson Welles for the stunt that fooled countless number of American citizens as well as some officials at the New York City Department of Health [3]. Ironically, the department was later revamped and renamed to the New York City Department of Health and Mental Hygiene [4].

9.2 Misinformation and Disinformation on Twitter and Facebook

Fast-forwarding 74 years from the old radio days to March 2012, American film director Spike Lee retweeted to his 250,000 followers the wrong address of George Zimmerman, the man who shot and killed 17-year-old Trayvon Martin in February [5]. The tweet took off on a life of its own. Consequentially, the homeowners at the address—Elaine McClain, 70, and her husband David McClain, 72—started receiving hate mail and death threats that eventually drove them out of their home and into a hotel [6]. Realizing his gross mistake, Lee apologized to the McClains and reached a settlement deal with them. The rush to judgment in the Trayvon Martin case in the world of immediacy via Twitter, Facebook, and other social networks can be chaotic and downright dangerous. Former U.S. Secretary of Education William J. Bennett warned about the behavior of influential people and celebrities, "The loudest voices should be particularly careful not to rush to conclusions" [7].

Users of Twitter, Facebook, and social networks often ignore the second half of the Japanese proverb "never let an opportunity pass by, *but always think twice before acting.*" In a world of immediacy, Twitter has become the perfect tool for instant gratification and rapid dissemination of information as well as misinformation.

Indeed, misinformation and disinformation abound in the digital information world. Every day, information is being circulated on the Internet without verification and clear thoughts. On May 8, 2012, Blogger Nate St. Pierre wrote an amusingly elaborate hoax article about U.S. President Abraham Lincoln filing a patent for Facebook in 1845 [8]. The story deliberately raised a few red flags by mentioning the infamous prankster P.T. Barnum and inserting a poorly Photoshopped copy of the December 24, 1845 newspaper *Springfield Gazette*.

St. Pierre put out one tweet and posted a link on Facebook. Within 36 h, he got 16,000 Facebook "Likes" and 104,463 unique page views to his blog. He was interviewed by reporters from *CNN*, *The Atlantic*, and *The Washington Post*.

On May 10, St. Pierre deconstructed the entire experience and expounded on the hoax, "It's a tip of the hat to P.T. Barnum's celebrated hoaxes (or humbugs) and Abe Lincoln's tall tales…. there are clues throughout the entire article telling you it's a hoax … I wanted to illustrate one of the drawbacks to our 'first and fastest' news aggregation and reporting mentality, especially online…. In addition to social media and bloggers, it ran as fact on a lot of big-name sites and news aggregators. That's the thing that surprised me the most…. I can tell you that virtually nobody checked with me to ask if it was true" [9].

In spite of the numerous red flags throughout St. Pierre's story, *Forbes* posted his story under the headline "Abraham Lincoln Filed a Patent for a Dead-Tree Facebook in 1845" for a day before pulling it down. "A Forbes contributor took Nate St. Pierre's story at face value," said a Forbes spokeswoman. "Once Forbes realized it was a prank, the article was pulled from the site" [10]. Nevertheless, *ZDNet* kept the story "Abraham Lincoln tried to patent Facebook in 1845, but failed?" on its website, but the *ZDNet* reporter Emil Protalinski crossed out some of the fake information and added an apology: "Update: Sorry everyone but this indeed a hoax" [11].

9.3 Serious Consequences of Misinformation and Disinformation

Misinformation and disinformation can lead to a more serious consequence than just a good laugh. In November 2010, a Nicaraguan general cited Google's map of the border with Costa Rica to justify a reported raid in a disputed area [12].

In May 2012, Iran threatened to sue Google for not labeling Persian Gulf, whereas nearby bodies of water—including the Gulf of Oman, Arabian Sea, Gulf of Aden and Red Sea—are labeled. "Toying with modern technologies in political issues is among the new measures by the enemies against Iran, (and) in this regard, Google has been treated as a plaything," said Iran Foreign Ministry spokesman Ramin Mehmanparast [13].

9.4 Trustworthiness of Wikipedia

When Encyclopedia Britannica decided in 2012 to cease production of its iconic multi-volume print book sets, Britannica president Jorge Cauz conceded, "Google's algorithm doesn't know what's fact or what's fiction. So Wikipedia is often the No. 1 or No. 2 result on search. But I'd bet a lot of money that most people would rather use Britannica than Wikipedia. Wikipedia is a wonderful technology for collecting everything from great insights to lies and innuendos. It's not all bad or all good, just uneven. It's the murmur of society, a million voices rather than a single informed one. As a result, consumers are craving accuracy and are willing to pay for it [Encyclopedia Britannica]" [14]. Prof. James S. O'Rourke at the University of Notre Dame concurred, "The problem with crowd-sourcing the answer to any particular question is, of course, that you're as likely to find ideologically driven opinion as hard fact. You also have little in the way of support for judgments about credibility, reliability, and accuracy"[15].

Wikipedia has become the de facto encyclopedia. Its online content is searchable, revisable, and up-to-date. Its credibility, reliability, and accuracy depend mostly on citations from trusted sources. Wikipedia flags articles for incompleteness and biases by displaying warning messages on the content pages. For example, "This biographical article needs additional citations for verification. Please help by adding reliable sources. Contentious material about living persons that is unsourced or poorly sourced must be removed immediately, especially if potentially libelous or harmful".

Given the open crowd-sourcing nature of Wikipedia, my own biographical article was vandalized on November 15, 2011 when someone by the login name "Newyorker1" revised the article. Apart from the vile changes that he made, he also updated my name to "Newton Shrimp Fried Rice Lee," my picture to that of President George Bush, and my book title *Disney Stories: Getting to Digital* to *Disney Stories: Getting to XXX Shop By Midnight* [16]. Fortunately, Wikipedia's ClueBot NG detected the vandalism almost immediately and reverted all the changes automatically. ClueBot NG's vandalism detection algorithm uses machine learning techniques, Bayesian classifiers, artificial neural network, threshold calculation, and post-processing filters [17].

9.5 Google Search Sabotage

Unlike Wikipedia, Google search sabotage is a lot trickier to deal with. For many years, former Pennsylvania Senator and 2012 GOP presidential hopeful Rick Santorum has been battling his Google search results. In November 2003, gay newspaper advice columnist Dan Savage created the blog "Spreading Santorum" in retaliation for Santorum's ultraconservative views and anti-gay comments [18]. Because of the prank, people saw a vulgar term for anal sex as the first result when they searched the word "Santorum" on Google. Santorum contacted Google to protest but to no avail.

In an e-mail to *CNN*, a Google spokeswoman said, "Google's search results are a reflection of the content and information that is available on the Web. Users who want content removed from the Internet should contact the webmaster of the page directly. Once the webmaster takes the page down from the Web, it will be removed from Google's search results through our usual crawling process" [19].

Obviously, contacting the webmaster Dan Savage is out of the question for Rick Santorum, who fired back at Google, "I suspect if something was up there like that about Joe Biden, they'd get rid of it. If you're a responsible business, you don't let things like that happen in your business that have an impact on the country" [20].

Nonetheless, Santorum's active political campaign activities in 2012 helped improve the rankings of his Wikipedia page and Google news just enough for them to be displaced above the "Spreading Santorum" blog in Google search results.

While Google, Microsoft's Bing, Facebook, Twitter, and other social media are excellent sources of information in the age of big data, it is up to the readers to decipher what is true and what is false. Information, misinformation, and disinformation are more mingled and harder to differentiate today than ever in the history of humankind. Pulitzer Prize nominee Nicholas Carr wrote an insightful article "Is Google Making Us Stupid?" in the July/August 2008 issue of the *Atlantic Magazine*:

> Thanks to the ubiquity of text on the Internet, not to mention the popularity of text-messaging on cell phones, we may well be reading more today than we did in the 1970s or 1980s, when television was our medium of choice. But it's a different kind of reading, and behind it lies a different kind of thinking—perhaps even a new sense of the self. 'We are not only what we read', says Maryanne Wolf, a developmental psychologist at Tufts University and the author of *Proust and the Squid: The Story and Science of the Reading Brain*. 'We are how we read.' Wolf worries that the style of reading promoted by the Net, a style that puts 'efficiency' and 'immediacy' above all else, may be weakening our capacity for the kind of deep reading that emerged when an earlier technology, the printing press, made long and complex works of prose commonplace. When we read online, she says, we tend to become 'mere decoders of information.' Our ability to interpret text, to make the rich mental connections that form when we read deeply and without distraction, remains largely disengaged [21].

9.6 Advertising Misinformation and Disinformation

A fashion trend is often the result of deliberate promotion of images online and in print to create a mass following—starting from runways, magazines, TV, movies, and the Internet to shopping malls. Like everything else, there are plenty of competitions.

Occidental University associate professor Caroline Heldman said, "The number of images out there means advertisers have a much more difficult time breaking through the clutter, causing the content to be much more violent and sexualized to get consumers' attention" [22].

As a result, misinformation and disinformation are widespread in advertisements. Between 2010 and 2012, the U.K. Advertising Standards Authority has banned eight misleading ads due to excessive Photoshop, social irresponsibility, and marketing deception [23]. The "misleadingly exaggerated" ads included Rachel Weisz's L'Oréal Revitalift Repair 10 and Julia Roberts' Lâncome Teint Miracle; the deceptive ad was for Reebok's EasyTone sneakers; and the "socially irresponsible" ads included Hailee Steinfeld for Miu Miu Fall 2011 collection, Dakota Fanning for Marc Jacobs Oh Lola! Perfume, and campaigns for Levi's Jeans "Go Forth" and Diesel "Be Stupid".

Some American teenagers are calling for an end to the digitally enhanced, unrealistic "beauty" in the pages of teen fashion magazines. In July 2012, 14-year-old Julia Bluhm from Maine hand-delivered a petition signed by 84,000 + people to the executive editor of *Seventeen* magazine, urging the publisher not to alter the body size or face shape of the girls and models in the magazine. Bluhm wrote on change.org, "*Seventeen* listened! They're saying they won't use Photoshop to digitally alter their models! This is a huge victory, and I'm so unbelievably happy. Another petition is being started by SPARK activists Emma [Stydahar] and Carina [Cruz], targeting *Teen Vogue* and I will sign it. If we can be heard by one magazine, we can do it with another. We are sparking a change!" [24].

9.7 Fake Information on Facebook, Twitter, and YouTube

Exaggerated images and sensationalized news are no strangers to mass media. The Internet, with its efficiency and immediacy, serves to exacerbate the potential danger of misinformation and disinformation. Sadly, the public is simply unaware of the authenticity of Facebook profiles, Twitter accounts, and YouTube videos:

- In 2006, "lonelygirl15" appeared as a home-schooled and confused 16-year-old teenager "Bree" on her wildly popular YouTube videos with over a million views. For four months, she fooled viewers into believing her real struggles with her estranged parents and dysfunctional family, until *Los Angeles Times* reporter Richard Rushfield revealed that Bree was a 19-year-old American-New Zealand actress Jessica Lee Rose. Rushfield reported, "Three lonelygirl15-obsessed amateur Web sleuths set up a sting using tracking software that appears to show that e-mails sent from a lonelygirl15 account came from inside the offices of the Beverly Hills-based talent agency Creative Artists Agency" [25].
- In 2009, a group of students at Millburn High School in New Jersey created a fake Facebook account for a fictional new student "Lauren" in their school, and almost 120 students and 55 others added her as a friend [26].
- In 2010, Indiana University professor Filippo Menczer and other researchers launched the Truthy project to detect political smears, astroturfing, misinformation, and other social pollution [27]. They found evidence that political campaigns and special interest groups are using fake Twitter accounts to create the false impression of grassroots movements. Repeated and retweeted messages from a score of fake users would show up as "trending" topics on Twitter and would ultimately influence Google's search results [28].
- In 2011, a student at Rancho Bernardo High School created a Facebook account using another teen's name, and posted threats of a mass shooting at the high school [29]. Police arrested the student for making terrorist threats and impersonating another on the Internet.
- In 2011, GOP Presidential hopeful Newt Gingrich had over 1.38 million Twitter followers, more than twice the number of Twitter followers for former Vice

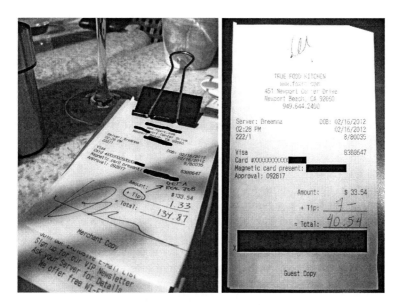

Fig. 9.1 "Get a real job" hoax—photoshopped receipt versus real receipt

Presidential candidate Sarah Palin, and 10 times more than that for his main GOP rival Mitt Romney. Gingrich's Twitter presence looked impressive, until a New York search company PeekYou discovered that only 8 % of Gingrich's Twitter followers were verifiable humans [30]. In other words, about 1.27 million phony Twitter accounts were created by Gingrich-hired campaign agencies.

- In 2012, media mogul Rupert Murdoch signed up for Twitter and started to follow four people on the social network including Google's co-founder and CEO Larry Page. Unbeknown to Murdoch, he followed a fake Larry Page—a parody account created by Virginia Tech for an university project [31].
- In 2012, one of the strangest receipts from America's restaurants went viral on Twitter and Facebook. Twitterer @FutureExBanker sent Receiptrocity at eater.com a picture of the receipt showing that his boss left the waitress a miniscule 1 % tip, $1.33, on a $133.54 bill with the message, "Get a real job" [32]. As it turned out, it was a Photoshoped hoax. The restaurant spokesperson was able to locate the merchant copy of the real receipt that showed a $7 tip for a $33.54 bill [33] (See Fig. 9.1).

In the amended S-1 filing on March 7, 2012, Facebook disclosed that 5–6 % of Facebook accounts were either fake or duplicated based on an internal review of a limited sample of accounts [34]. 5–6 % is probably a gross underestimate. Some industry watchers claimed that nearly 50 % of social network users could be fake or empty user accounts [35].

9.8 Facebook Account Verification

To help reduce spam, fake, and multiple accounts, Facebook encourages a user to "verify" their account by adding a mobile number to it [36]. The "Confirm Your Phone" page states, "Facebook uses security tests to ensure that the people on the site are real. Having a mobile phone helps us establish your identity. Please verify your account by confirming your phone here. We'll text you a confirmation code" [37]. After verification, a user may add a username (e.g. myusername) to the account and customize the Facebook web address (e.g. www.facebook.com/myusername) [38].

Facebook's mobile number verification constitutes a very basic security. Everyone in the U.S. can purchase a cheap, disposable prepaid cell phone for temporary use. In order for Facebook to step up its security, Facebook began to roll out in February 2012 "verified accounts" whose owners have submitted a government ID to prove their identities. However, the new security update is currently restricted to Facebook users with a large number of subscribers. "This update makes it even easier for subscribers to find and keep up with journalists, celebrities and other public figures they want to connect to", said a Facebook spokesman [39].

9.9 Twitter Verified Accounts

Unlike Facebook, Twitter does not accept public requests for account verification. Since the launch of verified accounts in June 2009, Twitter has stated on its help center, "Any account with a blue verified badge on their Twitter profile is a verified account. Verification is currently used to establish authenticity of identities on Twitter. The verified badge helps users discover high-quality sources of information and trust that a legitimate source is authoring the account's Tweets. Twitter proactively verifies accounts on an ongoing basis to make it easier for users to find who they're looking for. We concentrate on highly sought users in music, acting, fashion, government, politics, religion, journalism, media, advertising, business, and other key interest areas. We verify business partners from time to time and individuals at high risk of impersonation. We do not accept requests for verification from the general public. If you fall under one of the above categories and your Twitter account meets our qualifications for verification, we may reach out to you in the future" [40].

According to *Advertising Age*, Twitter reaches out to advertisers who have spent at least $15,000 over three months and get their accounts verified [41]. The Twitter business practice leaves many smaller businesses out in the cold. *The Wall Street Journal* reported that celebrities such as Britney Spears had their managers contacted the head of Twitter to obtain account verifications [42].

In spite of the verification process, Twitter has made quite a few mistakes in its nearly 17,000 verified accounts. In a high-profile error, Twitter apologized in

January 2012 for incorrectly verifying a false account for Wendi Deng, the wife of News Corp CEO Rupert Murdoch [43]. The @Wendi_Deng account had racked up more than 10,000 followers before it was discovered to be a faux one created by a British man to poke fun at Deng [44].

9.10 Abuse of Power

CNN reporter Todd Leopold wrote in his March 2012 article about online missteps and misinformation: "In an increasingly connected world where social networking has made us all news sources, that means missteps and misinformation get issued—and repeated—more quickly than ever. Gabrielle Giffords is declared dead, Chris Brown lets fly with profane rants, and it all makes the rounds before anyone has time to think" [45].

Frank Farley, Temple University professor and former president of the American Psychological Association, made this chilling conclusion: "Everyone now has a global platform on which they can shout their opinions and voice their beliefs. There's an old economic principle, that bad money drives out good. One thing that worries me is that bad information is driving out good" [46].

Information is power. Disinformation is abuse of power. *Los Angeles Times* playfully called the 2006 "lonelygirl15" YouTube mystery the "Web's Watergate" [47]. The real Watergate scandal culminated in the resignation of President Richard Nixon in August 1974 [48]. Watergate has had a profound influence on American journalism and politics. In the new era of digital information with the proliferation of Twitter, Facebook, and YouTube, inquisitive citizens and accidental journalists will radically transform the landscape of journalism and politics in the years to come.

References

1. Long, Tony. (October 30, 2007). Oct. 30, 1938: The Martians Have Landed in New Jersey! *Wired.* http://www.wired.com/science/discoveries/news/2007/10/dayintech_1030
2. Cantril, Hadley. (May 2, 2005). The Invasion from Mars: A Study in the Psychology of Panic. Transaction Publishers
3. Swan, Lisa. (October 30, 2008). 'War of the Worlds' terrified the nation 70 years ago. *New York Daily News.* http://www.nydailynews.com/entertainment/television/war-worlds-terrified-nation-70-years-article-1.304998
4. Hamilton, Gabrielle. (April 27, 2006). Good Enough to Fine. *The New York Times.* http://www.nytimes.com/2006/04/27/opinion/27hamilton.html
5. Picket, Kerry. (April 3, 2012). PICKET: Media misses the boat on Spike Lee Twitter story. *The Washington Times.* http://www.washingtontimes.com/blog/watercooler/2012/apr/3/picket-media-misses-boat-spike-lee-twitter-story/
6. Jacobson, Susan. (March 29, 2012). Elderly couple abandon their home after address is posted on Twitter as that of George Zimmerman. *Orlando Sentinel.* http://articles.orlandosentinel.com/

2012-03-29/news/os-trayvon-martin-wrong-zimmerman-20120327_1_spike-lee-william-zimmerman-retweeted

7. Bennett, William J. (March 30, 2012). Rush to judgment in Trayvon Martin case. *CNN.* http://www.cnn.com/2012/03/30/opinion/bennett-trayvon-martin/index.html

8. St. Pierre, Nate. (May 8, 2012). Abraham Lincoln Filed a Patent for Facebook in 1845. *Nate St. Pierre Blogs.* http://natestpierre.me/2012/05/08/abraham-lincoln-patent-facebook/

9. St. Pierre, Nate. (May 10, 2012). Anatomy of a Hoax: How Abraham Lincoln Invented Facebook. *Nate St. Pierre Blogs.* http://natestpierre.me/2012/05/10/hoax-abraham-lincoln-invented-facebook/

10. Gross, Doug. (May 10, 2012). Abraham Lincoln didn't invent Facebook (except on the Internet). *CNN.* http://www.cnn.com/2012/05/09/tech/web/abraham-lincoln-facebook/index.html

11. Protalinski, Emil. (May 8, 2012). Abraham Lincoln tried to patent Facebook in 1845, but failed? *ZDNet.* http://www.zdnet.com/blog/facebook/abraham-lincoln-tried-to-patent-facebook-in-1845-but-failed/12728

12. Sutter, John D. (November 5, 2010). Google Maps border becomes part of international dispute. *CNN.* http://articles.cnn.com/2010-11-05/tech/nicaragua.raid.google.maps_1_google-maps-google-spokeswoman-google-earth

13. Levs, Josh. (May 17, 2012). Iran threatens to sue Google for not labeling Persian Gulf. *CNN.* http://www.cnn.com/2012/05/17/world/meast/iran-google-gulf/index.html

14. Pepitone, Julianne. (March 13, 2012). Encyclopedia Britannica to stop printing books. *CNN.* http://money.cnn.com/2012/03/13/technology/encyclopedia-britannica-books/index.htm

15. O'Rourke, James S., IV. (March 15, 2012). Why Encyclopedia Britannica mattered. *CNN.* http://www.cnn.com/2012/03/14/opinion/orourke-encyclopedia/index.html

16. Wikipedia. (November 15, 2011). Newton Lee. Difference between revisions. *Wikipedia.* http://en.wikipedia.org/w/index.php?title=Newton_Lee&diff=460810113&oldid=458830548

17. Wikipedia. (October 20, 2010). User:ClueBot NG. *Wikipedia.* http://en.wikipedia.org/wiki/User:ClueBot_NG#Vandalism_Detection_Algorithm

18. Savage, Dan. (Retrieved April 5, 2012). Spreading Santorum. http://blog.spreadingsantorum.com/

19. Sutter, John D. (September 21, 2011). Santorum asks Google to clean up search results for his name. *CNN.* http://articles.cnn.com/2011-09-21/tech/tech_web_santorum-google-ranking_1_google-spokeswoman-google-ceo-eric-schmidt-google-places

20. Burns, Alexander. (September 20, 2011). Rick Santorum contacted Google, says company spreads 'filth.' *Politico.* http://www.politico.com/news/stories/0911/63952.html

21. Carr, Nicholas. (July/August 2008). Is Google Making Us Stupid? *The Atlantic Magazine.* http://www.theatlantic.com/magazine/archive/2008/07/is-google-making-us-stupid/6868/

22. Grinberg, Emanuella. (March 11, 2012). Sex, lies and media: New wave of activists challenge notions of beauty. *CNN.* http://www.cnn.com/2012/03/09/living/beauty-media-miss-representation/

23. Skarda, Erin. (February 3, 2012). Tough Standards: 8 'Misleading' Ads Banned by U.K. Officials. *Time Magazine.* http://newsfeed.time.com/2012/02/06/tough-standards-8-misleading-ads-banned-by-u-k-standards-board/

24. Bluhm, Julia. (July 3, 2012). Seventeen Magazine Gives Girls Images of Real Girls! *change.og.* http://www.change.org/petitions/seventeen-magazine-give-girls-images-of-real-girls

25. Rushfield, Richard; Hoffman, Claire. (September 8, 2006). Mystery fuels huge popularity of web's Lonelygirl15. *Los Angeles Times.* http://www.latimes.com/entertainment/news/la-et-lonelygirl15,0,241799.story

26. Podvey, Heather. (2009). Do you really KNOW your Facebook friends? *Applywise.* http://www.applywise.com/sep09_facebook.aspx

27. Indiana University Center for Complex Networks and Systems Research. (2010). About Truthy. *Indiana University.* http://truthy.indiana.edu/about

28. Kleiner, Kurt. (November 2, 2010). Bogus Grass-Roots Politics on Twitter. *MIT Technology Review.* http://www.technologyreview.com/computing/26666/

29. Repard, Pauline. (April 8, 2012). RB High threats on Facebook a hoax; teen arrested. *UT San Diego.* http://www.utsandiego.com/news/2011/oct/15/rb-high-threats-facebook-hoax-teen-arrested/
30. Taylor, Chris. (August 2, 2011). Newt Gingrich's Twitter Followers Are 8 % Human [INFOGRAPHIC]. *Mashable.* http://mashable.com/2011/08/02/newt-gingrich-twitter-followers/
31. Gross, Doug. (January 3, 2012). Twitter newbie Rupert Murdoch following fake account. *CNN.* http://www.cnn.com/2012/01/02/tech/social-media/murdoch-twitter-larry-page/index.html
32. Forbes, Paula. (February 24, 2012). Rich Jerk Tips 1 % and Advises Server to 'Get a Real Job'. *Eater.* http://eater.com/archives/2012/02/24/rich-jerk-tips-1-advises-server-to-get-a-real-job.php
33. Forbes, Paula. (February 28, 2012). The 'Get a Real Job' Receipt With a 1 % Tip Was a Hoax. *Eater.* http://eater.com/archives/2012/02/28/that-get-a-real-job-receipt-with-a-1-tip-was-a-hoax.php
34. Facebook. (March 7, 2012). Amendment No. 2 to Form S-1 Registration Statement. *U.S. Securities and Exchange Commission.* http://sec.gov/Archives/edgar/data/1326801/000119312512101422/d287954ds1a.htm
35. Foremski, Tom. (February 14, 2012). The hollow emptiness in social media numbers - most accounts are fake or empty. *ZdNet.* http://www.zdnet.com/blog/foremski/the-hollow-emptiness-in-social-media-numbers-most-accounts-are-fake-or-empty/2175
36. Facebook. (Retrieved April 8, 2012). Verifying Your Account. *Facebook.* http://www.facebook.com/help/verify
37. Facebook. (Retrieved April 8, 2012). Confirm Your Phone. *Facebook.* http://www.facebook.com/confirmphone.php
38. Facebook. (Retrieved April 8, 2012). General Information. Usernames. *Facebook.* http://www.facebook.com/help/usernames/general
39. Gross, Doug. (February 17, 2012). Facebook rolls out 'verified accounts,' celeb nicknames. *CNN.* http://www.cnn.com/2012/02/16/tech/social-media/facebook-verified-accounts/index.html
40. Twitter. (Retrieved April 8, 2012). FAQs about Verified Accounts. *Twitter help center.* http://support.twitter.com/groups/31-twitter-basics/topics/111-features/articles/119135-about-verified-accounts
41. Delo, Cotton. (January 10, 2012). One Way to Get a Twitter 'Verified Account': Buy Ads. *Advertising Age.* http://adage.com/article/digital/a-twitter-verified-account-buy-ads/231984/
42. Cheney, Alexandra. (March 7, 2011).How Does Twitter Verify Celebrity Accounts? *The Wall Street Journal.* http://blogs.wsj.com/speakeasy/2011/03/07/how-does-twitter-verify-celebrity-accounts/
43. Adegoke, Yinka. (January 4, 2012). Twitter embarrassed by fake Wendi Murdoch account. *Reuters.* http://www.reuters.com/article/2012/01/04/us-wendimurdoch-twitter-idUSTRE80305620120104
44. Swisher, Kara. (January 4, 2012). The Case of the Unfortunate Underscore: How Twitter Verified the Fake Wendi Over the Real Wendi. *All Things D.* http://allthingsd.com/20120104/the-case-of-the-unfortunate-underscore-how-twitter-verified-fake-wendi-over-real-wendi/
45. Leopold, Todd. (March 6, 2012). In today's warp-speed world, online missteps spread faster than ever. *CNN.* http://www.cnn.com/2012/03/06/tech/social-media/misinformation-social-media/index.html
46. Leopold, Todd. *Ibid.*
47. Rushfield, Richard. (September 4, 2006). On the Trail of lonelygirl15 Daily. *Los Angeles Times.* http://www.latimes.com/entertainment/news/la-et-lonelygirl5sep05,0,3933739.htmlstory
48. The Washington Post Special Reports. (Retrieved April 9, 2012). The Watergate Story. *The Washington Post.* http://www.washingtonpost.com/wp-srv/politics/special/watergate/

Chapter 10
E-Government and E-Activism

We are the nation that put cars in driveways and computers in offices; the nation of Edison and the Wright brothers; of Google and Facebook.
—President Barack Obama (2011 State of the Union Address)

In the face of everything else that's screwed up in Washington, we the American people can fix things.
—Reddit co-founder Alexis Ohanian (May 2012)

If there is an Internet connection, my camera is more powerful [than my AK-47].
—Syrian dissident Abu Ghassan (June 2012)

10.1 President Barack Obama and Web 2.0

John F. Kennedy's masterful images on television, the new medium in the 1960s, helped him defeated then Vice President and Republican candidate Richard Nixon in the 1960 U.S. presidential election. Those who heard their first debate on the radio pronounced Nixon the winner, but the majority of the 70 million Americans who watched the televised debate perceived Kennedy as the clear champion [1].

In 2008, Barack Obama ushered in a new Internet era in politics. With over 13 million addresses in his email list, 400,000 blog posts, 130,000 Twitter followers, and 5 million supporters on Facebook, Obama successfully raised half a billion dollars online for his 2008 presidential campaign [2]. The Triple O (Obama's Online Operation) used the World Wide Web to mobilize supporters and took advantage of YouTube for free advertising and fundraising [3].

Former Facebook spokesman Chris Hughes launched the networking site My.BarackObama.com (MyBO) for supporters to be actively involved in the 2008 presidential campaign. Volunteers on MyBO created more than 2 million profiles, planned 200,000 events, formed 35,000 groups, posted 400,000 blogs, and raised $30 million on 70,000 personal fund-raising pages. *Fast Company* featured Hughes on its April 2009 cover as "The Kid Who Made Obama President" [4].

"Were it not for the Internet, Barack Obama would not be president," said *Huffington Post* founder Arianna Huffington at the 2008 Web 2.0 Summit in San Francisco a few days after the election. "Were it not for the Internet, he wouldn't even have been the Democratic nominee. By contrast, the McCain campaign didn't have a clue. The problem wasn't the age of the candidate; it was the age of the idea" [5].

N. Lee, *Facebook Nation*, DOI: 10.1007/978-1-4614-5308-6_10,
© Springer Science+Business Media New York 2013

Fig. 10.1 WhiteHouse.gov

Immediately after winning the 2008 presidential election, President-Elect Barack Obama thanked his Twitter followers, "We just made history. All of this happened because you gave your time, talent and passion. All of this happened because of you. Thanks" [6].

Obama also launched the website change.gov to inform the American public about the Obama-Biden transition and to encourage people to share their ideas with the government [7]. The website reads, "To change this country, we're counting on Americans from every walk of life to get involved. Tell us how an experience in your life showed you something that is right or something that is wrong with this country—and share your ideas for how to make it better" [8].

After the transition, President Obama continued to leverage the power of the Internet via the government website whitehouse.gov as well as holding online town hall meetings via Google+, Facebook, and YouTube [9]. When we visit the whitehouse.gov, we see something familiar to some commercial business websites—we are prompted to enter our email address to get periodic updates (from President Obama and other administration officials in the case of whitehouse.gov) [10]. (See Fig. 10.1).

In 1966, the U.S. Congress enacted the Freedom of Information Act (FOIA) to give the American public greater access to the federal government's records [11]. The Electronic Freedom of Information Act Amendments of 1996 broadens the scope of FOIA to encompass electronic records and to make government's records more easily and widely available to the public by placing more material online [12]. All government agencies are required to have their websites provide the function of "electronic reading rooms" [13]. In addition, the U.S. Congress passed the

E-Government Act of 2002 intended to improve the management and promotion of electronic government services and processes [14]. In 2009, President Obama created Data.gov to "increase public access to high value, machine readable datasets generated by the Executive Branch of the Federal Government" [15].

Instead of a passive electronic reading room as described in 1996, however, the Internet has evolved into a proactive medium, or Web 2.0, for governments, politicians, and citizens in the 21st century. *Web* 2.0 is the title of a book by Dermont McCormack published in 2002 [16]. Nevertheless, the term "Web 2.0" was popularized by Dale Dougherty, Vice President of O'Reilly Media, to describe the present, evolutionary stage of the Internet since the do-com bust in 2001 [17]. With the advent of Web 2.0 social media tools and applications, Government 2.0 (or Gov 2.0) fosters a two-way communication between citizens and governments.

In his 2011 State of the Union Address, President Barack Obama said, "30 years ago, we couldn't know that something called the Internet would lead to an economic revolution. What we can do—what America does better than anyone—is spark the creativity and imagination of our people. We are the nation that put cars in driveways and computers in offices; the nation of Edison and the Wright brothers; of Google and Facebook. In America, innovation doesn't just change our lives. It's how we make a living" [18].

In September 2011, the Obama administration launched "We the People on WhiteHouse.gov," a new online platform for Americans to create and sign petitions on a range of issues affecting the United States [19]. When a petition gathers enough online signatures, it will be reviewed by government policy experts who will then issue an official response.

Steven VanRoekel, U.S. Chief Information Officer, said in October 2011 that America has become a "Facebook nation" that demands increased transparency and interactivity from the federal government [20]. His solution is to bring startup culture to the bureaucracy. He argues that the ubiquity of social media has created a "Facebook nation" that expects the same kinds of interactivity from commercial websites as it does from the federal government.

10.2 Gov 2.0 Apps

In a June 2012 interview with *CNN*, U.S. Chief Technology Officer Todd Park said that he wanted to unleash the power of data, technology, and innovation. Park explained the power of government data: "It's the notion of government taking a public good, which is this data—say weather data, or the global-positioning system or health-related knowledge and information—making it available in electronic, computable form and having entrepreneurs and innovators of all stripes turn it into an unbelievable array of products and services that improves lives and create jobs" [21].

Indeed, the White House has been promoting the Open Data Initiatives program to "stimulate a rising tide of innovation and entrepreneurship that utilizes government data to create tools that help Americans in numerous ways—e.g., apps and services that help people find the right health care provider, identify the college that provides the best value for their money, save money on electricity bills through smarter shopping, or keep their families safe by knowing which products have been recalled" [22]. The Open Data Initiatives program will also support the Health Data Initiative launched in 2010 by the Institute of Medicine and the U.S. Department of Health and Human Services.

In addition to the federal government, state and local government officials have also been active in promoting Government 2.0. With more than a million Twitter followers, mayor Cory Booker of Newark, New Jersey is an exemplary government official who actively uses Twitter to help citizens who are in need and to keep them informed. On New Year's Eve 2009, for example, Mayor Booker and his volunteers shoveled the driveway of a 65-year-old Newark man after receiving a tweet from the man's concerned daughter [23].

To facilitate communication between citizens and local governments, technologies have created an assortment of Gov 2.0 applications such as "SeeClickFix" and "Street Bump." "SeeClickFix" allows anyone to file a public report online or via a mobile phone with GPS location about a non-emergency issue [24]. Their website claims to have fixed 75,000 issues as of April 2012. "Street Bump" is an Android app piloted by Boston's Mayor's Office of New Urban Mechanics to catch potholes using the smartphone's built-in accelerometer [25]. As of April 2012, "Street Bump" works in four cities: Boston, Austin, New York City, and London.

"I see [the Gov 2.0 applications] as the death of a passive relationship with government," said Clay Johnson, director of Sunlight Labs and author of *The Information Diet*. "Instead of people saying, 'Well, it's the government's job to fix that,' … people are taking ownership and saying, 'Hey, wait a minute. Government is us. We are government. So let's take a responsibility and start changing things ourselves'" [26]. Reddit's co-founder Alexis Ohanian voiced a similar opinion, "In the face of everything else that's screwed up in Washington, we the American people can fix things" [27].

As local government releases more community-specific data to the public, new Gov 2.0 utility apps are popping up. Among them are "EcoFinder," "Are You Safe," "DiscoverBPS," and "Adopt a Hydrant." "EcoFinder" informs its users where to recycle and properly dispose of hazardous materials in San Francisco [28]. "Are You Safe" displays a safety level on the Threat Meter along with up-to-date crime data in the immediate vicinity of the smartphone user traveling in various cities including Atlanta, Washington D.C., Sacramento, Indianapolis, Milwaukee, Chicago, San Francisco, Dallas, and Cincinnati [29]. "DiscoverBPS" assists parents in finding eligible schools for students in grade K0 through 12 in the Boston area [30]. "Adopt a Hydrant" encourages Boston residences to help shovel out a fire hydrant after it snows [31].

Jennifer Pahlka, founder and executive director of Code for America, spoke at the TED2012 conference in February 2012, "Code for America … it's a little bit like a Peace Corps for geeks. We select a few fellows every year, and we have them work with city governments. … One of the applications the Code for America fellows wrote last year is called Adopt-a-Hydrant. It lets Bostonians sign up to dig out fire hydrants when they're covered in snow. ... It's open-source, so anyone can take the code. Forest Frizzell in the IT department of the City of Honolulu found it and realized he could use it to recruit citizens to check on the tsunami sirens in his city to make sure they're functioning. Seattle is planning to use it to get citizens to clear clogged storm drains. Chicago has rolled it out to let people sign up to shovel sidewalks when it snows. There are now nine cities we know of looking to use this app, and it's happening organically, frictionlessly" [32]. Pahlka suggested how government might work more like the Internet itself: "permission less, open, generative."

Mark Zuckerberg echoed Jennifer Pahlka's ambition in his letter from the Facebook IPO filing in 2012. Zuckerberg expounded his hope to change how people relate to their governments and social institutions:

> We believe building tools to help people share can bring a more honest and transparent dialogue around government that could lead to more direct empowerment of people, more accountability for officials and better solutions to some of the biggest problems of our time. By giving people the power to share, we are starting to see people make their voices heard on a different scale from what has historically been possible. These voices will increase in number and volume. They cannot be ignored. Over time, we expect governments will become more responsive to issues and concerns raised directly by all their people rather than through intermediaries controlled by a select few [33].

10.3 The Kony 2012 Phenomenon

"Kony 2012" is a perfect exemplification of social networks empowering people in voicing their concerns over injustice in the world. Uploaded to YouTube on March 5, 2012, the "Kony 2012" video has garnered over 87 million views within a month [34]. With the goal of capturing the notorious criminal Joseph Kony, Invisible Children's 30-min documentary film about the Ugandan warlord has been shared all over Facebook and mentioned incessantly on Twitter. The video went viral almost instantly after Invisible Children shared the YouTube link on Facebook, Tmblr, and Twitter [35].

As shown in Fig. 10.2, the "Kony 2012" video statistics retrieved on March 8, 2012 from YouTube indicated the following significant discovery events over a four-day period:

1. More than 2.6 million views came from mobile devices.
2. Over 1 million views came from the embedded YouTube video on Facebook.
3. Additional 1 million views came from referrals on Facebook.
4. Almost 300,000 views came from referrals on Twitter.
5. A combination of 150,000 views came from YouTube search and Google search.
6. More than 50,000 views came from the embedded video on Twitter.

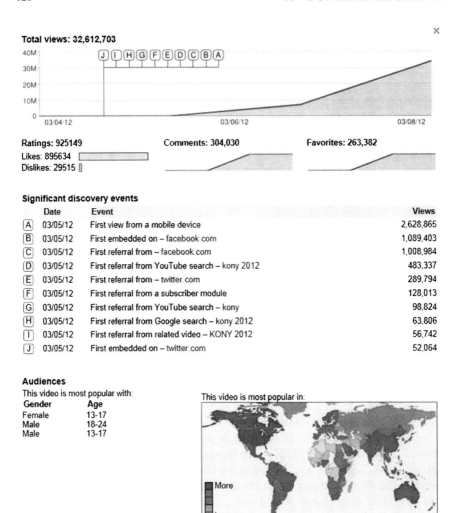

Fig. 10.2 Kony 2012 Video Statistics from YouTube on March 8, 2012

The discovery events confirmed that Facebook and Twitter were instrumental in spreading the "Kony 2012" video around the world with lightning speed.

Moreover, the audiences' breakdown in Fig. 10.2 showed that among the 32.6 million views between March 5 and 8, the video was most popular in the United States with female ages 13–17, followed by male ages 18–24 and 13–17. Columbia University professor Emily Bell found out about the "Kony 2012" video from her 11-year-old [36]. The City University of New York journalism professor discovered the video from his daughter's Facebook page [37]. Mark C. Toner, deputy spokesman at the State Department, had the video brought to his attention by his 13-year-old. Stories like these abounded.

Soon enough, Hollywood celebrities and entertainers joined in and ignited more chatter on Facebook, Twitter, and other social networks with their millions of fans [38]. Some of the notable tweets included [39]:

- Oprah Winfrey to her 10 million followers: "Thanks tweeps for sending me info about ending #LRAviolence. I am aware. Have supported with $'s and voice and will not stop. #KONY2012" (March 6, 2102)
- Ryan Seacrest to his 6 million followers: "Was going to sleep last night and saw ur tweets about #StopKony… watched in bed, was blown away. If u haven't seen yet on.fb.me/zClYoj" (March 7, 2012)
- Justin Bieber to his 18 million followers: "it is time to make him known. Im calling on ALL MY FANS, FRIENDS, and FAMILY to come together and #STOPKONY—youtu.be/Y4MnpzG5Sqc" (March 7, 2012)
- Kim Kardashian to her 14 million followers: "#Kony2012 Wow just watched! What a powerful video! Stop Kony!!! RT @KendallJenner: please WATCH THIS… vimeo.com/37119711" (March 7, 2012)

The ripple effect reached all the way to the U.S. government. State Department spokeswoman Victoria Nuland answered reporters' questions at a daily press briefing on March 8, 2012 [40]:

QUESTION: *Toria, have you seen this video that's going around the web, the Kony 2012 video, and does the State Department have a reaction to that or a comment on it?*

MS. NULAND: *We have. It's had some 25 million tweets. In fact, Mark had it brought to his attention by his 13-year-old, I think, earlier this morning.* Well, certainly we appreciate the efforts of the group, Invisible Children, to shine a light on the horrible atrocities of the LRA. As you know, there are neighboring states, there are NGO groups who have been working on this problem for decades, and we, of course, are very much involved in trying to support all the states of East and Central Africa. We have a multifaceted strategy to work on this, including, as you know, we now have special forces advisors working to train some of the neighboring states in their efforts to get a handle on this awful, awful problem.

QUESTION: And if I could just follow up, *the film makes a point that they are doing this now because the U.S.—they say the U.S. could pull out these advisors that you cited at any moment. So they're trying to keep up the momentum.* Is that a concern—a right concern on their part that these advisors could be moved out of Uganda?

MS. NULAND: I don't have any information to indicate that we are considering that, but that would be a question for the Pentagon. As you know, they've only been in for a couple of months, and we consider them a very important augmentation of our effort to help the East and Central African countries with this problem.

As you know, hundreds of people—*hundreds and thousands of people around the world, especially young people, have been mobilized to express concern for the communities in Central Africa that have been placed under siege by the LRA. So the degree to which this YouTube video helps to increase awareness and increase support for the work that governments are doing, including our own government, that can only help all of us.*

QUESTION: And just one more, if I may. Would an update on what these advisors are doing currently be more of a question for the Pentagon, or do you have a summary?

MS. NULAND: Well, we've spoken about this in general terms. If you need a detailed briefing, I'd send you to them. But we are not part of the fight ourselves. We're involved in training and supporting and providing advice to the forces of the governments of East and Central Africa that are engaged in the fight.

QUESTION: *Are you concerned that this type of call, which takes viral form on the web and so on, might increase pressure for direct U.S. involvement in the fight for Kony rather than just providing the support that you mentioned?*

MS. NULAND: *I don't think anybody in the region favors that.* What they have asked for is this logistical technical training support, and that is what we are providing. We are also helping them with their public information campaign. We are trying to get the word into these communities that if members of the LRA, whether they're pressed into service or whether they're volunteers, are ready to defect, that they'll have support in doing that, et cetera.

The March 8th daily press briefing demonstrated that the "Kony 2012" video did prompt the U.S. State Department to address the issue of American apathy in the past and the recent involvement of the U.S. government in finding a solution to the problem. The Department's spokeswoman even acknowledged that a 13-year-old brought the video to the attention of her colleague at the State Department.

A little over a month later on April 13, 2012, the "Kony 2012" video statistics from YouTube indicated a slight change in the audiences' demographics: the video was still most popular in the United States (and Canada) with female ages 13–17, but the second latest group was male ages 45–54, larger than the previous groups of male ages 18–24 and 13–17. (See Fig. 10.3).

The new data implied that on the Internet, news of "Kony 2012" spread from the younger generation to the older generation. It explained why male ages 45–54 replaced male ages 18–24 as the second largest group of viewers after a month.

"No one wants a boring documentary on Africa," said filmmaker Jason Russell, co-founder of Invisible Children who spent years in making the documentary. "Maybe we have to make it pop, and we have to make it cool. We view ourselves as the Pixar of human rights stories" [41].

Ben Keesey, Invisible Children's CEO, acknowledged to *The Wall Street Journal* that the video was made to appeal to children. Kessey admitted in an interview, "How do we make this translate to a 14-year-old who just walked out of algebra class?" [42].

Notwithstanding the video's serious subject matter, "Kony 2012" succeeded in drawing the initial massive wave of attention from the younger generation, mostly teenagers and college students ages 13 and above, who do care about human rights and social issues to the extent that they want to share the news with all their friends on Facebook and Twitter.

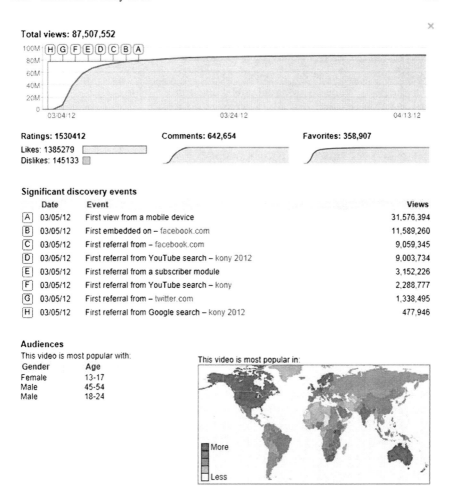

Fig. 10.3 Kony 2012 Video Statistics from YouTube on April 13, 2012

10.4 Reactions to Kony 2012

Skeptic Andrew Keen voiced his concerns on *CNN*, "In a post-era era world of 'Kony2012,' with its harrypotterfication of reality and its transformation of Africa from a complex, infinitely nuanced society into a manichaean Madison Avenue fantasy of good and evil, are we all now becoming teenagers? Should we really be empowering children to make moral decisions about a world in which they have little experience? Should we entrust the innocent, that 'bunch of littles' who have made 'Kony 2012' such an instant hit, to architect our brave new connected world?" [43].

No amount of skepticism can change the fact that the younger generation is a powerful force to be reckoned with in the Internet age. Nevertheless, both children and adults can be equally susceptible to well-crafted propagandas and disinformation, as Journalist Matthew Ingram thoughtfully questioned, "Is Kony 2012 a sign of how powerful social media can be as a news distribution mechanism, a sign of how dangerous it can be, or both?" [44].

On the heels of the phenomenal public attention of "Kony 2012," Sheila Lyall Grant and Huberta von Voss-Wittig, wives of the British and German ambassadors to the United Nations, posted a 4-min video on YouTube to ask the viewers to petition Asma al-Assad for peace in Syria [45]. The April 16, 2012 video juxtaposed glamorous pictures of Syria's first lady Asma al-Assad against disturbing images of dead and injured Syrian children [46]. Grant and Voss-Wittig urged Asma to help end the bloodshed in her country [47]: "Stand up for peace ... for the sake of your people. ... No one cares about your image. We care about your action" [48]. The YouTube video encouraged the public to sign the petition and spread the word on Facebook, Twitter, and LinkedIn [49].

Social media has become a powerful information distribution mechanism. Information is power; and with power comes responsibility.

10.5 SOPA/PIPA Blackout Day

The MPAA and RIAA called the SOPA/PIPA blackout on January 18, 2012 an "abuse of power" when Wikipedia, Reddit, WordPress, *Wired*, *Boing Boing*, Mozilla, Google, Flickr, and other websites went dark or posting anti-SOPA/PIPA messages on their homepages that reach out to more than 1 billion people [50].

In May 2011, Vermont Senator Patrick Leahy and 15 bipartisan co-sponsors in the U.S. Senate introduced PIPA, the PROTECT IP (Preventing Real Online Threats to Economic Creativity and Theft of Intellectual Property) Act [51]. PIPA would enhance enforcement against rogue websites operated and registered overseas, and would eliminate the financial incentive to steal intellectual property online.

The Senate Judiciary Committee unanimously passed the PIPA bill, but Oregon Senator Ron Wyden placed a hold on it, citing that the overreaching legislation poses a significant threat to Internet commerce, innovation, and free speech. Wyden issued a press release on May 26, 2011, "I understand and agree with the goal of the legislation, to protect intellectual property and combat commerce in counterfeit goods, but I am not willing to muzzle speech and stifle innovation and economic growth to achieve this objective. At the expense of legitimate commerce, PIPA's prescription takes an overreaching approach to policing the Internet when a more balanced and targeted approach would be more effective. The collateral damage of this approach is speech, innovation and the very integrity of the Internet" [52].

A group of 55 high-profile venture capitalists also opposed the PIPA bill. They wrote a letter to the U.S. Congress in June 2011 to express their concerns: "As investors in technology companies, we agree with the goal of fostering a thriving digital content market online. Unfortunately, the current bill will not only fail to achieve that goal, it will stifle investment in Internet services, throttle innovation, and hurt American competitiveness. ... The entire set of issues surrounding copyright in an increasingly digital world are [sic] extremely complex, and there are no simple solutions. These challenges are best addressed by imagining, inventing, and financing new models and new services that will allow creative activities to thrive in the digital world. There is a new model for financing, distributing, and profiting from copyrighted material and it is working—just look at services like iTunes, Netflix, Pandora, Kickstarter, and more. Pirate web sites will always exist, but if rights holders make it easy to get their works through innovative Internet models, they can and will have bright futures" [53].

Undeterred by the oppositions, the U.S. Chamber of Commerce sent a letter to the U.S. Congress in support of the PIPA legislation. Signed in September 2011 by an impressive list of 360 businesses and professional organizations, the letter read, "IP-intensive industries are a cornerstone of the U.S. economy, employing more than 19 million people and accounting for 60 percent of exports. Rampant online counterfeiting and piracy presents a clear and present threat to American jobs and innovation. A study examined approximately 100 rogue sites and found that these sites attracted more than 53 billion visits per year, which average out to approximately nine visits for every man, woman, and child on Earth. Global sales of counterfeit goods via the Internet from illegitimate retailers reached $135 billion in 2010. The theft of American IP is the theft of American jobs" [54].

The U.S. Chamber of Commerce list of 360 included industry heavyweights and household names such as 3 M, American Society of Composers, Authors and Publishers (ASCAP), Broadcast Music, Inc. (BMI), Dolby Laboratories, Electronic Arts, Harley-Davidson, Motion Picture Association of America (MPAA), National Basketball Association (NBA), National Football League (NFL), Nike, Nintendo, Pfizer, Philip Morris, Ralph Lauren, Recording Industry Association of America (RIAA), Reebok, Revlon, Rite Aid, Rolex, SESAC, Sony, The Dow Chemical Company, The Walt Disney Company, Tiffany & Co., Time Warner, Toshiba, Viacom, Walmart, World Wrestling Entertainment (WWE), and Xerox.

Texas Representative Lamar S. Smith agreed with the U.S. Chamber of Commerce. In October 2011, Smith and a bipartisan group of lawmakers in the U.S. House of Representatives introduced the Stop Online Piracy Act (SOPA), a bill that would expand the authority of U.S. law enforcement to shut down websites that offer pirated content such as music, films, software, and other intellectual properties [55]. SOPA's goal was "to promote prosperity, creativity, entrepreneurship, and innovation by combating the theft of U.S. property, and for other purposes" [56]. The bill would also provide immunity for a service provider, payment network provider, Internet advertising service, advertiser, Internet search engine, domain name registry, or domain name registrar for voluntarily blocking access to or ending financial affiliation with an Internet site that offers pirated content.

Although the objective of SOPA was indisputable, the content of the bill generated a huge backlash. "There is no need for a bill this sweeping and this Draconian," said Gigi B. Sohn, president and co-founder of Public Knowledge. "There are simple, easily implemented solutions on which industry and others agree—such as cutting off the ability of credit-card companies to fulfill payments to sites that traffic in copyright infringement. At a time when Congress and the Obama Administration are trying to cut back on sweeping, overbroad regulation, we are disappointed that House Judiciary Committee Chairman Lamar Smith and his co-sponsors have chosen this means of establishing a vast new regulatory regime over the Internet" [57].

In November 2011, AOL, eBay, Facebook, Google, LinkedIn, Mozilla, Twitter, Yahoo!, and Zynga sent a joint letter to the U.S. Congress and placed a full-page ad in *The New York Times*:

> We support the bills' stated goals—providing additional enforcement tools to combat foreign 'rogue' websites that are dedicated to copyright infringement or counterfeiting. Unfortunately, the bills as drafted would expose law-abiding U.S. Internet and technology companies to new and uncertain liabilities, private rights of action, and technology mandates that would require monitoring of websites. We are concerned that these measures pose a serious risk to our industry's continued track record of innovation and job creation, as well as to our nation's cybersecurity. One issue merits special attention. We are very concerned that the bills as written would seriously undermine the effective mechanism Congress enacted in the Digital Millennium Copyright Act (DMCA) to provide a safe harbor for Internet companies that act in good faith to remove infringing content from their sites. Since their enactment in 1998, the DMCA's safe harbor provisions for online service providers have been a cornerstone of the U.S. Internet and technology industry's growth and jeopardize a foundational structure that has worked for content owners and Internet companies alike information lawfully online [58].

Vint Cerf, one of the fathers of the Internet and now Google's vice president, provided scientific explanations for his objection to SOPA. In December 2011, Vint Cerf wrote Lamar S. Smith an open letter:

> I appreciate the opportunity to express my concerns about and opposition to the managers' amendment to the Stop Online Piracy Act (SOPA) and, in particular, the 'technological solutions' related to the Domain Name System (DNS) and search engines. … Even with the proposed manager's amendment, SOPA's site-blocking provisions remain problematic. They would undermine the architecture of the Internet and obstruct the 15 year effort by the public and private sectors to improve cybersecurity through implementation of DNSSEC, a critical set of extensions designed to address security vulnerabilities in the DNS. This collateral damage of SOPA would be particularly regrettable because site blocking or redirection mechanisms are unlikely to make a significant dent in the availability of infringing material and counterfeits online, given that DNS manipulation can be defeated by simply choosing an offshore DNS resolution provider, maintaining one's own local DNS cache or using direct IP address references. The search engine remedy also suffers from the fact that it will not be effective in preventing users' access to illegal, offshore websites. A congressional 'tech mandate' on search engines to delete a domain name from search results does not result in the website disappearing. Users can and do today find their way to these websites largely without the help of search engines. Relative to the questionable efficacy of this proposed remedy, requiring search engines to delete a domain name begins a worldwide arms race of unprecedented 'censorship' of the Web [59].

Go Daddy, the world's largest ICANN-accredited registrar with 47 million domain names under its management, had been working with federal lawmakers for months to help craft revisions to SOPA. In contrast to Vint Cerf's viewpoints, Go Daddy's Executive Vice President and General Counsel Christine N. Jones testified before the U.S. House of Representatives Committee on the Judiciary on April 6, 2011:

> In 2010 alone, Go Daddy suspended approximately 150,000 websites found to be engaged in illegal or malicious activity. ... We believe that DNS blocking, as opposed to DNS filtering, is a much more effective vehicle for removing illegal content from the Internet. DNS blocking is different from DNS filtering in that DNS blocking is action taken at the 'authoritative' or 'response' level of the DNS cycle. As such, it needs to be done by the registrar (which provides the authoritative DNS response), or, in cases where the registrar is unable or unwilling to comply, by the registry (which provides the Root zone file records—the database—for the entire TLD [Top-Level Domain]). Though a very similar technical process to DNS filtering, DNS blocking provides a much more thorough solution because it applies to all Internet users, regardless of which ISP they are a customer of or whether proxy services are used. Where DNS blocking is imposed, Internet users will not be able to access a ParaSite by any common means [60].

Nonetheless, no revisions of SOPA and PIPA could quench the fierce opposition to the bills. After all, legislators are not scientists, and lawmakers are not expected to propose technical solutions to copyright infringement and counterfeiting.

Wikipedia's CEO Jimmy Wales announced that the Wikipedia domain names would move away from Go Daddy [61]. Cheezburger's CEO Ben Huh announced they would be moving their 1,000 + registered domains elsewhere [62]. As a result of the aggressive anti-Go Daddy campaign, 21,000 domains transferred out of Go Daddy in just 1 day [63]. Bowing to boycott and criticism from high-profile clients, Go Daddy reluctantly reversed their stance and rescinded their support of SOPA on December 23, 2011 [64]:

"Fighting online piracy is of the utmost importance, which is why Go Daddy has been working to help craft revisions to this legislation – but we can clearly do better," said Go Daddy CEO Warren Adelman, "It's very important that all Internet stakeholders work together on this. Getting it right is worth the wait. Go Daddy will support it when and if the Internet community supports it" [65].

The "when and if" did not happen. Instead, Internet businesses, big and small, were preparing for a "blackout" day on January 18, 2012 to protest SOPA and PIPA.

Chris Dodd, Connecticut Senator and CEO of the Motion Picture Association of America (MPAA), issued the following statement on January 17, 2012 to criticize the impending blackout [66]:

> Only days after the White House and chief sponsors of the legislation responded to the major concern expressed by opponents and then called for all parties to work cooperatively together, some technology business interests are resorting to stunts that punish their users or turn them into their corporate pawns, rather than coming to the table to find solutions to a problem that all now seem to agree is very real and damaging. It is an irresponsible response and a disservice to people who rely on them for information and use their services. It is also an abuse of power given the freedoms these companies enjoy in the marketplace today. It's a dangerous and troubling development when the platforms that serve as gateways to information intentionally skew the facts to incite their users in order to further their corporate interests. A so-called 'blackout' is yet another gimmick, albeit a dangerous one, designed to punish elected and administration officials who are working diligently to protect American jobs from foreign criminals. It is our hope that the White

House and the Congress will call on those who intend to stage this 'blackout' to stop the hyperbole and PR stunts and engage in meaningful efforts to combat piracy.

Dodd's pleading went unheeded. On January 18, 2012, the Internet revolted by staging the largest online protest in history. Over 115,000 websites participated in the strike by going dark and/or posting anti-SOPA messages on their homepages that reach out to more than 1 billion people [67]. The largest participants included Google, Reddit, Craigslist, Wikipedia, WordPress, Mozilla, Tumblr, Cheezburger, Imgur, Pinterest, Flickr, and Amazon. (See Fig. 10.4).

Wikipedia displayed on its homepage, "Imagine a World Without Free Knowledge: For over a decade, we have spent millions of hours building the largest encyclopedia in human history. Right now, the U.S. Congress is considering legislation that could fatally damage the free and open Internet. For 24 h, to raise awareness, we are blacking out Wikipedia."

WordPress and *Wired* placed black "censored" bars over their blogs and stories. WordPress wrote, "Many websites are blacked out today to protest proposed U.S. legislation that threatens internet freedom: the Stop Internet Piracy Act (SOPA) and the Protect IP Act (PIPA). From personal blogs to Wikipedia, sites all over the web—including this one—are asking you to help stop this dangerous legislation from being passed."

Google added a black "censored" bar atop its logo as well as a link "Tell Congress: Please don't censor the web!" to the Google Public Policy Blog that said, "You might notice many of your favorite websites look different today. Wikipedia is down. WordPress is dark. We're censoring our homepage logo and asking you to petition Congress. So what's the big deal? Right now in Washington D.C., Congress is considering two bills that would censor the web and impose burdensome regulations on American businesses. They're known as the PRO-TECT IP Act (PIPA) in the Senate and the Stop Online Piracy Act (SOPA) in the House. … Fighting online piracy is extremely important. We are investing a lot of time and money in that fight. … Because we think there's a good way forward that doesn't cause collateral damage to the web, we're joining Wikipedia, Twitter, Tumblr, Reddit, Mozilla and other Internet companies in speaking out against SOPA and PIPA" [68].

Reddit remarked on its website, "SOPA and PIPA damage reddit. Today we fight back. Today, for 12 h, reddit.com goes dark to raise awareness of two bills in congress: H.R.3261 'Stop Online Piracy Act' and S.968 'PROTECT IP', which could radically change the landscape of the Internet. These bills provide overly broad mechanisms for enforcement of copyright which would restrict innovation and threaten the existence of websites with user-submitted content, such as reddit. Please take today as a day of focus and action to learn about these destructive bills and do what you can to prevent them from becoming reality."

Boing Boing displayed a "503: Service Unavailable" message with an explanation, "Boing Boing is offline today, because the US Senate is considering legislation that would certainly kill us forever. The legislation is called the PROTECT IP Act (PIPA), and would put us in legal jeopardy if we linked to a site anywhere

Fig. 10.4 Homepages of Wikipedia, WordPress, Wired, Google, Firefox, Cheezburger, Reddit, and Boing Boing on January 18, 2012

online that had any links to copyright infringement. This would unmake the Web, just as proposed in the Stop Online Piracy Act (SOPA). We don't want that world."

Cheezburger popped up a huge panel with the message: "CHEEZBURGER NEEDS YOUR HELP. This and millions of other sites could be censored by the US government. A bill called PIPA proposed in the US Senate will cripple the Web—one of the biggest job-creating engines in America—and censor our online freedoms. It could mean the censoring of Cheezburger, Facebook, Wikipedia, and millions of others. It will mean censoring you. We need to tell our Senators that this bill needs to be stopped."

Mozilla redirected traffic from the Mozilla.org and Mozill.com for 12 h to an action page that said, "Today Mozilla joins with other sites in a virtual strike to protest two proposed laws in the United States, called SOPA and the PROTECT IP Act. On January 24th, the U.S. Senate will vote on the PROTECT IP Act to censor the Internet, despite opposition from the vast majority of Americans. Join us to protect our rights to free speech, privacy, and prosperity."

The wide-scale Internet protest was a triumph. Two days after the blackout, the U.S. Congress shelved the PIPA and SOPA bills on January 20 [69].

10.6 Reactions to SOPA/PIPA Blackout

"The SOPA/PIPA blackout … was a whole new form of engagement and protest. I know that a lot of people in Hollywood were absolutely shocked at the effectiveness of that," said Marc Andreessen, co-founder of Netscape and venture capital firm Andreessen Horowitz that funded Facebook, Twitter, Zynga, Groupon, and Pinterest, and other Internet companies [70].

"With SOPA and PIPA," Google's co-founder Sergey Brin opined, "fears of piracy had reduced the entertainment industry to shooting itself in the foot, or maybe worse than in the foot" [71].

Google fights piracy in its own way by processing removal requests from copyright holders. In May 2012, Google's Transparency Report online indicated that in the past month more than 1.25 million URLs from 24,374 domains were removed from the Google search results [72].

Fred von Lohmann, senior copyright counsel at Google, said, "We believe that the time-tested 'notice-and-takedown' process for copyright strikes the right balance between the needs of copyright owners, the interests of users and our efforts to provide a useful Google Search experience" [73]. For YouTube videos, copyright holders can submit copyright infringement notifications online or sign up for YouTube's Content Verification Program [74].

Sean Parker, co-founder of Napster and founding president of Facebook, told an audience at the 2012 South by Southwest conference in Austin, Texas, "The way online communities rose up to ultimately derail the Stop Online Piracy Act is heartening. … SOPA awakened that sleeping giant. There are a lot of really smart hackers in this audience. We need to put our heads together and take control of this [political] system … before the slow-thinking incumbents … know what's happening" [75].

Indeed, the effectiveness of the SOPA/PIPA blackout took Vermont Senator Patrick Leahy by surprise. As U.S. senators and representatives dropped their support of the anti-piracy bills after the blackout [76], Leahy retorted, "I understand and respect Majority Leader Reid's decision to seek consent to vitiate cloture on the motion to proceed to the PROTECT IP Act. But the day will come when the senators who forced this move will look back and realize they made a knee-jerk reaction to a monumental problem. Somewhere in China today, in Russia today, and in many other countries that do not respect American intellectual property, criminals who do nothing but peddle in counterfeit products and stolen American content are smugly watching how the U.S. Senate decided it was not even worth debating how to stop the overseas criminals from draining our economy" [77].

Cary H. Sherman, CEO of the Recording Industry Association of America (RIAA) that represents music labels, criticized the blackout tactic in *The New York Times*: "Wikipedia, Google and others manufactured controversy by unfairly equating SOPA with censorship. ... The hyperbolic mistruths, presented on the home pages of some of the world's most popular Web sites, amounted to an abuse of trust and a misuse of power. ... The violation of neutrality is a patent hypocrisy. ... What the Google and Wikipedia blackout showed is that it's the platforms that exercise the real power. Get enough of them to espouse Silicon Valley's perspective, and tens of millions of Americans will get a one-sided view of whatever the issue may be, drowning out the other side" [78].

Whether we are for or against SOPA and PIPA, January 18, 2012 will forever be remembered as a historic day when the new-age Internet technology companies triumphed over the age-old entertainment industry.

10.7 Battles over Internet Legislations: OPEN, ACTA, CISPA

With more than 50,000 people petitioned the Obama administration to veto the SOPA bill [79], the White House issued an official response on "We the People on WhiteHouse.gov:"

"While we believe that online piracy by foreign websites is a serious problem that requires a serious legislative response, we will not support legislation that reduces freedom of expression, increases cybersecurity risk, or undermines the dynamic, innovative global Internet. ... Moving forward, we will continue to work with Congress on a bipartisan basis on legislation that provides new tools needed in the global fight against piracy and counterfeiting, while vigorously defending an open Internet based on the values of free expression, privacy, security and innovation" [80].

While SOPA and PIPA have stalled indefinitely, California Representative Darrell Issa and Oregon Senator Ron Wyden have introduced the OPEN (Online Protection and Enforcement of Digital Trade) Act in the U.S. House of Representatives and the U.S. Senate respectively [81]. The new bills are meant to deliver stronger intellectual property rights for American copyright holders while protecting the openness of the Internet.

Back in December 2011, AOL, eBay, Facebook, Google, LinkedIn, Mozilla, Twitter, Yahoo!, and Zynga sent an endorsement letter to Issa and Wyden to express their support of the OPEN Act [82]. These were the same nine companies that opposed SOPA and PIPA.

In March 2012, Tiffiniy Cheng of Fight for the Future and Reddit co-founder Alexis Ohanian registered the domain name internetdefenseleague.org. Their new entity, Internet Defense League, announced in May their plan to defeat ACTA (Anti-Counterfeiting Trade Agreement) and CISPA (Cyber Intelligence Sharing and Protection Act).

Ohanian said, "You can only cry 'Oh my gosh, they're going to shut down the Internet' so often. We've scared [Congress] from doing anything as egregious as SOPA and PIPA again. But the new challenge is this endless series of smaller bills that try to unravel internet rights" [83].

To Obanian's disappointment, Facebook is one of the supporters of CISPA. Ohanian told *CNN's* Soledad O'Brien in a May 2012 interview, "One of the big issues that a lot of us in the tech community have had of late has been their support for bills like CISPA that make it really easy for companies like Facebook to hand over private data about us without any due process" [84]. The Internet Defense League ensures that the battles over Internet legislations rage on.

Notwithstanding the ongoing battles over government legislations, America's largest Internet Service Providers (ISPs) have quietly begun implementing a "graduated response" antipiracy program on July 1, 2012 [85]. The program requires Comcast, Cablevision, Time Warner Cable, Verizon, AT&T, and others ISPs to send out an educational notice to subscribers who download copyrighted content illegally. If a repeat infringer does not stop pirating, an ISP can apply "mitigation measures" such as throttling down the customer's Internet connection speed or suspending his or her account altogether.

10.8 Internet Activism

Facebook's mission is "to give people the power to share and make the world more open and connected" [86]. In the realm of world peace, Facebook has a dedicated website https://peace.facebook.com/ to highlight Friends Without Borders, Invisible Children, One Million Voices Against FARC, Stanford University's Peace Innovation, and other activism [87]. The site also displays statistics on friend connections created each day since November 5, 2011 between people of different regions, religions, and political affiliations. Figure 10.5 shows the daily friendships statistics on August 25, 2012.

Besides world peace, Facebook has been involved with the rally against bullying (since 2011) [88], alerting Facebook users in the United States of their voting

Fig. 10.5 Facebook Daily
Friendships Statistics on
August 25, 2012

Geographic Friendships	Connections
India-Pakistan	180,625
Israel-Palestine	19,155
Albania-Serbia	19,109
Greece-Turkey	6,767

Religious Friendships	Connections
Muslim-Christian	118,454
Christian-Atheist	32,131
Muslim-Jewish	554
Sunni-Shiite	132

Political Friendships	Connections
U.S.	7,885
Conservative/Liberal	

activities on the election day (since 2010) [89], and issuing AMBER Alerts in response to child abductions (since 2009) [90].

In partnership with Donate Life America, Mark Zuckerberg announced on May 1, 2012 that Facebook users could now identify themselves as potential organ donors on Facebook under the "Health & Wellness" section of the Life Event. "The Facebook partnership is an opportunity for people to share decisions," said David Fleming, CEO of Donate Life America, "The most important part of this is actually registering to be a donor so that your wishes can be carried out. Sharing that decision through Facebook is an opportunity to encourage your friends and family to also register" [91].

There are many other examples of Internet activism (aka Web activism) in the United States:

- Co-founded by Sean Parker, former Facebook president, and Joe Green, former Harvard roommate of Mark Zuckerberg, Causes claims to be the world's largest online platform for activism and philanthropy [92]. Since 2007, Causes has brought together 170 million members and raised $40 million dollars for 27,000 nonprofits and 500,000 causes.
- Votizen is a website whose 1.24 million registered users can unlock the potential of their social networks (Facebook, LinkedIn, and Twitter) to see how their friends vote, and to campaign for the candidates by making endorsements and bringing their friends to their side [93]. Votizen has been collecting data from 200 million registered American voters. Co-founder Jason Putorti told *Business Insider*, "Votizen allows people to find voters in their social networks. Only half of people are registered, so it's actually non-trivial to know who votes, as well as see how they're registered and how frequently they vote in their districts. You can then campaign with them to elect the candidates you want to win in 2012 up and down ticket. The way I explain it to people is you're moving votes around that you can influence, so you can have a real impact not just where you live, but all over the country" [94].

- Silicon Valley entrepreneurs Joan Blades and Wes Boyd founded MoveOn.org in 1998 in response to the impeachment of President Bill Clinton by the U.S. House of Representatives. With 5 million members, the online activist group "gives real Americans a voice in a political process dominated by big money and armies of lobbyists" [95]. In 2007, MoveOn.org launched a paid ad campaign on Facebook to protest against Facebook's Beacon advertisements for "glaring violation of [Facebook's] users' privacy" [96].

Internet activism is growing stronger by the number of causes, advocates, supporters, and philanthropists each day. Inspired by the grassroots Occupy Movement against social and economic inequality, former Vice President Al Gore told an overcrowded audience at the South by Southwest conference in Austin, Texas, in March 2012, "Our democracy has been hacked. It no longer works, in the main, to serve the best interests of the people of this country. I would like to see a new movement called Occupy Democracy, where people who have Internet savvy remedy this situation" [97]. Former U.S. Secretary of Labor Robert Reich concurred, "Our democracy is increasingly being taken over by big money and that's wrong. ... We need to occupy democracy" [98].

10.9 Transnational (Arab–Israeli) Facebook Nation

The Internet has empowered individuals to start their own grassroots movements. Amid the longstanding Arab–Israeli conflict since 1920 that has taken more than 107,000 lives [99] and has cost more than $12 trillion dollars [100], Ronny Edry, an Israeli graphic designer based in Tel Aviv, reached out to the people of Iran on Facebook in March 2012. Edry and his wife uploaded posters on Facebook page of Pushpin Mehina with the resounding message "IRANIANS. We will never bomb your country. We *Heart* You" [101].

Edry shared his Facebook experience: "My idea was simple, I was trying to reach the other side. There are all these talks about war, Iran is coming to bomb us and we bomb them back, we are sitting and waiting. I wanted to say the simple words that this war is crazy. In a few hours, I had hundreds of shares and thousands of likes. ... I think it's really amazing that someone from Iran poked me and said 'Hello, I'm from Iran, I saw your poster on Facebook.' ... I got a private message from Iran: 'We love you too. Your word reaches out there, despite the censorship. And Iranian people, aside from the regime, have no hard feelings or animosity towards anybody, particularly Israelis'" [102].

Iran's neighbor Pakistan has also banned Facebook for "hosting competitions featuring blasphemous caricatures." On the first annual "Draw Muhamad Day" on May 20, 2010, the Facebook ban was temporary and lasted for 12 days [103]. On the second annual event on May 20, 2011, however, the Lahore High Court ordered permanent blockage to Facebook and all websites that "spread religious hatred" [104].

10.10   Internet Censorship in Western Democracies and China

Google released a Transparency Report in June 2012 showing an alarming rise in government censorship around the world. Google's senior policy analyst Dorothy Chou wrote, "We've been asked to take down political speech. It's alarming not only because free expression is at risk, but because some of these requests come from countries you might not suspect—Western democracies not typically associated with censorship" [105]. Those countries included Canada, Czech Republic, Germany, Poland, Spain, the United Kingdom, and the United States. During the second half of 2011, the number of content removal requests from the U.S. government increased by a whopping 103 % compared to the first half of 2011 [106].

Twitter released its first Transparency Report on July 2, 2012 [107]. Inspired by Google, Twitter aims to shed more light on government requests received for user information, government requests received to withhold content, and Digital Millennium Copyright Act (DMCA) takedown notices received from copyright holders. With data from January 1 to June 30, 2012, the Transparency Report revealed that an overwhelming 80 % of the user information requests came from the United States, and Twitter provided the requested data 75 % of the time. Japan came in a distant second, followed by Canada and the United Kingdom.

Unlike Western democracies, China made no content removal request to Google during the second half of 2011. Instead, China opts for preemptive measures and imposes severe Internet censorship by banning Facebook, YouTube, and Twitter as well as censoring search results from Google, Yahoo!, MSN, and Baidu [108].

In June 2006, Paris-based Reporters Without Borders identified Yahoo! as the "strictest" search engine censor in China [109]. In March 2010 when Google ceased filtering its search results in China [110], the search giant had to scale back operations in China and redirect users from Google.cn to its uncensored Google.com.hk in Hong Kong [111]. In May 2011, eight New York residents filed a lawsuit against Baidu for aiding Chinese censorship in spite of the fact that Baidu is operating in China in full compliance with the Chinese laws [112].

Weibo, a Chinese counterpart of Twitter, has 300 million registered users as of April 2012 [113], two times the number of Twitter users worldwide. The Chinese authorities are censoring the rumbustious micro blogs by 24/7 monitoring, blacklisting users, deleting illegal or harmful posts, and intercepting messages with Deep Packet Inspection [114]. In response, Weibo users have become skillful at evading censorship by inventing codewords and nicknames such as "Teletubby" for China's Prime Minister Wen Jiabao [115].

Dissident artist Ai Weiwei, who was jailed for 81 days for supporting Arab-style protests in China, wrote in *The Guardian*, "Chairman Mao used to say: 'As communists we gain control with the power of the gun and maintain control with the power of the pen.' You can see propaganda and the control of ideology as an authoritarian society's most important task. … Censorship is saying: 'I'm the one who says the last sentence. Whatever you say, the conclusion is mine.' But the internet is like a tree that is growing. The people will always have the last word —even if someone has a very weak, quiet voice. ... The internet is a wild land with its own games, languages and gestures through which we are starting to share common feelings. But the [Chinese] government cannot give up control. It blocks major internet platforms—such as Twitter and Facebook—because it is afraid of free discussion. And it deletes information. ... China may seem quite successful in its controls, but it has only raised the water level. It's like building a dam: it thinks there is more water so it will build it higher. But every drop of water is still in there. It doesn't understand how to let the pressure out. ... But in the long run, its leaders must understand it's not possible for them to control the internet unless they shut it off—and they can't live with the consequences of that. The internet is uncontrollable. And if the internet is uncontrollable, freedom will win" [116].

One big country did shut down the Internet and suffer the consequences.

10.11   Arab Spring Uprisings and Egypt Shutting Down the Internet

Social media has played a vital role in Arab Spring uprisings including the 2011 Egyptian revolution [117]. Activists organized through Facebook and Twitter the nationwide protests on January 28, 2011 to call for an end to President Hosni Mubarak's government [118].

Mubarak reacted by blocking social media sites and mobile phone networks. A day before the planned demonstrations, the Egyptian government began to shut down the Internet access nationwide. By midnight January 28, virtually all of Egypt's Internet addresses were unreachable [119]. Google responded to the Internet blockade by working with Twitter and SayNow to unveil a web-free speak-to-tweet service, allowing anyone to send and receive tweets by calling a phone number [120].

The unprecedented totalitarian action failed to thwart the planned demonstrations. Fourteen days later on February 11, 2011, Mubarak resigned as president. In May 2011, a judge in Cairo found Mubarak and two officials guilty of "causing damage to the national economy" for cutting cellphone and Internet services during the protests in January [121]. Mubarak was fined $33.6 million. About $16.8 million would be paid to telecommunications companies that were forced to suspend their services during the revolution.

10.12   The Rise of Facebook Nation

Elsewhere in Norway, Christine Bar and Lili Hjonnevag posted on Facebook a call to assemble a choir in downtown Oslo in protest against mass murderer Anders Behring Breivik [122]. Bar and Hjonnevag expected a few dozen responses, but 4,000 people accepted their Facebook invitation, and a mass choir of 40,000 braved the pouring rain and gathered at Oslo's Youngstorget square on April 26, 2012 [123]. Artist Lillebjørn Nilsen led the choir to sing the song "Children of the Rainbow" (Barn av regnbuen) in protest of Breivik who cited in court that the song was an example of Marxist influence on Norwegian children.

On April 30, 2012, 9-year-old Martha Payne in Scotland started blogging about her school lunches, rating and photographing each meal [124]. Payne's blog, NeverSeconds, attracted international attention from schoolchildren, parents, and even British celebrity chef Jamie Oliver who sent a tweet to Payne's father, "Shocking but inspirational blog. Keep going, Big love from Jamie x" [125]. Payne also raises money for Mary's Meals that sets up school feeding projects in the world's poorest communities. However, Scotland local government Argyll and Bute Council banned Payne from taking pictures in the dining hall for the reason of "unwarranted attacks on its schools catering service which culminated in national press headlines which have led catering staff to fear for their jobs" [126]. Payne's supporters wrote many encouraging comments such as "you are an inspiration, bless you for being upfront and honest and not afraid to speak up" and "the world needs your voice; don't let a couple of frightened adults silence you." Amid mounting public criticism of government censorship, Argyll and Bute Council eventually withdrew the ban.

In May 2012, Manal al-Sharif, co-founder of the Women2Drive campaign, received the Václav Havel Prize for Creative Dissent at the Oslo Freedom Forum [127]. Advocating for women's right to drive in Saudi Arabia, Al-Sharif filmed herself a year earlier in May 2011 driving through the Saudi city of Khobar, and posted the video on YouTube and Facebook. In her Havel Prize acceptance speech, Al-Sharif said, "The rain begins with a single drop" [128].

In June 2012, *Time Magazine*'s congressional correspondent Jay Newton-Small asked the Syrian dissident Abu Ghassan whether his AK-47 or his video camera was the more powerful weapon. Ghassan replied, "My AK!" But he paused for a few seconds, and said, "Actually, if there is an Internet connection, my camera is more powerful" [129]. Partially aided by the Internet Freedom Grants from the U.S. State Department, Syrian rebels have been filming the protests and posting them on the Internet [130].

The social networks have been playing an important role everywhere in the world with no exception. With the rise of Facebook nation with over 955 million cybercitizens and 2 billion people connected to the Internet, the World Wide Web is an open platform for debates of opposing views and an outlet for unpopular voices. Internet activism, spearheaded by private individuals as well as organizations, is becoming a driving force for peace and justice around the world regardless of the ruling regimes.

10.13   Electoral College and Social Network Constitution

Grassroots campaigns can help put issues and people on the public agenda. Although Web activism has generated public awareness and achieved some significant results, believing that the Internet empowers each and every individual is somewhat naive.

In the United States of America, the Electoral College, not the American voters, directly elects the President and Vice President of the United States. Known as indirect election, 538 electors from 50 states and the District of Columbia represent some 200 million registered American voters in a U.S. presidential election. Unbeknownst to many voters, Americans cast their ballots for presidential and vice presidential candidates by voting for correspondingly pledged electors. Despite its rarity, some electors can be either unpledged or faithless, and they can ignore the popular votes altogether.

Similarly, the Internet is becoming the online equivalent of the Electoral College. Google, Facebook, Twitter, Wikipedia, YouTube, and other high-traffic websites are the online electors representing the voices of individuals, businesses, and special interest groups. These electors are capable of exerting great influences on politics, as we have witnessed in the SOPA/PIPA blackout.

Cary H. Sherman, CEO of the Recording Industry Association of America (RIAA), described the SOPA/PIPA blackout as "the digital tsunami that swept over the Capitol … forcing Congress to set aside legislation to combat the online piracy of American music, movies, books and other creative works, raised questions about how the democratic process functions in the digital age" [131].

Political strategist and Internet consultant Wesley Donehue warned of the influence of social media in America: "Well for starters, we don't live in a democracy. We never have, nor should we. We live in a republic, where we elect people to take the tough votes and make the tough decisions for us. … Too many politicians aren't voting their conscience, they're voting to placate blog commenters, and that's no way to run government. … Technology has expedited our descent toward a political system devoid of real ideas and bold, controversial thought" [132].

Why is it that technology is often the one to blame? On the contrary, social media encourages people to "think aloud" and come up with bold, new, controversial, or opposing ideas. Bloggers make certain that the political process is no longer confined to "backroom deal-making in a smoke-filled room." Chinese scholar Chen Zhiwu at Yale University wrote, "Microblogs are the best weapon to reduce corruption, improve social governance and make officials behave well" [133]. The United States is light years ahead of China in democracy. Facebook nation will certainly transform the republic in the years to come. Nonetheless, Donehue's controversial and thought-provoking statement is a wake-up call for Americans to examine and comprehend the all-important U.S. Constitution.

Prof. Lori B. Andrews at Chicago-Kent College of Law suggested that since Facebook has become as big and powerful as a country, it is high time that its citizens got a "Social Network Constitution" that governs in minute detail what a social network should or should not do [134]:

> We the people of Facebook Nation, in order to form a more Perfect Internet, to protect our fundamental rights and freedoms, to explore our identities, dreams, and relationships, to safeguard the sanctity of our digital selves, to ensure equal access to technology, to lessen discrimination and disparities, and to promote democratic principles and the general welfare, declare these truths to be self-evident:

1. The Right to Connect.
2. The Right to Free Speech and Freedom of Expression.
3. The Right to Privacy of Place and Information.
4. The Right to Privacy of Thoughts, Emotions and Sentiments.
5. The Right to Control One's Image.
6. The Right to Fair Trial.
7. The Right to an Untainted Jury.
8. The Right to Due Process of Law and the Right to Notice.
9. Freedom from Discrimination.
10. Freedom of Association [135].

The Social Network Constitution would give us the ammunition to mandate Internet businesses to behave constitutionally. Moreover, government legislations affecting Facebook nation would be tested on the ground of being constitutional. Take the case of Malcolm Harris as an example. In February 2012, the District Attorney's Office in Manhattan issued Twitter a subpoena to ask for three months of information connected to the Twitter account that belongs to Harris, who was arrested and charged with disorderly conduct on the Brooklyn Bridge for the Occupy Wall Street protest [136]. In May 2012, Twitter filed a motion in New York state court seeking to quash the court order for turning over the requested information: "If the Fourth Amendment's warrant requirement applies merely to surveillance of one's location in public areas for 28 days, it also applies to the District Attorney's effort to force Twitter to produce over three months worth of a citizen's substantive communications, regardless of whether the government alleges those communications are public or private" [137].

American Civil Liberties Union (ACLU) applauded Twitter's decision: "This is a big deal. ... If Internet users cannot protect their own constitutional rights, the only hope is that Internet companies do so. ... That is why it is so important to encourage those companies that we all increasingly rely on to do what they can to protect their customers' free speech and privacy rights" [138].

ACLU proposes that companies who are stewards of our digital lives should [139]:

- Tell you when the government is asking for your information so that you can protect yourself;
- Disclose how often they share information with the government;
- Stand up for user privacy in the courts and in Congress;
- Advocate for an update to the outdated Electronic Privacy Communications Act (ECPA) which was passed in 1986 before the Internet as we know it today existed.

Although the call for a Social Network Constitution is a tall order, we can rest assured that the pen is mightier than the sword.

References

1. Allen, Erika Tyner. (Retrieved April 10, 2012). The Kennedy-Nixon Presidential Debates, 1960. The Museum of Broadcast Communications. http://www.museum.tv/eotvsection. php?entrycode=kennedy-nixon
2. Vargas, Jose Antonio. (November 20, 2008). Obama Raised Half a Billion Online. The Washington Post. http://voices.washingtonpost.com/44/2008/11/20/obama_raised_half_a_billion_on.html
3. Vargas, Jose Antonio. (August 20, 2008). Obama's Wide Web: From YouTube to Text Messaging, Candidate's Team Connects to Voters. The Washington Post. http://www.washingtonpost.com/wp-dyn/content/story/2008/08/19/ST2008081903613.html
4. McGirt, Ellen. (April 1, 2009). How Chris Hughes Helped Launch Facebook and the Barack Obama Campaign. Fast Company. http://www.fastcompany.com/magazine/134/boy-wonder.html
5. Schiffman, Betsy. (November 7, 2008). The Reason for the Obama Victory: It's the Internet, Stupid. Wired. http://www.wired.com/epicenter/2008/11/the-obama-victo/
6. Obama, Barack. (November 5, 2008). @BarackObama. Twitter. http://twitter.com/#!/barackobama/statuses/992176676
7. Weiner, Rachel. (December 7, 2008). Change.Gov Launched. The Huffington Post. http://www.huffingtonpost.com/2008/11/06/changegov-launched_n_141822.html
8. The Office of the President-Elect. (November 2008). change.gov. Open Government. http://change.gov/content/home
9. Lothian, Dan; Brittain, Becky. (January 30, 2012). Obama hosts Google 'hangout.' CNN. http://www.cnn.com/2012/01/30/politics/obama-google/index.html
10. The White House. (Retrieved April 9, 2012). The White House. http://www.whitehouse.gov
11. United States Department of Justice. (Retrieved April 9, 2012). FOIA. FOIA.gov http://www.foia.gov/
12. FOIA Update. Vol. XVII, No. 4. (Fall 1996). The Freedom of Information Act 5 U.S.C. § 552, As Amended By Public Law No. 104−231, 110 Stat. 3048. FOIA Update. Vol. XVII, No. 4. http://www.justice.gov/oip/foia_updates/Vol_XVII_4/page2.htm
13. FOIA Update. Vol. XVII, No. 4. (Fall 1996). Congress Enacts FOIA Amendments. http://www.justice.gov/oip/foia_updates/Vol_XVII_4/page1.htm
14. United States Senate. (Retrieved April 10, 2012). E-Government Act of 2002. National Archives. http://www.archives.gov/about/laws/egov-act-section−207.html
15. Data.gov. (Retrieved March 23, 2012). About data.gov. http://www.data.gov/about
16. McCormack, Dermont; Aspatore Books Staff. (June 15, 2002). Web 2.0: 2003-'08 AC (After Crash): The Resurgence of the Internet & E-Commerce. Aspatore Books.
17. O'Reilly, Tim. (September 30, 2005). What Is Web 2.0. Design Patterns and Business Models for the Next Generation of Software. O'Reilly. http://oreilly.com/web2/archive/what-is-web−20.html
18. Obama, Barack. (January 25, 2011). 2011 State of the Union Address. PBS. http://www.pbs.org/newshour/interactive/speeches/4/2011-state-union-address/
19. Sabochik, Katelyn. (September 22, 2011). Petition the White House with We the People. The White House. http://www.whitehouse.gov/blog/2011/09/22/petition-white-house-we-people
20. Ferenstein, Gregory. (October 24, 2011). Inspired By "Facebook Nation," Obama's Chief Disruptor Brings Startup Culture To The Gov't. Fast Company. http://www.fastcompany.com/1790016/steven-vanroekel-cio
21. Ferenstein, Gregory. (June 14, 2012). Obama's chief tech officer: Let's unleash ingenuity of the public. CNN. http://www.cnn.com/2012/06/14/tech/web/white-house-tech-officer/index.html
22. The White House. (Retrieved June 14, 2012). Presidential Innovation Fellows: Open Data Initiatives. WhiteHouse.gov. http://www.whitehouse.gov/innovationfellows/opendata

23. Kuhn, Eric. (January 3, 2010). Mayor digs in after Twitter appeal. CNN. http://politicalticker.blogs.cnn.com/2010/01/03/mayor-digs-in-after-twitter-appeal/
24. SeeClickFix. (Retrieved April 10, 2012). SeeClickFix. http://www.seeclickfix.com/
25. The Mayor's Office of New Urban Mechanics in Boston. (Retrieved April 10, 2012). Street Bump. http://streetbump.org/
26. Sutter, John D. (December 29, 2009). Cities embrace mobile apps, 'Gov 2.0'. CNN. http://www.cnn.com/2009/TECH/12/28/government.web.apps/index.html
27. Greenberg, Andy. (May 25, 2012). Reddit's Alexis Ohanian And Activists Aim To Build A 'Bat-Signal For The Internet'. Forbes. http://www.forbes.com/sites/andygreenberg/2012/05/25/reddit-founder-and-activists-aim-to-build-a-bat-signal-for-the-internet/
28. ecofindeRRR. (Retrieved April 10, 2012). EcoFinder for iPhone. http://ecofinderapp.com/
29. Are You Safe. (Retrieved April 10, 2012). Are You Safe. http://areyousafeatlanta.com/
30. DiscoverBPS. (Retrieved April 28, 2012). DiscoverBPS. http://discoverbps.org/
31. Adopt a Hydrant. (Retrieved April 28, 2012). Adopt a Hydrant. http://adoptahydrant.org/
32. Pahlka, Jennifer. (March 25, 2012). To fix government, call in the geeks. CNN. http://www.cnn.com/2012/03/25/opinion/pahlka-code-government/index.html
33. Benoit, David. (February 1, 2012). Mark Zuckerberg's Letter From The Facebook Filing. The Wall Street Journal. http://blogs.wsj.com/deals/2012/02/01/mark-zuckerbergs-letter-from-the-facebook-filing/
34. Invisible Children Inc. (March 5, 2012). KONY 2012. YouTube. http://www.youtube.com/watch?v=Y4MnpzG5Sqc
35. Fantz, Ashley. (March 7, 2012). 'Stop Kony' video goes viral, puts spotlight on Ugandan warlord. CNN. http://news.blogs.cnn.com/2012/03/07/viral-video-puts-spotlight-on-ugandan-warlord/
36. Bell, Emily. (March 8, 2012). Twitter. https://twitter.com/#!/emilybell/status/177736783289794560
37. Jarvis, Jeff. (March 8, 2012). Twitter. https://twitter.com/#!/jeffjarvis/status/177743392942473217
38. Goodman, David J.; Preston, Jennifer. (March 9, 2012). How the Kony Video Went Viral. The New York Times. http://thelede.blogs.nytimes.com/2012/03/09/how-the-kony-video-went-viral/
39. NBC Universal. (March 8, 2012).Hollywood Reacts To 'Kony 2012' Video. Access Hollywood. http://www.accesshollywood.com/justin-bieber/kim-kardashian-justin-bieber-and-more-tweet-support-for-kony−2012-movement_article_61715
40. Nuland, Victoria. (March 8, 2012). Daily Press Briefing. Washing, DC. March 8, 2012. U.S. Department of State. http://www.state.gov/r/pa/prs/dpb/2012/03/185423.htm
41. Kron, Josh; Goodman, David J. (March 8, 2012). Online, a Distant Conflict Soars to Topic No. 1. The New York Times. http://www.nytimes.com/2012/03/09/world/africa/online-joseph-kony-and-a-ugandan-conflict-soar-to-topic-no−1.html
42. Orden, Erica; Steel, Emily. (March 9, 2012). How 'Kony' Clip Caught Fire Online. The Wall Street Journal. http://online.wsj.com/article/SB10001424052970204781804577271692294533870.html
43. Keen, Andrew. (March 14, 2012). Opinion: After Kony, should kids decide our morals? CNN. http://www.cnn.com/2012/03/14/opinion/keen-kony−2012/index.html
44. Ingram, Matthew. (March 12, 2012). Kony2012: New Media Success Story or Cautionary Tale? Bloomberg Businessweek. http://www.businessweek.com/articles/2012−03−12/tc-gigaom−0312-kony2012-new-media-success-story-or-cautionary-tale/
45. Roth, Richard. (April 18, 2012). Wives of U.N. diplomats tell Syria's first lady to 'stop being a bystander'. CNN. http://www.cnn.com/2012/04/18/world/meast/syria-un-wives/index.html
46. Women of the World. (April 16, 2012). International Letter & Petition to Asma al-Assad. YouTube. http://www.youtube.com/watch?v=SzUViTShIAo
47. Kekeh, Nicole. (April 18, 2012). After Kony 2012, Now Asma 2012? Forbes. http://www.forbes.com/sites/worldviews/2012/04/18/after-kony−2012-now-asma−2012/

48. Associated Press. (April 17, 2012). Ambassadors' wives urge Syrian president's wife to 'stop your husband,' lobby for peace. The Washington Post. http://www.washing tonpost.com/world/middle_east/ambassadors-wives-urge-syrian-presidents-wife-to-stop-your-husband-lobby-for-peace/2012/04/17/gIQAvSbEOT_story.html
49. Women of the World. (April 18, 2012). Asma Al-Assad: Call for peace in Syria. Change.org. http://www.change.org/petitions/asma-al-assad-call-for-peace-in-syria
50. PC Magazine editors. (Retrieved April 17, 2012). SOPA/PIPA Blackout Day. PC Magazine. http://www.pcmag.com/slideshow_viewer/0,3253,l%253D292984%2526a%253D292997%2526po%253D1,00.asp
51. Senate Judiciary Committee. (May 26, 2011). To prevent online threats to economic creativity and theft of intellectual property, and for other purposes. U.S. Government Printing Office (GPO). http://www.gpo.gov/fdsys/pkg/BILLS−112s968rs and http://www.gpo.gov/fdsys/pkg/BILLS−112s968rs/pdf/BILLS−112s968rs.pdf
52. Wyden, Ron. (May 26, 2011). Wyden Places Hold on Protect IP Act. Overreaching Legislation Still Poses a Significant Threat to Internet Commerce, Innovation and Free Speech. U.S. Senate. http://wyden.senate.gov/newsroom/press/release/?id=33a39533−1b25−437b-ad1d−9039b44cde92
53. 55 Venture Capitalists. (June 23, 2011). Letter to U.S. Congress in Opposition of Legislation. Net-VCLetterRePIPA. https://docs.google.com/document/d/14CkX3zDyAxShrqUqEkewtUCjvvFdciIbKjC18_eUHkg/edit?hl=en_US&authkey=CNHr3I4L&pli=1
54. U.S. Chamber of Commerce. (September 22, 2011). Letter to Congress in Support of Legislation. U.S. Chamber of Commerce Global Intellectual Property Center. http://www.theglobalipcenter.com/sites/default/files/pressreleases/letter−359.pdf
55. Kang, Cecilia. (October 26, 2011). House introduces Internet piracy bill. The Washington Post. http://www.washingtonpost.com/blogs/post-tech/post/house-introduces-internet-piracy-bill/2011/10/26/gIQA0f5xJM_blog.html
56. House Judiciary Committee. (October 26, 2011). H.R. 3261 - Stop Online Piracy Act. U.S. House of Representatives. http://judiciary.house.gov/hearings/pdf/112%20HR%203261.pdf
57. Sohn, Gigi B. (October 26, 2011). Public Knowledge Sees Dangers In New Intellectual Property Bill. Public Knowledge. http://www.publicknowledge.org/public-knowledge-sees-dangers-new-intellectual-pro
58. Doctorow, Cory. (November 16, 2011). Internet giants place full-page anti-SOPA ad in NYT. BoingBoing. http://boingboing.net/2011/11/16/internet-giants-place-full-pag.html
59. McCullagh, Declan. (December 15, 2011). Vint Cerf: SOPA means 'unprecedented censorship' of the Web. CNet. http://news.cnet.com/8301−31921_3−57344028−281/vint-cerf-sopa-means-unprecedented-censorship-of-the-web/
60. Statement of Christine N. Jones. (April 6, 2011). Hearing on "Promoting Investment and Protecting Commerce Online: Legitimate Sites v. Parasites, Part II". U.S. House of Representatives. Committee on the Judiciary. http://judiciary.house.gov/hearings/pdf/Jones04062011.pdf
61. Wales, Jimmy. (December 23, 2011). @jimmy_wales. Twitter. https://twitter.com/#!/jimmy_wales/status/150287579642740736
62. Kumparak, Greg. (December 22, 2011). Cheezburger's Ben Huh: If GoDaddy Supports SOPA, We're Taking Our 1000+ Domains Elsewhere. TechCrunch. http://techcrunch.com/2011/12/22/cheezburgers-ben-huh-if-godaddy-supports-sopa-were-taking-our−1000-domains-elsewhere/
63. Weinstein, Natalie. (December 24, 2011). 21,000 domains transfer out of Go Daddy in 1 day. CNet. http://news.cnet.com/8301−1023_3−57348183−93/21000-domains-transfer-out-of-go-daddy-in−1-day/
64. McCullagh, Declan. (December 29, 2011). GoDaddy bows to boycott, now 'opposes' SOPA copyright bill. CNet. http://news.cnet.com/8301−31921_3−57349913−281/godaddy-bows-to-boycott-now-opposes-sopa-copyright-bill/
65. Go Daddy. (December 23, 2011). Go Daddy No Longer Supports SOPA. Go Daddy News Releases. http://www.godaddy.com/newscenter/release-view.aspx?news_item_id=378

66. Dodd, Chris. (January 17, 2012). A statement by Senator Chris Dodd, Chairman and CEO of the Motion Picture Association of America, Inc. (MPAA) on the so-called "Blackout Day" protesting anti-piracy legislation. http://www.mpaa.org/resources/c4c3712a−7b9f−4be8-bd70−25527d5dfad8.pdf
67. Fight For The Future 2012. (Retrieved April 17, 2012). http://sopastrike.com/numbers/
68. Drummond, David. (January 18, 2012). Don't censor the web. Google Public Policy Blog. http://googlepublicpolicy.blogspot.com/2012/01/dont-censor-web.html
69. Yu, Roger. (January 20, 2012). Congress shelves anti-piracy bills. USA Today. http://www.usatoday.com/tech/news/story/2012−01−20/anti-piracy-bills-halted/52698192/1
70. Taylor, Colleen. (February 2, 2012). How Marc Andreessen makes Silicon Valley magic. Gigaom. http://gigaom.com/2012/02/02/marc-andreessen-horowitz-silicon-valley-startups/
71. Katz, Ian. (April 15, 2012). Web freedom faces greatest threat ever, warns Google's Sergey Brin. The Guardian. http://www.guardian.co.uk/technology/2012/apr/15/web-freedom-threat-google-brin
72. Google. (Retrieved May 25, 2012). Google Removal Requests. http://www.google.com/transparencyreport/removals/copyright/
73. Goldman, David. (May 24,2012). Google kills 250,000 search links a week. CNN Money. http://money.cnn.com/2012/05/24/technology/google-search-copyright/index.htm
74. Google. (Retrieved May 27, 2012). Copyright Infringement Notification. YouTube. http://www.youtube.com/t/dmca_policy
75. Gross, Doug. (March 12, 2012). Gore, Parker urge Web to 'Occupy Democracy'. CNN. http://www.cnn.com/2012/03/12/tech/web/gore-parker-sxsw/index.html
76. OpenCongress. (January 24, 2012). Protect IP Act Senate whip count. The OpenCongress Wiki. http://www.opencongress.org/wiki/Protect_IP_Act_Senate_whip_count
77. Leahy, Patrick. (January 20, 2012). Comment Of Senator Patrick Leahy On Postponement Of The Vote On Cloture On The Motion To Proceed To The PROTECT IP Act. U.S. Senate Press Releases. http://www.leahy.senate.gov/press/press_releases/release/?id=467fb8f0−828d−403c−9b7b−8bf42d583c3e
78. Sherman, Cary H. (February 7, 2012). What Wikipedia Won't Tell You. The New York Times. http://www.nytimes.com/2012/02/08/opinion/what-wikipedia-wont-tell-you.html
79. U.S. Petitioners. (December 18, 2011). VETO the SOPA bill and any other future bills that threaten to diminish the free flow of information. We the People. Your Voice in Our Government. https://wwws.whitehouse.gov/petition-tool/petition/veto-sopa-bill-and-any-other-future-bills-threaten-diminish-free-flow-information/g3W1BscR
80. Espinel, Victoria; Chopra, Aneesh; Schmidt, Howard. (Retrieved April 17, 2012).Combating Online Piracy while Protecting an Open and Innovative Internet. We the People. Your Voice in Our Government. https://wwws.whitehouse.gov/petition-tool/response/combating-online-piracy-while-protecting-open-and-innovative-internet
81. DesMarais, Christina. (January 21, 2012). SOPA, PIPA Stalled: Meet the OPEN Act. PCWorld. http://www.pcworld.com/article/248525/sopa_pipa_stalled_meet_the_open_act.html
82. Keeptheweb#OPEN (December 13, 2011). Big Web Companies OPEN Endorsement Letter. Keeptheweb#OPEN. http://keepthewebopen.com/assets/pdfs/12−13−11%20Big%20Web%20Companies%20OPEN%20Endorsement%20Letter.pdf
83. Greenberg, Andy. (May 25, 2012). Reddit's Alexis Ohanian And Activists Aim To Build A 'Bat-Signal For The Internet'. Forbes. http://www.forbes.com/sites/andygreenberg/2012/05/25/reddit-founder-and-activists-aim-to-build-a-bat-signal-for-the-internet/
84. Greenberg, Andy. (May 7, 2012). Reddit Founder Says He Won't Buy Facebook's Stock Due To Its CISPA Support. Forbes. http://www.forbes.com/sites/andygreenberg/2012/05/07/reddit-founder-says-he-wont-buy-facebooks-stock-due-to-its-cispa-support/
85. Sandoval, Greg. (March 14, 2012). RIAA chief: ISPs to start policing copyright by July 1. CNet. http://news.cnet.com/8301−31001_3−57397452−261/riaa-chief-isps-to-start-policing-copyright-by-july−1/
86. Facebook. (February 4, 2004). About Facebook. https://www.facebook.com/facebook/info

87. Facebook. (Retrieved May 2, 2012). Peace on Facebook. Facebook. https://peace. facebook.com/
88. Time Warner Inc. (September 19, 2011). Facebook and Time Warner Inc. Launch Stop Bullying: Speak Up App. Time Warner Press Releases. http://www.timewarner.com/ newsroom/press-releases/2011/09/ Facebook_and_Time_Warner_Inc_Launch_Stop_Bullying_Speak_Up_App_09–19– 2011.php
89. Chang, Jonathan. (November 4, 2010). How voters turned out on Facebook. Facebook Data Team. http://www.facebook.com/notes/facebook-data-team/how-voters-turned-out-on-facebook/451788333858
90. AMBER Alert. (December 30, 2009). About AMBER Alert on Facebook. Facebook. http:// www.facebook.com/AMBERalert/info
91. Almasy, Steve. (May 1, 2012). Facebook encouraging organ donations. CNN. http:// www.cnn.com/2012/05/01/health/facebook-organ-donors/index.html
92. Causes. (Retrieved April 20, 2012). About Causes. Causes. http://www.causes.com/about
93. Votizen. (Retrieved April 20, 2012). Votizen. https://www.votizen.com/
94. Dickinson, Boonsri. (April 9, 2012). Votizen Wants To Use Social Networks To Revolutionize Politics. Business Insider. http://articles.businessinsider.com/2012–04–09/ tech/31311939_1_politics-social-networks-users
95. MoveOn.org. (Retrieved April 20, 2012). About the MoveOn Family of Organizations. MoveOn.org. http://www.moveon.org/about.html
96. McCarthy, Caroline. (November 20, 2007). MoveOn.org takes on Facebook's 'Beacon' ads. CNet. http://news.cnet.com/8301–13577_3–9821170–36.html
97. Healey, Jon. (March 13, 2012). Al Gore, Sean Parker call for 'Occupy Democracy' movement online. Los Angeles Times. http://opinion.latimes.com/opinionla/2012/03/al-gore-and-sean-parker-do-sxsw.html
98. #OccupyDemocracy. (Retrieved April 20, 2012). http://occupydemocracy.org/
99. The American-Israeli Cooperative Enterprise. (Retrieved April 20, 2012). The Arab-Israeli Conflict: Total Casualties (1920–2012). Jewish Virtual Library. http:// www.jewishvirtuallibrary.org/jsource/History/casualtiestotal.html
100. Strategic Foresight Group. (January 2009). Cost of Conflict in the Middle East. Strategic Foresight Group Report Excerpts. http://www.strategicforesight.com/Cost%20of%20 Conflict%20-%206%20pager.pdf
101. Mehina, Pushpin. (Retrieved April 20, 2012). Facebook. http://www.facebook.com/pushpin
102. Said, Samira. (March 20, 2012). Peace-minded Israeli reaches out to everyday Iranians via Facebook. CNN. http://www.cnn.com/2012/03/19/world/meast/israel-iran-social-media/ index.html
103. Khan, Habibullah. (May 19, 2010). ABC News. http://abcnews.go.com/Technology/ International/facebook-banned-pakistan-prophet-muhammad-sketch-competition/story?id= 10688625
104. Staff Report. (September 19, 2011). Facebook to be blocked. Pakistan Today. http://www. pakistantoday.com.pk/2011/09/19/uncategorized/facebook-to-be-blocked/
105. Chou, Dorothy. (June 17, 2012).More transparency into government requests. Google Official Blog. http://googleblog.blogspot.com/2012/06/more-transparency-into-government. html#!/2012/06/more-transparency-into-government.html
106. Google. (Retrieved June 28, 2012). Google Transparency Report. July to December 2011. http://www.google.com/transparencyreport/removals/government/
107. Kessel, Jeremy. (July 2, 2012). Twitter Transparency Report. Twitter Blog. http://blog. twitter.com/2012/07/twitter-transparency-report.html
108. Foley, Kathryn. (July 7, 2009). China Bans Access to Facebook and Twitter Due to Riots. Yahoo! http://voices.yahoo.com/china-bans-access-facebook-twitter-due-riots–3755708. html
109. Milchman, Eli. (June 15, 2006). Yahoo 'Strictest' Censor in China. Wired. http://www. wired.com/politics/onlinerights/news/2006/06/71166

110. Helft, Miguel; Barboza, David. (March 22, 2010). Google Shuts China Site in Dispute Over Censorship. The New York Times. http://www.nytimes.com/2010/03/23/technology/23google.html

111. Drummond, David. (March 22, 2010). A new approach to China: an update. Google Official Blog. http://googleblog.blogspot.com/2010/03/new-approach-to-china-update.html

112. Fletcher, Owen. (May 19, 2011). Baidu Accused of Aiding Chinese Censorship in U.S. Suit. The Wall Street Journal. http://online.wsj.com/article/SB10001424052748703482104576332073063272688.html

113. Cao, Belinda; Lazaroff, Leon. (April 2, 2012). Sina Drops to 5-Week Low After Suspending Weibo Commentary. Bloomberg Businessweek. http://www.businessweek.com/news/2012-04-02/sina-tumbles-to-5-week-low-after-suspending-weibo-user-comments

114. Henochowicz, Anne. (February 29, 2012). Big Brother Gets Tough on Weibo, Sina Balks. China Digital News. http://chinadigitaltimes.net/2012/02/big-brother-gets-tough-on-weibo-sina-balks/

115. Branigan, Tania. (March 22, 2012). China's microbloggers turn to Teletubbies to discuss politics. The Guardian. http://www.guardian.co.uk/world/2012/mar/22/china-microbloggers-teletubbies

116. Weiwei, Ai (April 15, 2012). China's censorship can never defeat the internet. The Guardian. http://www.guardian.co.uk/commentisfree/libertycentral/2012/apr/16/china-censorship-internet-freedom

117. Alexander, Anne. (February 9, 2011). Internet role in Egypt's protests. BBC. http://www.bbc.co.uk/news/world-middle-east-12400319

118. Fathi, Yasmine. (January 27, 2011). In Egypt, nationwide protests planned for January 28. Ahram Online. http://english.ahram.org.eg/News/4953.aspx

119. Cowie, James. (January 27, 2011). Egypt Leaves the Internet. Renesys Blog. http://www.renesys.com/blog/2011/01/egypt-leaves-the-internet.shtml

120. AFP. (January 31, 2011). Google unveils Web-free 'tweeting' in Egypt move. Google. http://www.google.com/hostednews/afp/article/ALeqM5h8de3cQ8o_S2zg9s72t7sxNToBqA?docId=CNG.ddc0305146893ec9e9e6796d743e6af7.c81

121. Hennessy-Fiske, Molly; Hassan, Amro. (May 29, 2011). Mubarak, other former Egypt officials fined $91 million for blocking cellphones, Internet. Los Angeles Times. http://articles.latimes.com/2011/may/29/world/la-fg-egypt-mubarak-fines-20110529

122. Lendon, Brad. (April 26, 2012). Norwegians sing to annoy mass killer. CNN. http://news.blogs.cnn.com/2012/04/26/norwegians-sing-to-annoy-mass-killer/

123. Solholm, Rolleiv. (April 26, 2012). Mass choir of 40,000 sang in Breivik protest. The Norway Post. http://www.norwaypost.no/news/mass-choir-to-sing-in-breivik-protest-26832.html

124. Payne, Martha. (Retrieved July 9, 2012). One primary school pupil's daily dose of school dinners. NeverSeconds. http://neverseconds.blogspot.com.es/

125. Hough, Andrew; Johnson, Simon. (June 15, 2012). Victory for Martha Payne as Argyll and Bute council backs down on school dinner blog ban. The Telegraph http://www.telegraph.co.uk/education/educationnews/9333975/Victory-for-Martha-Payne-as-Argyll-and-Bute-council-backs-down-on-school-dinner-blog-ban.html

126. Hough, Andrew; Johnson, Simon. Ibid.

127. Oslo Freedom Forum. (May 2012). About Manal al-Sharif. Oslo Freedom Forum. http://www.oslofreedomforum.com/speakers/manal-al-sharif.html

128. Havel Prize. (May 30, 2012). Manal al-Sharif - 2012 Havel Prize Acceptance Speech. YouTube. http://www.youtube.com/watch?v=xECB8Xyagnk

129. Newton-Small, Jay. (June 13, 2012). Hillary's Little Startup: How the U.S. Is Using Technology to Aid Syria's Rebels. Time Magazine. http://world.time.com/2012/06/13/hillarys-little-startup-how-the-u-s-is-using-technology-to-aid-syrias-rebels/

130. CNN Editors. (June 14, 2012). Syria's 'cyber warriors' choose cameras over guns. CNN. http://globalpublicsquare.blogs.cnn.com/2012/06/14/syrias-cyber-warriors-choose-cameras-over-guns/

131. Sherman, Cary H. (February 7, 2012). What Wikipedia Won't Tell You. The New York Times. http://www.nytimes.com/2012/02/08/opinion/what-wikipedia-wont-tell-you.html
132. Donehue, Wesley. (April 24, 2012). The danger of Twitter, Facebook politics. CNN. http://www.cnn.com/2012/04/24/opinion/donehue-social-media-politics/index.html
133. Branigan, Tania. (April 15, 2012). China's censors tested by microbloggers who keep one step ahead of state media. The Guardian. http://www.guardian.co.uk/technology/2012/apr/16/internet-china-censorship-weibo-microblogs
134. Andrews, Lori B. (December 31, 2011). The rise of Facebook Nation. Salon. http://www.salon.com/2011/12/31/the_rise_of_facebook_nation/singleton/
135. Andrews, Lori. (Retrieved April 23, 2012). The Social Network Constitution. http://www.socialnetworkconstitution.com/the-social-network-constitution.html
136. Moynihan, Colin. (February 6, 2012). Protester's Lawyer Challenges Twitter Subpoena. The New York Times. http://cityroom.blogs.nytimes.com/2012/02/06/protesters-lawyer-challenges-twitter-subpoena/
137. Fitzpatrick, Alex. (May 9, 2012). Twitter fights court order for user's data. CNN. http://www.cnn.com/2012/05/09/tech/social-media/twitter-court-order/index.html
138. Fine, Aden. (May 8, 2012). Twitter Stands Up For One Of Its Users. American Civil Liberties Union. http://www.aclu.org/blog/technology-and-liberty-national-security-free-speech/breaking-news-twitter-stands-one-its-users
139. ACLU. (Retrieved May 12, 2012). Hey! Do you use the Internet? American Civil Liberties Union. https://secure.aclu.org/site/SPageServer?pagename=110419_Internet_Privacy

Part IV
Total Information Awareness
in Facebook Nation

Chapter 11
Living in Facebook Nation

On the Internet, nobody knows you're a dog.
—Cartoonist Peter Steiner (July 5, 1993)

We are our real identities online.
—Facebook's chief operating officer Sheryl Sandberg
(January 2012)

The things we do and say online leave behind ever-growing trails of personal information.
—American Civil Liberties Union

11.1 Digital Personalities and Identities

It used to be that "on the Internet, nobody knows you're a dog"—as it was cleverly depicted by Peter Steiner in his famous cartoon published on July 5, 1993 in *The New Yorker* [1]. Six years later on May 7, 2009, a real dog named "Boo" joined Facebook [2]. Three years later in May 2012, Boo has garnered 4.4 million "Likes" on Facebook, surpassing the popularity of most humans on the social network. Everyone can have his or her own digital personality and identity online.

IBM released a new study in April 2012 that identified four emerging digital personalities—efficiency experts, content maestros, social butterflies, and content kings—respectively representing 41, 35, 15, and 9 % of the online population [3]. Efficiency experts are proficient Internet users; content maestros are media consumers and gamers on the web and on mobile devices; social butterflies are Facebook and Twitter addicts; and content kings are both consumers and creators of rich media.

Prof. Mitja Back of Johannes Gutenberg University in Mainz, Germany, studied a group of Facebook users and concluded, "Online social networks are so popular and so likely to reveal people's actual personalities because they allow for social interactions that feel real in many ways. ... Facebook is so true to life that encountering a person there for the first time generally results in a more accurate personality appraisal than meeting face to face" [4].

On the other hand, *Consumer Reports* magazine conducted a survey of 2002 online households, including 1,340 that are active on Facebook. The findings based on the January 2012 survey showed that 25 % of Facebook users falsified information in their profiles to protect their identity [5].

N. Lee, *Facebook Nation*, DOI: 10.1007/978-1-4614-5308-6_11,
© Springer Science+Business Media New York 2013

Moreover, a Facebook profile may represent the alter ego of a person. UCLA Prof. Patricia Greenfield and researcher Adriana Manago published their research on Facebook and MySpace in the November–December 2008 issue of the *Journal of Applied Developmental Psychology* [6]. "You can manifest your ideal self", said Manago, "You can manifest who you want to be and then try to grow into that. We're always engaging in self-presentation; we're always trying to put our best foot forward. Social networking sites take this to a whole new level. You can change what you look like, you can Photoshop your face, you can select only the pictures that show you in a perfect lighting. These websites intensify the ability to present yourself in a positive light and explore different aspects of your personality and how you present yourself. You can try on different things, possible identities, and explore in a way that is common for emerging adulthood. It becomes psychologically real. People put up something that they would like to become—not completely different from who they are but maybe a little different—and the more it gets reflected off of others, the more it may be integrated into their sense of self as they share words and photos with so many people".

"People are living life online," Greenfield added to Manago's statements. "Identity, romantic relations and sexuality all get played out on these social networking sites. All of these things are what teenagers always do, but the social networking sites give them much more power to do it in a more extreme way. In the arena of identity formation, this makes people more individualistic and more narcissistic; people sculpt themselves with their profiles".

In the case of Boo the dog on Facebook, Boo is the living alter ego of his behind-the-scene owner who never appears in any of the Facebook pictures. Facebook's chief operating officer Sheryl Sandberg said at the January 2012 Digital Life Design (DLD) conference in Munich, "We are our real identities online" [7].

11.2 Intertwining Lives, Online and Offline

For many people, life online is as real as life offline. The two lives are intertwined; each of them affects the other, both in the psychological and physical sense. On one hand, some people utilize social media to help them stay in shape. Social apps that track and share their fitness habits make them feel accountable and more likely to follow through with their fitness plans. On the other hand, Prof. Lori B. Andrews at Chicago-Kent College of Law pointed out that "virtually every interaction a person has in the offline world can be tainted by social network information" [8]. The following are some examples of the adverse effects of online life that made headline news:

1. 24 year-old public high school English teacher Ashley Payne went to Europe for a summer vacation in 2009. She posted her vacation photos on Facebook. One of the pictures showed a smiling Payne holding a glass of wine and a mug

of beer. She also used the "B" word on Facebook and thought that only her closest friends could access her Facebook page. Payne did not realize that despite the Facebook privacy settings, no one could ever guarantee the absolute privacy of content posted on the Internet. When the school principal found out about the Facebook photo and profanity, Payne was forced to resign [9].

2. A high school graduate applied for a job in 2011 as security guard for the local Port Authority. The recruiter asked the applicant if he or any of his friends had ever been incarcerated. He honestly answered "no". However, the recruiter pulled out a copy of his Facebook page, with two of his "friends" highlighted; and those two "friends" were indeed in jail for their convicted crimes. Although the applicant denied knowing those two people at all, he did not get the job [10].

3. In 2012, Marine Sgt. Gary Stein posted on his Facebook pages derogatory comments about President Barack Obama. As a direct consequence, a military board recommended that Stein be discharged for violating "good order and discipline" required by all U.S. military service members [11].

There are many similar stories that did not make national news, but the potential impact of our digital personalities and identities on our real life should not be understated.

In 2008, educational company Kaplan conducted an annual survey of 500 top colleges and found that 10 % of admissions officers acknowledged looking at social networking sites to evaluate applicants, and 38 % of them said that what they saw "negatively affected" their views of the applicants. Thomas Griffin, director of undergraduate admissions at North Carolina State University in Raleigh, disclosed that several applicants a year had been rejected partly due to the information on Facebook and other social media sites [12].

In 2011, Kaplan Test Prep's annual survey found that 24 % of admissions officers have gone to an applicant's Facebook or other social network sites to learn more about them. The percentage has more than doubled in 3 years. The growing practice of exploring applicants' digital trails is evident, as Kaplan Test Prep reported, "More prevalent is the use of social media for outreach purposes. ... Facebook and YouTube are increasingly important recruiting tools for colleges— 85 % use Facebook (up from 82 % in the 2010 survey) and 66 % use YouTube (up from 52 % in the 2010 survey) to vie for the interest of prospective students" [13].

Aside from college admissions, employment decisions are also affected by our digital personalities and identities. *Consumer Reports* in June 2012 stated that 69 % of human-resource officers have rejected job applicants based on social media reviews that turned up any of the red flags such as sexually explicit photos or videos, racist remarks, and evidence of illegal activities.

As more employers are turning to Facebook to check on the job applicants, both American Civil Liberties Union (ACLU) and Facebook have voiced their oppositions. In March 2012, ACLU attorney Catherine Crump said, "It's an invasion of privacy for private employers to insist on looking at people's private Facebook pages as a condition of employment or consideration in an application process.

People are entitled to their private lives. You'd be appalled if your employer insisted on opening up your postal mail to see if there was anything of interest inside. It's equally out of bounds for an employer to go on a fishing expedition through a person's private social media account" [14].

At the same time, Facebook's chief privacy officer Erin Egan wrote on the company's official blog, "In recent months, we've seen a distressing increase in reports of employers or others seeking to gain inappropriate access to people's Facebook profiles or private information. This practice undermines the privacy expectations and the security of both the user and the user's friends. It also potentially exposes the employer who seeks this access to unanticipated legal liability. ... For example, if an employer sees on Facebook that someone is a member of a protected group (e.g. over a certain age, etc.) that employer may open themselves up to claims of discrimination if they don't hire that person" [15].

Nonetheless, from the standpoint of employers and college admission officers, looking up an applicant on Facebook, Google, and Linked In can be regarded as a type of background check. It is up to the applicant to keep his or her own private life private by not uploading any inappropriate materials online.

11.3 Digital Footprint and Exhaust Data

At the 2011 South by Southwest Interactive conference in Austin, Texas, LinkedIn founder Reid Hoffman spoke of the web of "real identities generating massive amounts of data" [16]. The exhaust data—the output of human beings using the Internet—contains the digital footprint of the past and current user activities and interactions.

When we go to a night club, the bouncer checks our IDs. We are not anonymous. Likewise, when we log onto Facebook, Twitter, YouTube, and Google, among others, we are not Jane/John Doe. There is plenty of personally identifiable information (PII) online such as our full name, IP address, phone number, and date of birth. Furthermore, government-issued IDs are required to establish verified accounts on Facebook and Twitter. Is the online world moving towards PII instead of anonymity?

American Civil Liberties Union (ACLU) expresses their concerns: "The things we do and say online leave behind ever-growing trails of personal information. With every click, we entrust our conversations, emails, photos, location information and much more to companies like Facebook, Google and Yahoo. But what happens when the government asks these companies to hand over their users' private information?" [17].

In 2012, ACLU launched a new campaign—Demand Your dot Rights (Privacy 2.0)—to educate the public about digital footprint and exhaust data [18]:

To the Members of the California State Assembly:

I am returning Assembly Bill 1176 without my signature.

For some time now I have lamented the fact that major issues are overlooked while many unnecessary bills come to me for consideration. Water reform, prison reform, and health care are major issues my Administration has brought to the table, but the Legislature just kicks the can down the alley.

Yet another legislative year has come and gone without the major reforms Californians overwhelmingly deserve. In light of this, and after careful consideration, I believe it is unnecessary to sign this measure at this time.

Sincerely,

Arnold Schwarzenegger

Fig. 11.1 Gov. Arnold Schwarzenegger's acrostic poem

- Search Engines: When you browse through online stacks of information, you are leaving a trail that reveals a lot about you: interests, hobbies, habits, and concerns.
- Location Information: Location data from your cell phone or laptop can tell more than just where you travel, but also what you do and even who you know.
- Social Networking: Replacing interactions in the coffee shop with connections online leaves behind a lot of information about you, friends, and activities.
- Webmail: Online email services make it easy to keep in touch with friends and family. But every email creates a record of who you write, what you write, and when you send and read it.
- Photo Sites: The pictures you develop, store, or share online can tell many thousands of words to others about you and who you know, where you've gone, and what you've done.
- Media Sites: Reading a book or watching a video is a great way to learn and explore new things. But a lot of information can be collected about who you are and what you read and watch.
- Cloud Computing: Moving files from your hard drive to an online service or accessing applications through the Internet can be convenient. But, those documents and files you store or produce online can say a lot about you.

Not everyone is as talented as former California Governor Arnold Schwarzenegger who sent lawmakers a "F*ck You" message through an acrostic poem in 2010 (See Fig. 11.1). Hip-hop singer Chris Brown lashed out against his critics after his Grammy performance in February 2012. He sent a series of missives ending with a "F*ck You" on Twitter. A few minutes later, he attempted to delete all the offensive tweets, but it was too late. Some bloggers took screenshots of his tweets and posted them online for the whole world to see [19].

"We now have entered a phase where every single thing you say—the way you say it, how you say it—is now all exposed," said Gavin Newsom, former San Francisco Mayor and 49th Lieutenant Governor of California. "I have to watch myself now singing 'I left my heart in San Francisco' on YouTube, and it can't go away. I am desperate to get it to go away" [20].

Chris Brown and Gavin Newsom are among the majority of people who wish they could erase their digital foot print and eliminate their exhaust data. We all have said to ourselves at one point, "Oh, I wish I hadn't sent that email". Gmail and AOL Mail enable users to unsend their emails under some circumstances, but we cannot be certain if the unsent emails may be stored in some mail servers for an unknown period of time. Once data is uploaded to the Internet via email, Twitter, Facebook, YouTube, et cetera, they can potentially take on a life of their own regardless of whether the data is meant to be public or private.

In June 2012, Sunlight Foundation launched the U.S. edition of Politwoops in order to expose tweets that politicians shared and then promptly deleted [21]. "It's kind of a fiction to pretend that you can put something out on the Internet, and then delete it", said Tom Lee, director of the technical arm of the Sunlight Foundation [22].

11.4 Facebook Knows Who, When, Where

In February 2012, Jacqui Cheng, Senior Apple Editor at Ars Technica, recounted her own experience and 3-year investigation that even if a Facebook user decides to delete uploaded photos for whatever reasons, the "deleted" Facebook photos may still be online indefinitely and are accessible via direct links (URLs) [23]. Cheng first contacted Facebook in 2009 about the issue [24]. She did a follow up with Facebook in 2010. Over three years later, her "deleted" Facebook photos were still online.

Facebook responded to Cheng defensively, "For all practical purposes, the photo no longer exists, and we wouldn't be able find it if we were asked or even compelled to do so. ... It's possible that someone who previously had access to a photo and saved the direct URL from our content delivery network partner could still access the photo" [25]. Facebook blamed the problem on their legacy database systems, and promised to work with their content delivery network (CDN) partner to "significantly reduce the amount of time that backup copies persist." In other words, no one can tell how long a deleted Facebook photo will linger in the online universe before it is ultimately purged, if ever.

Moreover, *The New York Time* reported in February 2012, "Facebook can calculate your location information from different sources, including your computer's Wi-Fi connection or phone's GPS feature. When it finds you, it adds a small tag on the updates you post to your Facebook wall, like 'near New Orleans, LA' or wherever you are" [26].

In June 2012, *Consumers Report* made public another startling revelation: "Regulators in Germany found that such information [user's IP address and activities] was being collected on Facebook users for up to two years even after they deactivated their accounts" [27]. An IP address can be traced back to a company's datacenter or a residential address in some circumstances. Facebook explained that their policy of collecting IP addresses and user activities was required to "enhance Facebook security."

The massive amount of data each online company keeps about us can inadvertently expose not only our real identity but also our activities, habits, likes, dislikes, and, as Thelma Arnold puts it, "the whole personal life".

Thelma Arnold is a 62 year-old widow in Lilburn, Georgia. Arnold was the anonymous user No. 4417749 among more than 650,000 users whose 20 million web search queries were collected by AOL and released to academic researchers in August 2006. Although the user's logs were associated with random ID numbers, several users' identities were readily discovered based on their search queries. Over a three-month period, Arnold conducted hundreds of searches such as "numb fingers", "60 single men", "dog that urinates on everything", and "landscapers in Lilburn, Ga". A *New York Times* reporter was able to follow the data trail to Thelma Arnold in Lilburn. "My goodness, it's my whole personal life," said Arnold to the reporter. "I had no idea somebody was looking over my shoulder" [28].

Based on the 1990 U.S. Census summary data, researcher Latanya Sweeney at Carnegie Mellon University found that combinations of few characteristics often uniquely or nearly uniquely identify some individuals in geographically situated populations [29]. In fact, 53 % of the U.S. population had reported characteristics that likely made them uniquely identifiable based only on their city of residence, gender, and date of birth. The number increased to a startling 87 % if their zip code was also included.

11.5 Online Births in Facebook Nation

A September 2010 study by Internet security company AVG found that almost a quarter (23 %) of children have online births before their actual birth dates, as today's parents are building digital footprints for their children prior to and from the moment they are born. In the U.S., 92 % of children have an online presence by the time they are two.

J.R. Smith, CEO of AVG, commented on the report, "It's completely understandable why proud parents would want to upload and share images of very young children with friends and families. At the same time, we urge parents to think… you are creating a digital history for a human being that will follow him or her for the rest of their life. What kind of footprint do you actually want to start for your child, and what will they think about the information you've uploaded in future?" [30] Parenting columnist Aisha Sultan and University of Michigan researcher Jon Miller concurred, "Never before have parents had the ability to publish the details of their children's lives in such a widespread manner. A potentially embarrassing anecdote won't faze a toddler, but how does the unilateral flow of information affect a tween or teenager?" [31].

References

1. Fleishman, Glenn. (December 14, 2000). Cartoon Captures Spirit of the Internet. The New York Times. http://www.nytimes.com/2000/12/14/technology/cartoon-captures-spirit-of-the-internet.html
2. Boo. (Retrieved May 8, 2012). Boo Facebook Timeline. Facebook. http://www.facebook.com/Boo
3. Guildhary, Fabienne. (April 16, 2012). IBM Survey Reveals Digital Behavioral Trends for Consumers: What is your Digital Personality? IBM News Releases. http://www−03.ibm.com/press/us/en/pressrelease/37423.wss
4. Bower, Bruce. (February 26, 2010). No Lie! Your Facebook Profile Is the Real You. Wired. http://www.wired.com/wiredscience/2010/02/no-lie-your-facebook-profile-is-the-real-you/
5. Consumer Reports magazine editors. (June 2012).Facebook & your privacy. Who sees the data you share on the biggest social network? Consumer Reports. http://www.consumerreports.org/cro/magazine/2012/06/facebook-your-privacy/index.htm
6. Wolpert, Stuart. (November 17, 2008). Crafting your image for your 1,000 friends on Facebook or MySpace. UCLA Newsroom. http://newsroom.ucla.edu/portal/ucla/crafting-your-image-for-your−1−71910.aspx
7. Keen, Andrew. (January 25, 2012). Battle Lines Drawn as Data Becomes Oil of Digital Age. DLD (Digital Life Design).http://www.dld-conference.com/news/digital-business/battle-lines-drawn-as-data-becomes-oil-of-digital-age_aid_3097.html
8. Andrews, Lori. (January 10, 2012). I Know Who You Are and I Saw What You Did: Social Networks and the Death of Privacy. Free Press.
9. CBSNews. (February 6, 2011). Did the Internet Kill Privacy? http://www.cbsnews.com/2100−3445_162−7323148.html
10. Gregory, Corinne. (June 28, 2011). The unforseen impact of online "friendships". ResumeBear. http://blog.resumebear.com/career-book-authors/the-unforseen-impact-of-online-%E2%80%9Cfriendships%E2%80%9D/
11. Obeidallah, Dean. (April 25, 2012). Marine's Facebook posts on Obama go too far. CNN. http://www.cnn.com/2012/04/14/opinion/obeidallah-marine-obama-facebook/index.html
12. Hechinger, John. (September 8, 2008). College Applicants, Beware: Your Facebook Page Is Showing. The Wall Street Journal. http://online.wsj.com/article/SB122170459104151023.html#ixzz1i3OJLjmd
13. Kaplan Test Prep. (September 21, 2011). Facebook Checking is No Longer Unchartered Territory in College Admissions: Percentage of Admissions Officers Who Visited An Applicant's Profile On the Rise. Kaplan Test Prep. http://press.kaptest.com/press-releases/facebook-checking-is-no-longer-unchartered-territory-in-college-admissions-percentage-of-admissions-officers-who-visited-an-applicant%E2%80%99s-profile-on-the-rise
14. ACLU. (March 20, 2012). Your Facebook Password Should Be None of Your Boss' Business. American Civil Liberty Union. http://www.aclu.org/blog/technology-and-liberty/your-facebook-password-should-be-none-your-boss-business
15. Egan, Erin. (March 23, 2012). Protecting Your Passwords and Your Privacy. Facebook and Privacy. https://www.facebook.com/note.php?note_id=326598317390057
16. Ha, Anthony. (March 15, 2011). LinkedIn's Reid Hoffman explains the brave new world of data. Venture Beat. http://venturebeat.com/2011/03/15/reid-hoffman-data-sxsw/

17. ACLU. (Retrieved May 12, 2012). Hey! Do you use the Internet? American Civil Liberties Union. https://secure.aclu.org/site/SPageServer?pagename=110419_Internet_Privacy

18. ACLU. (Retrieved May 12, 2012). Demand Your dotRights (Privacy 2.0). American Civil Liberties Union.http://www.dotrights.org/education

19. Warren, Christina. (February 14, 2012). Chris Brown Curses Out Twitter Critics Then Tries to Delete the Evidence. Mashable. http://mashable.com/2012/02/14/chris-brown-twitter−2/

20. Allday, Erin. (November 7, 2011). Nowhere to hide from the Internet. San Francisco Chronicle. http://blog.sfgate.com/cityinsider/2008/11/07/nowhere-to-hide-from-the-internet/

21. Politwoops. (Retrieved June 11, 2012). Politwoops. Deleted tweets from politicians. http://politwoops.sunlightfoundation.com/

22. National Public Radio. (June 6, 2012). The Deleted Tweets Of Politicians Find A New Home. NPR. http://www.npr.org/2012/06/06/154432624/the-deleted-tweets-of-politicians-find-a-new-home

23. Cheng, Jacqui. (February 7, 2012). Over 3 years later, "deleted" Facebook photos are still online. CNN. http://www.cnn.com/2012/02/06/tech/social-media/deleted-facebook-photos-online/index.html

24. Cheng, Jacqui. (July 3, 2009). Are "deleted" photos really gone from Facebook? Not always. Ars Technica. http://arstechnica.com/business/2009/07/are-those-photos-really-deleted-from-facebook-think-twice/

25. Cheng, Jacqui. (October 11, 2010). "Deleted" Facebook photos still not deleted: a followup. Ars Technica. http://arstechnica.com/business/2010/10/facebook-may-be-making-strides/

26. Biersdorfer, J. D. (February 13, 2012). Q&A: When Facebook Marks Your Spot. The New York Times. http://gadgetwise.blogs.nytimes.com/2012/02/13/qa-when-facebook-marks-your-spot/

27. Consumer Reports magazine editors. (June 2012).Facebook & your privacy. Who sees the data you share on the biggest social network? Consumer Reports. http://www.consumerreports.org/cro/magazine/2012/06/facebook-your-privacy/index.htm

28. Barbaro, Michael; Zeller, Tom Jr. (August 9, 2006). A Face Is Exposed for AOL Searcher No. 4417749. The New York Times. http://www.nytimes.com/2006/08/09/technology/09aol.html

29. Sweeney, Latanya. (2000). Simple Demographics Often Identify People Uniquely. Carnegie Mellon University, Data Privacy Working Paper 3. Pittsburgh.

30. AVG. (October 6, 2010). Digital Birth: Welcome to the Online World. Business Wire. http://www.businesswire.com/news/home/20101006006722/en/Digital-Birth-Online-World

31. Sultan, Aisha; Miller, Jon. (May 25, 2012). 'Facebook parenting' is destroying our children's privacy. CNN. http://www.cnn.com/2012/05/25/opinion/sultan-miller-facebook-parenting/index.html

Chapter 12
Personal Information Management

Awareness is an effective weapon against many forms of identity theft.

—U.S. Federal Trade Commission

As we go through our lives we create vast amounts of data. It's more than just data. It represents our actions, interests, intentions, communications, relationships, locations, behaviors and creative and consumptive efforts.

—The Locker Project

12.1 Identity Theft Prevention

With the abundance of our digital footprint and exhaust data online, we must manage our personal data better. First and foremost, we need to address identify theft prevention. Even if companies are doing their best to protect our private information, hackers are hard at work to steal our valuable data online.

In June 2012, more than six million LinkedIn users had their account passwords stolen [1]. Between January 21 and February 25, 2012, thieves cracked into the Global Payments administrative account and stole more than 10 million credit and debit card transaction records [2]. Earlier in December 2011, hackers affiliated with the Anonymous Group broke into the private intelligence analysis firm Strategic Forecasting (Stratfor) and obtained private information of about 860,000 people including former U.S. Vice President Dan Quayle, former Secretary of State Henry Kissinger, and former CIA Director Jim Woolsey [3]. The group went on to publish the stolen emails and thousands of credit card numbers on the Internet.

According to Javelin Strategy and Research, more than 11.6 million Americans were victims of identity fraud in 2011, up 13 % from 2010 [4]. I was one of the victims many years ago. In attempt to find the best mortgage deal, I disclosed to several brokers my personal information including social security number, copy of my driver license, and bank statements. A few months later, an identity thief opened a new online bank account and transferred all the money from my bank to his account. I immediately reported the incident to the police and my bank reimbursed me the financial loss.

The Federal Trade Commission (FTC) advised us, "Awareness is an effective weapon against many forms of identity theft. Be aware of how information is stolen and what you can do to protect yours, monitor your personal information to

N. Lee, *Facebook Nation*, DOI: 10.1007/978-1-4614-5308-6_12,
© Springer Science+Business Media New York 2013

uncover any problems quickly, and know what to do when you suspect your identity has been stolen" [5].

Although we can never completely eradicate identity theft, we can protect ourselves to a large extent by taking the necessary steps to deter identity thieves, detect suspicious activity, and defend against identity theft [6]. Expanding on the FTC recommendations, we can:

1. Deter identity thieves by safeguarding your information:

    a. Shred financial documents and paperwork with personal information before you discard them.
    b. Sign up for paperless statements from your banks and utility companies.
    c. Do not carry your Social Security card or write your Social Security number on a check.
    d. Use hard-for-anyone-to-guess but easy-for-you-to-remember passwords with a combination of letters, numbers, and special characters.
    e. Set a passcode on your smartphone for protection.
    f. Keep the anti-virus software up-to-date on your computers.
    g. Do not access sensitive information or install any software through public WiFi or Internet connections in hotels, restaurants, and other public venues. (The FBI issued a warning on May 8, 2012 about travelers' laptops being infected with malicious software while using hotel Internet connections [7].)
    h. Opt out pre-screened credit and insurance offers to prevent potential thieves from intercepting and accepting the offers in your name. Opting out can be done online at https://www.optoutprescreen.com/

2. Detect suspicious activity by monitoring your information:

    a. Review financial accounts and billing statements regularly.
    b. Examine your Google Account Activity for any suspicious activities with your account sign-ins, visited places, emails, web history, etc. [8].
    c. Set up Google Alerts at http://www.google.com/alerts to monitor the web 24/7 for any news and videos about you or someone with the same name as you [9]. You can receive an alert once a week, once a day, or as-it-happens.
    d. Obtain your free annual credit reports from TransUnion, Equifax, and Experian; and look for abnormalities or inaccuracies.

3. Defend against identity theft by proactive measures:

    a. Place a fraud alert and a credit freeze on your credit reports at TransUnion, Equifax, and Experian. Fraud alerts and credit freezes help prevent an identity thief from opening new financial accounts, applying for loans, and seeking employment in your name.
    b. Report all identity theft incidences to the police and the FTC at 1-877-ID-THEFT.

12.2 Privacy Protection

We all have dealt with annoying cold calls from telemarketers. Since 2004, the National Do Not Call Registry has allowed us to register a phone number to limit the telemarketing calls we receive [10]. As for unsolicited text spam, we can reply "STOP" and forward the text to the shortcode 7726 (which spells "SPAM") [11].

Financial companies have the freedom to choose how they share our personal information. U.S. Federal law gives consumers the right to limit some but not all sharing. Federal law also requires financial companies to inform us how they collect, share, and protect our personal information.

Take the Target REDcard credit card as an example, its February 2012 privacy policy states that the types of personal information they collect and share can include: social security number, income, purchase history, payment history, credit history, and credit scores. These information may be used for their everyday business purposes, marketing purposes, joint marketing with other financial companies, affiliates' everyday business purposes, and non-affiliates to market to us. Under Federal law, consumers can limit the sharing of information for non-affiliates only by informing Target.

Some financial companies provide consumers more privacy choices than what the Federal law mandates. In February 2012, the JPMorgan Chase credit card, for instance, allowed their customers to restrict information sharing with Chase's affiliates as well as non-affiliates with whom Chase does business. Consumers can opt out the information sharing by phone, postal mail, or logging onto the Chase website.

Facebook and Google privacy policies, on the other hand, are more confusing to users than credit card agreements. A survey released in April 2012 by strategic branding firm Siegel+Gale revealed that the majority of Facebook and Google users do not fully comprehend the privacy policies and are ignorant of personal data management [12]. Among the 400+ respondents, the survey found that:

1. Less than 40 % of Facebook users understand how an Application Programming Interface (API) can be used to access their information on Facebook.
2. Only 15 % of users know what will happen to their Facebook accounts after they delete them.
3. Just 20 % of respondents know how to block outside applications and websites from accessing their information on Facebook.
4. Only 23 % of Google users realize that their profile is visible to anyone online.
5. Less than 50 % of Google users are aware that the same Google privacy policy applies to Google Talk, Google Maps, YouTube, and Blogger.
6. Just 38 % of people realize that Google connects search activity to a user's IP address whether or not they sign into a Google account.

12.3 Privacy on Facebook

1. Think twice before uploading anything to Facebook.

Even if you delete a Facebook account, the deleted photos may still be accessible through other means. The old content may be stored on Facebook servers for a month to three years or longer [13]. Deleting a Facebook account does not remove the messages that you post on other people's timeline.

2. Review and set individual privacy settings carefully to control who sees your contact information, posts, and timeline, etc.

In general, the choices are public (everyone), friends of friends, friend only, and only me. The most open setting is "public (everyone)" and the most private is "only me." Facebook Help Center offers the comprehensive privacy controls by feature [14], and you can control sharing and finding you on Facebook [15].

3. Turn on the option to review tagged posts and tagged photos.

Facebook allows you to use the privacy settings to turn on the option to "review posts friends tag you in before they appear on your timeline" [16]. You can also turn off "suggest photos of me to friends" in the privacy settings [17], but your friends can still tag you manually. As for tags from non-friends, Facebook automatically requires your approval before they go on your timeline.

4. Always check the privacy policy of a Facebook app before installing.

Facebook apps have access to your personal information on Facebook. The apps can keep your data even after you delete the apps [18]. Do not install a Facebook app that you do not feel comfortable sharing your personal data with. Keep in mind that Facebook's "frictionless sharing" facilitates someone to find out something about you without you telling them. *Mashable* editor Lauren Hockenson offered a detail account of what to look out for with the new Facebook Open Graph [19] that enables third-party apps to integrate deeply into the Facebook experience [20]. On Facebook, you can control the sharing of information with other websites and applications [21].

5. Adjust public search listing when appropriate.

Facebook by default creates a public search listing for all accounts that belong to users 18 years of age and older. If you do not want people to find your Facebook page on Google, Yahoo!, and other search engines, you can use the privacy settings to turn off "public search" [22].

6. Accept friend requests only from friends that you know.

For socializing with people other than your own friends, Facebook offers non-personal pages for building relationship with your audience and customers [23]. The categories include entertainment, artist or public figure, cause or community, brand or product, company or organization, and local business or place.

12.4 Privacy on Google

1. Control personalized ads on Google search and Gmail.

Google allows you to opt out of Google search ads and Gmail ads that are personalized based on your Google search strings and email content respectively [24]. While unsolicited ads can be as annoying as junk mail, the right kind of targeted ads can be beneficial to consumers.

2. Turn off location services on your Android devices.

The location services function can be turned on or off in Android's setting menu. It is off by default. However, Apple, Microsoft, and RIM turn on location services by default. However, your cell phone registers its location with cell phone networks several times a minute, and this function cannot be turned off when the phone is getting a wireless signal. American Civil Liberties Union reported in April 2012 that most police track phones' locations without warrants [25].

3. Remove Carrier IQ on your Android devices.

A free Android app "Voodoo Carrier IQ Detector" can be used to detect the presence of Carrier IQ on your smartphone [26]. In December 2011, Federal Bureau of Investigation director Robert Mueller testified before US Congress, "We may obtain information that in some way Carrier IQ may have been involved with. ... [but the FBI] has neither sought nor obtained any information from Carrier IQ in any one of our investigations" [27].

4. Turn off Find my Face.

Find my Face offers name tag suggestions to you and people you know to quickly tag photos. Google+ uses the photos you are tagged into create a model of your face. If you turn off Find my Face, your face model is deleted. However, any name tags already added are not deleted. By default, Find my Face is turned off [28].

5. Turn on "Do Not Track" on your Internet browser.

Much like the popular Do Not Call registry, Do Not Track gives you the choice to opt out of tracking by third-party websites, applications, and advertising networks. The Federal Trade Commission (FTC) has asked the industry for their voluntary compliance of Do Not Track. FTC chairman Jon Leibowitz said in March 2012, "Do Not Track from our perspective certainly means 'do not collect'—not 'do not advertise back. If a real Do Not Track option doesn't come to fruition by the end of the year, there will be, I don't want to say a tsunami of support for Do Not Track legislation next Congress, but certainly a lot of support" [29]. You can check to see if your Internet browser supports Do Not Track and if it has been enabled or not, by visiting http://donottrack.us/ [30]. Some popular anti-virus software such as AVG has Do Not Track feature that is enabled by default. Microsoft announced in May 2012 that IE10 in Windows 8 would send the "Do Not Track" signal to web sites by default to help consumers protect their privacy [31].

6. Accept only session cookies and block all other cookies.

Session cookies are short-lived cookies that last only as long as your browser is open. Cookies are small chunks of information that websites can put on your computer to track your activities, also known as your web history. When you create a Google Account, web history is automatically turned on [32]. You can remove you web history at https://www.google.com/history, but it does not stop Google from recording your search activity. A word of caution: some websites may not work without enabling both session cookies and first-party cookies.

7. Set up Google Alerts and send Google removal requests when necessary.

In addition to Googling yourself periodically, set up Google Alerts at http://www.google.com/alerts to monitor the web 24/7 for any news and videos about yourself [33]. You can receive an alert once a week, once a day, or as-it-happens. If a Google search reveals anything inappropriate, you can send Google a request at https://www.google.com/webmasters/tools/removals to remove search links to web pages, images, and blogs for legal reasons [34]. For YouTube videos, you can initiate a privacy complaint process online [35].

8. Use Google SSL search.

Use https://encrypted.google.com/ to conduct Google search over Secure Sockets Layer (SSL). SSL encrypts your search queries and results between your computer and Google, protecting them from being intercepted and read by a third party [36].

9. Consider using web proxies and anonymizing software.

Since search activity is connected to a user's IP address, web proxies such as Privoxy [37] and anonymizing software like Tor [38] hide the user's real IP address. Anonymizer's Anonymous Surfing [39] is more user-friendly but their servers will have access to your original IP address. Blogger Jared Newman discussed in *Time Magazine* a list of applications and services to help you stay anonymous online: PrivacyScore, Disconnect, SafeShepherd, Cocoon, AnchorFree HotspotShield, LBE Privacy Guard, Tor, and Burn Note [40].

12.5 Data Vault: Data is the New Oil

Absolute privacy is unattainable whenever we need to conduct business with a financial institution, an online shop, or a government agency. The Locker Project elaborates, "As we go through our lives we create vast amounts of data. Emails, phone calls, social network posts, photos, utility bills, health monitoring devices, text messages, browsing data, purchase receipts and more are all born out of the regular course of our actions. It's more than just data. It represents our actions, interests, intentions, communications, relationships, locations, behaviors and creative and consumptive efforts" [41]. The Locker Project provides open-source application programming interfaces (APIs) for developers to build applications to access and control personal data.

While Facebook, Google, and other online businesses collect information about us and make billions of dollars from selling our data, what if we can organize our own information online in a secure "data vault" so that we may even be compensated for sharing that information? [42].

A data vault is the digital counterpart of a bank vault where money, valuables, and important documents can be stored. Our individual data vault will contain the photos we take, the places we visit, the links we share, contact details for the people we communicate with, and many other personal information.

Founded by Kaliya Hamlin in June 2011, Personal Data Ecosystem Consortium brings together startup companies that are developing tools and systems for personal control over personal data. Hamlin wrote, "Privacy protections are just the tip of the iceberg; the industry of managing these assets wisely is in the process of creating new economic opportunities and is a magnet for talent and capital. ... Our vision for the ecosystem is inclusive of a wide range of potential services and business models, while holding true to the core non-negotiable that people are ultimately in control of the sum of their data" [43].

Singly is one of the startups. It offers an open platform where people can store their personal data after pulling it in from multiple sources such as Facebook posts, purchase histories from Amazon, past search queries from Google, and email contacts [44]. Singly supports the open source The Locker Project and the new protocol TeleHash that enables lockers connect with one another to share things [45].

Another startup—Personal—states that "small data is the new oil" as big data is rapidly becoming a commodity [46]. Personal allows users to enter their personal information in structured data fields within categories ranging from banking to shopping to babysitting. "What we envisioned was effectively creating a matchmaking marketplace, and it's very predicated on online dating," said Personal's president and CEO Shane Green, "Consumers will assume the role of women, who are typically the choosier sex on dating sites, and the marketplace will employ a ranking methodology to show which deals a user is most compatible" [47].

Steve McNally, CTO at True/Slant, wrote on *Forbes* about our lives online, "All that time spent and an unprecedented level of detail about how we've spent it—and it's mostly detail others have about you but you don't see yourself" [48].

By collecting and analyzing our own digital footprint and exhaust data online, we will eventually get a more complete picture of our lives. For financial gains, we can sell the data to businesses who want us to be their customers. For personal analytics, we can use the data to help us make better life decisions and self-improvements.

12.6 Personal Analytics and Social Networks

Martin Blinder, founder and CEO of Tictrac, spoke at the 2011 Intelligence Squared's If Conference, "We leave a data residue everywhere. ... New formats are enabling us to bring data sets together and drive compelling insights. ... What if I could compare myself to others? I could understand if certain activities in my life are normal, above average, etc. Does my daughter catch too many colds? Do I spend too much on shoes given my salary? Is my sex life normal for my age, job and location? A lot of these questions are in the back of my mind. We think about, but we don't talk about them. The benefit of this is that we are able to improve ourselves. ... Personal analytics means we can stop lying to ourselves and start leading healthier lives, making better choices, fewer mistakes and have control over our wellbeing" [49].

Reports have shown that social networks can help people stay on the path to physical fitness. Social apps that track and share their fitness habits make them feel more accountable. Fitocracy, a 500 Startups accelerator program alum, is a fitness social network and online game on iPhone with almost half a million users. Canadian Virginia Champoux told *CNN* that Fitocracy kept her diligent about her workouts, "It is motivational and it offers me support. It's the social aspect that helps" [50].

The Nike+ sports community has more than 5 million members who share their runs and profiles with friends online. Nike's Global Digital Brand and Innovation Director Jesse Stollak said, "The Nike+ community has grown tremendously in past couple years with the addition of new products like the Nike+ GPS App and Nike+ GPS Sportwatch. We've added new features like the new Maps site, which leverages a wealth of run route data to provide recommendations. We also included the 'cheer me on' functionality inside the Nike+ GPS app, which taps into the runners' friends on Facebook for additional motivation and support. When they are running, they hear applause on top of their music when friends 'cheer' them" [51].

Personal analytics combined with social networks provide a high-tech mechanism for self-help and self-improvement. The success in physical fitness applications is only the beginning.

References

1. Ingraham, Nathan. (June 6, 2012). LinkedIn confirms that member passwords have been compromised. The Verge. http://www.theverge.com/2012/6/6/3068652/linkedin-member-passwords-stolen
2. Acohido, Byron. (March 30, 2012). Credit card processor hit by hackers. USA Today. http://www.usatoday.com/money/industries/banking/story/2012-03-30/mastercard-security-breach/53887854/1
3. Zakaria, Tabassum; Hosenball, Mark. (December 30, 2011). Stratfor Hack: Anonymous-Affiliated Hackers Publish Thousands Of Credit Card Numbers. Huffington Post. http://www.huffingtonpost.com/2011/12/30/stratfor-hack-anonymous_n_1176726.html
4. Better Business Bureau. (May 10, 2012). Consumers Get Smart and Shred, Shred, Shred to Prevent Fraud. Better Business Bureau. http://www.bbb.org/us/article/consumers-get-smart-and-shred--shred--shred-to-prevent-fraud-34226
5. Federal Trade Commission. (Retrieved May 14, 2012). About Identity Theft. Federal Trade Commission. http://www.ftc.gov/bcp/edu/microsites/idtheft/consumers/about-identity-theft.html

6. Federal Trade Commission. (Retrieved May 14, 2012). Deter. Detect. Defend. Fighting Back Against Identity Theft. http://www.ftc.gov/bcp/edu/pubs/consumer/idtheft/idt01.pdf
7. Federal Bureau of Investigation. (May 8, 2012). Malware Installed on Travelers' Laptops Through Software Updates on Hotel Internet Connections. Federal Bureau of Investigation. http://www.fbi.gov/scams-safety/e-scams
8. Tuerk, Andreas. (March 28, 2012). Giving you more insight into your Google Account activity. Google Official Blog. http://googleblog.blogspot.com/2012/03/giving-you-more-insight-into-your.html#!/2012/03/giving-you-more-insight-into-your.html
9. Google. (Retrieved May 25, 2012). What are Google Alerts? Google Alerts. https://support.google.com/alerts/bin/answer.py?hl=en&answer=175925
10. National Do Not Call Registry. (Retrieved May 29, 2012). National Do Not Call Registry. https://www.donotcall.gov/
11. Gahran, Amy. (March 19, 2012). Getting text spam? New service helps you report it. CNN. http://www.cnn.com/2012/03/19/tech/mobile/text-spam-gahran/index.html
12. Siegel + Gale. (April 24, 2012). Survey Finds Facebook and Google Privacy Policies Even More Confusing Than Credit Card Bills and Government Notices. Siegel + Gale Press Releases.   http://www.siegelgale.com/media_release/survey-finds-facebook-and-google-privacy-policies-even-more-confusing-than-credit-card-bills-and-government-notices/
13. Cheng, Jacqui. (February 7, 2012). Over 3 years later, "deleted" Facebook photos are still online. CNN. http://www.cnn.com/2012/02/06/tech/social-media/deleted-facebook-photos-online/index.html
14. Facebook Privacy. (Retrieved May 14, 2012). Facebook Basics. Manage Your Account. Privacy. Facebook Help Center. http://www.facebook.com/help/?page=187475824633454
15. Facebook. (Retrieved May 15, 2012). Sharing and finding you on Facebook. Facebook Data Use Policy. http://www.facebook.com/about/privacy/your-info-on-fb
16. Facebook Privacy. (Retrieved May 15, 2012). How do I turn on the option to review posts and photos I'm tagged in before they appear on my profile? Facebook Help Center. http://www.facebook.com/help/?faq=223100381057791
17. Mitchell, Justin. (June 30, 2011). Making Photo Tagging Easier. The Facebook Blog. http://blog.facebook.com/blog.php?post=467145887130
18. Johnston, Casey. (May 13, 2012). On Facebook, deleting an app doesn't delete your data from their system. Ars Technica. http://arstechnica.com/gadgets/2012/05/on-facebook-deleting-an-app-doesnt-delete-your-data-from-their-system/
19. Hockenson, Lauren. (January 27, 2012). 7 Big Privacy Concerns for New Facebook and the Open Graph. Mashable. http://mashable.com/2012/01/27/facebook-privacy-open-graph/
20. Facebook. (Retrieved May 15, 2012). Open Graph. Facebook Developers. https://developers.facebook.com/docs/opengraph/
21. . (Retrieved May 15, 2012). Sharing with other websites and applications. Facebook Data Use Policy. http://www.facebook.com/about/privacy/your-info-on-other
22. Facebook Privacy. (Retrieved May 15, 2012). How do I prevent search engines (e.g., Google) from showing my public search listing? Facebook Help Center. http://www.facebook.com/help/?faq=131026496974464
23. Facebook. (Retrieved June 29, 2012). Create a Facebook Page to build a closer relationship with your audience and customers. Facebook. http://www.facebook.com/pages/create.php
24. Google. (Retrieved May 15, 2012). About personalized ads on Google Search and Gmail. Google Inside Search. http://support.google.com/websearch/bin/answer.py?hl=en&answer=1634057
25. Gahran, Amy. (April 3, 2012). ACLU: Most police track phones' locations without warrants. CNN. http://www.cnn.com/2012/04/03/tech/mobile/police-phone-tracking-gahran/index.html
26. Mello, John P. (December 2, 2011). Carrier IQ Test: Android App Detects Controversial Software. PC World. http://www.pcworld.com/article/245371/carrier_iq_test_android_app_detects_controversial_software.html

27. Vijayan, Jaikumar. (December 14, 2011). FBI never sought Carrier IQ data, director says. Computerworld.   http://www.computerworld.com/s/article/9222678/FBI_never_sought_ Carrier_IQ_data_director_says

28. Google + . (Retrieved May 15, 2012). Find my Face. Google + . http://support.google.com/ plus/bin/answer.py?hl=en&p=name_suggest_promo&answer=2370300

29. Vega, Tanzina; Wyatt, Edward. (March 26, 2012). U.S. Agency Seeks Tougher Consumer Privacy Rules. New York Times. http://www.nytimes.com/2012/03/27/business/ftc-seeks-privacy-legislation.html

30. Mayer, Jonathan; Narayanan, Arvind. (Retrieved May 15, 2012). Do Not Track. Universal Web Tracking Opt Out. http://donottrack.us/

31. Hachamovitch, Dean. (May 31, 2012). Windows Release Preview: The Sixth IE10 Platform Preview. MSDN Blogs. http://blogs.msdn.com/b/ie/archive/2012/05/31/windows-release-preview-the-sixth-ie10-platform-preview.aspx

32. Google. (Retrieved May 16, 2012). Google Accounts & Web History. Google. http:// www.google.com/goodtoknow/data-on-google/web-history/

33. Google. (Retrieved May 25, 2012). What are Google Alerts? Google Alerts. https:// support.google.com/alerts/bin/answer.py?hl=en&answer=175925

34. Google. (February 15, 2012). Remove content from someone else's site. Google Webmaster Tools. https://support.google.com/webmasters/bin/answer.py?hl=en&answer=1663688

35. Google. (Retrieved May 27, 2012). Privacy Complaint Process. YouTube. http:// support.google.com/youtube/bin/answer.py?hl=en&answer=142443

36. Google. (Retrieved June 1, 2012). SSL Search. Google Inside Search. http:// support.google.com/websearch/bin/answer.py?hl=en&answer=173733

37. Privoxy Developers. (Retrieved May 15, 2012). Privoxy. http://www.privoxy.org/

38. Tor Developers. (Retrieved May 15, 2012). Tor. https://www.torproject.org/

39. Anonymizer Developers. (Retrieved May 15, 2012). Anonymizer. http://www. anonymizer.com/

40. Newman, Jared. (May 4, 2012). 8 Tools for the Online Privacy Paranoid. Time Magazine. http://techland.time.com/2012/05/04/8-tools-for-the-online-privacy-paranoid/

41. The Locker Project. (Retrieved May 17, 2012). About The Locker Project. http:// lockerproject.org/

42. Gross, Doug. (February 27, 2012). Manage (and make cash with?) your data online. CNN. http://www.cnn.com/2012/02/24/tech/web/owning-your-data-online/index.html

43. Hamlin, Kaliya. (June 1, 2011). What is the Personal Data Ecosystem? Personal Data Ecosystem Consortium. http://personaldataecosystem.org/category/about/

44. Singly. (Retrieved May 17, 2012). Singly exists for you. http://blog.singly.com/about-singly/

45. Shute, Tish. (February 11, 2011). The Locker Project: data for the people. O'Reilly Radar. http://radar.oreilly.com/2011/02/singly-locker-project-telehash.html

46. Personal. (Retrieved May 17, 2012). A new kind of company. http://www.personal.com/who-we-are/a-new-kind-of-company

47. Delo, Cotton. (November 28, 2011). Here's My Personal Data, Marketers. What Do I Get For it? Advertising Age. http://adage.com/article/digital/web-data-startups-bank-consumers-controlling-data/231208/

48. McNally, Steve. (June 30, 2011). The Locker Project and Your Digital Wake. Forbes. http:// www.forbes.com/sites/smcnally/2011/06/30/your-digital-wake/

49. Solon, Olivia. (November 28, 2011). Personal analytics could lead to 'designed' lifestyles. Wired. http://www.wired.co.uk/news/archive/2011-11/28/martin-blinder-personal-analytics

50. Imam, Jareen. (June 29, 2012). Want to get fit? Pull out your phone. CNN. http:// www.cnn.com/2012/06/29/tech/social-media/tech-fitness-irpt/index.html

51. Swallow, Erica. (September 22, 2011). How Nike Outruns the Social Media Competition. Mashable. http://mashable.com/2011/09/22/nike-social-media/

Chapter 13
Total Information Awareness

You can have data without information, but you cannot have information without data.
—Facebook Data Team (2008)

I think that big data is going to become humanity's dashboard.
—Photographer Rick Smolan (2012)

He didn't know if he was Zhuangzi who had dreamt he was a butterfly, or a butterfly dreaming he was Zhuangzi. Between Zhuangzi and a butterfly there must be some distinction! This is a case of what is called the transformation of things.
—Chinese philosopher Zhuangzi (circa 300 AD)

13.1 Humanity's Dashboard

In Francis Ford Coppola's *The Godfather Part II* (1974), Michael Corleone said, "There are many things my father taught me here in this room. He taught me: keep your friends close, but your enemies closer" [1]. Ironically, the biggest blows to the mafia in America have been due to the efficacious FBI infiltration. Undercover FBI agents have been able to penetrate the mafia families as wiseguys and "made men", leading to the arrests and convictions of notorious mob figures [2].

Although there are Facebook apps like "EnemyGraph" that bond like-minded haters online, in reality the real "enemies" are actually Facebook "friends" who are bullying their classmates or applying peer pressure on their weaker counterparts. School bullying has gotten so out of hand that in April 2012, 13-year-old Rachel Ehmke in Minnesota committed suicide after months of school bullying [3], and a mother sent her 17-year-old son Darnell Young to school in Indiana armed with a stun gun for his protection against bullies. Young's mother Chelisa Grimes said, "I do not promote violence—not at all—but what is a parent to do when she has done everything that she felt she was supposed to do ... at the school?" [4].

In Steven Spielberg's *Minority Report* (2002), "Pre-Crime" is a specialized police department that apprehends criminals based on foreknowledge provided by three psychics named "precogs" in the year 2054 [5]. Although the notion of "Pre-Crime" is overarching Orwellian, who would not want to know if a criminal out there was planning to abduct our children or shoot up our schools?

We were appalled by the senseless massacres at Columbine High School in 1999 and at Virginia Tech in 2007. What if these atrocities could have been prevented? We were equally horrified by the kidnapping of 14-year-old Elizabeth Smart in 2002 and of 11-year-old Jaycee Dugard, who was abducted in 1991 and held captive for 18 years. What if the abductees could have been rescued in a matter of hours or days instead of years or decades?

The answers rely heavily on the collection, interpretation, and usage of big data—the avalanche of personal data driven by social networks and other existing infrastructures. As the Facebook Data Team wrote on their official Facebook profile, "You can have data without information, but you cannot have information without data" [6].

"When people hear of big data, they think Big Brother", said Photographer Rick Smolan, co-founder of The Day in the Life photography series. "The general public and the media tend to immediately think, 'Oh, this is all invasive. People are trying to sell us stuff or spy on us, or it's the government trying to control us'. But I think that data will become one of the ways that we can finally start addressing some of the biggest challenges facing humanity—of poverty, and crime, and pollution, and overcrowding, and the use of resources, and environmental problems. Right now, I feel like the human race is like driving a car around this twisty road, and we have no idea whether our tires are inflated, how much gas we have left. We have no headlights. … It's like no dashboard in front of us. And I think that big data is going to become humanity's dashboard" [7].

Facebook nation exists in the intersection of humanities and sciences, somewhere in between the fictional worlds of *The Godfather Part II* and *Minority Report*. We saw in *Minority Report* that in 2054 computers scan human faces and display targeted advertisements to individuals as they walk down the street. It turns out that since 2010 there have been billboards in Tokyo subway stations and London bus stops that employ cameras and face recognition software to determine the gender and age of passersby. Gesture-control interfaces [8], retina scanners [9], insect robots [10], augmented-reality glasses [11], and electronic paper [12] are some of the other cutting-edge technologies that are already available today. Ericsson's human USB [13], Nokia's vibrating tattoo alerts [14], Disney's touch-sensing furniture [15], NeuroSky's mind-controlled videogames [16], and Google's self-driving cars [17] are just a few of the many new products in the works. The future is arriving sooner than we imagine.

In the age of big data, Facebook nation is progressing towards Total Information Awareness whether or not we are ready for it. A whole new world of possibilities, either good or bad, has been bestowed on us. What we opt to do or not do in this brave new world will have a significant impact on our future.

13.2 Ambient Awareness and Suicide Prevention

Social scientists use the term "ambient awareness" to describe the incessant online contact on Facebook, Twitter, and other social networks. Prof. Andreas Kaplan at ESCP Europe Business School in France defines ambient awareness as "awareness created through regular and constant reception, and/or exchange of information fragments through social media" [18]. Clive Thompson of the *New York Times* wrote, "Ambient awareness is very much like being physically near someone and picking up on his mood through the little things he does—body language, sighs, stray comments—out of the corner of your eye" [19].

Ambient social apps and Facebook's "frictionless sharing" greatly facilitate ambient awareness among friends nearby and far away. We can find out something about others without them telling us. We can be more vigilant only by becoming more aware of people, our surroundings, and happenings around us.

Friend's awareness can save lives. Frank Warren founded PostSecret in 2004 to collect secrets mailed to him on postcards anonymously. He scans the postcards and posts them on the blog www.postsecret.com. Warren shared his testimony at the TED2012 conference, "When I posted a secret from someone who confesses to thinking about jumping from the Golden Gate Bridge, Post-Secret Blog readers sprang to action creating a Facebook group page called, Please Don't Jump. They posted encouraging pictures and shared their own inspiring stories of hope. 60,000 people joined the group in 10 days. The next week the San Francisco City Council proclaimed the first annual 'Please Don't Jump Day'" [20].

The public's reaction was in sharp contrast to the bystander effect or "Genoverse syndrome," named after Catherine Susan (Kitty) Genovese whose cry in the night went unanswered by 38 of her neighbors in Queens, New York, on March 13, 1964 [21]. Diffusion of responsibility is a sociopsychological phenomenon whereby a person is less likely to take responsibility for an action or inaction when others are present. In 1968, John M. Darley of New York University and Bibb Latané of Columbia University performed experiments to verify their hypothesis that "the more bystanders to an emergency, the less likely, or the more slowly, any one bystander will intervene to provide aid" [22]. In 2008, Mark Levine and Simon Crowther of Lancaster University conducted four new experiments, which concluded that "increasing group size inhibited intervention in a street violence scenario when bystanders were strangers but encouraged intervention when bystanders were friends" [23]. The key here is "friends."

Facebook friends can make a difference in people's lives, for better or worse. In December 2009, John T. Cacioppo of University of Chicago, James H. Fowler of UC San Diego, and Nicholas A. Christakis of Harvard University showed that loneliness spreads through a contagious process in a large social network. A person is 52 % more likely to be lonely if a direct connection in the social network is lonely [24]. In August 2011, the National Center on Addiction and Substance Abuse at Columbia University found that teens that spend time on the social networks are likely to see images of their peers drinking or using drugs—images that could help to convince them that substance abuse is a normal, acceptable activity [25].

On the positive side, Pew Internet Project in February 2012 released the research results by Keith N. Hampton of Rutgers University, Lauren Sessions Goulet of University of Pennsylvania, and Cameron Marlow of Facebook. The researchers combined server logs of Facebook activity with survey data to explore the structure of Facebook friendship networks and measures of social well-being. The results showed that most Facebook users receive more from their Facebook friends than they give—they receive more messages than they send, they are tagged in a photo more than they tag a friend in a photo, and their content is "liked" more often than they "like" their friend's content. Lee Rainie, Director of the Pew Internet Project, said, "This examination of people's activities in a very new realm affirms one of the oldest truths about the value of friendship: Those who are really active socially have a better shot at getting the help and emotional support they need. The Golden Rule seems to rule digital spaces, too" [26].

Sometimes help might have come too late. In September 2010, 18-year-old Rutgers University freshman Tyler Clementi killed himself after his roommate Dharun Ravi and Ravi's friend Molly Wei secretly video streamed him kissing another man using a webcam. Clementi felt alone and helpless during the ordeals. His final message on Facebook read, "Jumping off the gw bridge sorry" [27]. His friends and Ravi's apologetic text message were too late to help [28].

On Christmas Day 2010, 42-year-old Simone Back in Brighton told her 1,048 friends on Facebook: "Took all my pills, be dead soon, bye bye everyone" [29]. Of the 150 online responses, one Facebook friend called her a liar, another said, "she does it all the time, takes all her pills", and yet another said, "It's her choice". No one who lived nearby contacted the police or sought her out in time to save her. Back's friend Samantha Pia Owen said, "Everyone just carried on arguing with each other on Facebook ... Some of those people lived within walking distance of Simone. If one person just left their computer and went to her house, her life could have been saved. These so-called friends are a waste of air. If someone has got problems you don't go around adding to them, you don't start attacking people who are already vulnerable ... Facebook should put up a flag or button so that a post can be flagged up as a suicide threat and Facebook should be able to contact the police" [30].

While Facebook could not tell people how to choose their friends, Facebook in March 2011 added Samaritans suicide risk alert system [31]. If someone is posting depressing photos or writing about killing themselves, their Facebook friends can click on the "report suicidal content" link to alert Facebook staff members who are monitoring these reports 24/7 [32]. Other social media follows suit. Google provides a feature in the U.S. search engine that displays a picture of a red telephone and the National Suicide Prevention Lifeline phone number when people are searching for suicide-related topics [33]. Twitter and Tumblr also allow their users to report suicidal behavior.

Surgeon General Regina Benjamin wrote on Facebook in December 2011, "The Action Alliance brings together public, private and nonprofit partners to engage every sector of society with a vision of ending the tragic experience of suicide in America. Facebook is an important part of that partnership, and I'm excited about the new initiative to augment its response to potentially suicidal members by offering the opportunity for a private chat with a trained crisis representative from the Suicide Prevention Lifeline in addition to providing the

Lifeline's phone number. This service will be available to people who use Facebook in the United States and Canada. The new service enables Facebook users to report a suicidal comment they see posted by a friend to Facebook using either the Report Suicidal Content link or the report links found throughout the site. The person who posted the suicidal comment will then immediately receive an e-mail from Facebook encouraging them to call the National Suicide Prevention Lifeline 1-800-273-TALK (8255) or to click on a link to begin a confidential chat session with a crisis worker."

13.3 Parental Awareness and (Cyber) Bullying

In April 2012, 17-year-old Darnell Young went to Arsenal Technical High School in Indianapolis with a stun gun. "I brought the stun gun 'cause I wasn't safe", said Young who was taunted and bullied for months. "I was at my wit's end. I didn't know what to do and I thought about suicide". He was kicked out of school for bringing the weapon. Young's mother Chelisa Grimes protested, "I do not promote violence—not at all—but what is a parent to do when she has done everything that she felt she was supposed to do … at the school? I think that the self-protection device is what's making the news, but the big picture is that my child is not the only one who does not feel safe at our school" [34].

It is a tragedy that some victims of school bullying took their own lives. For example, 13-year-old Rachel Ehmke in Minnesota committed suicide in April 2012 after months of bullying by her schoolmates in Kasson/Mantorville Middle School [35]. A note that her parents found after her death read, "I'm fine = I wish I could tell you how I really feel", alongside a picture of a broken heart.

Cyber bullying only exacerbates the danger. Victims are constantly being stalked by bullies even after school. In January 2010, 15-year-old Phoebe Prince, an immigrant from Ireland, took her own life in order to escape vicious bullying on Facebook, via text messages, and in her school. After her death, one student wrote "Done" on Facebook while another wrote that "She got what she deserved" [36]. Darby O'Brien, a high school parent and friend of Prince's family, wondered why the bullies who tormented Prince were still in school. O'Brien said, "Instead of confronting the evil among us, the reality that there are bullies roaming the corridors at South Hadley High, people are blaming the victim, looking for excuses why a 15-year-old girl would do this. People are in denial" [37]. The South Hadley police chief responded, "We've subpoenaed records from Facebook, we've subpoenaed web pages from Facebook, hoping to track down perpetrators of some of this criminal threatening" [38].

In September 2011, Facebook collaborated with Cartoon Network in launching the "Stop Bullying: Speak Up" social pledge application. "The Stop Bullying: Speak Up Social Pledge App is rooted in the fact that students, educators and parents have the power to stop bullying by speaking up when they see it occur", said Marne Levine, Vice President of Global Public Policy at Facebook. "The launch of this campaign reinforces our deep commitment to the safety and security of kids everywhere. By working with Time Warner, our hope is to inspire millions of people who witness bullying to take action" [39].

Bullying has become such an epidemic that some schools have been going for a shock-and-awe approach by hiring The Scary Guy (a real legal name for Earl Kenneth Kaufmann) to deliver anti-bullying messages in an unconventional manner. Covered with tattoos all over his face and body, The Scary Guy pokes fun at the audience and yet gets serious about the harm of bullying. His message is to "show [kids] they have the power to make the choice to be who they want to be and not become what they see and hear around them. … [The letters from the kids] just tell me what it's like to make a difference, to make a change—to wake up to the idea that they don't have to live with stress and negative behavior around them" [40].

Indeed, children and teens need to learn that they are who they are and they can be what they want to be, regardless of what other people call them or try to hurt them. 13-year-old Faye Gibson is constantly bullied by schoolmates who call her ugly. In January 2012, Gibson made a YouTube video "Am I pretty or ugly" in order to get a second opinion from strangers on the Internet [41]. Her mother Naomi Gibson told *ABC Good Morning America*, "I took away her Facebook and Twitter account because of bullying. She needs to stop putting herself out there. Now people are walking around asking her if she's pretty to her face. It's hurting her more in the long run, I think" [42].

Keeping children away from Facebook and Twitter may not be the right thing to do. Instead, parents should monitor their kid's Facebook messages and tweets to make sure that they are not being bullied as well as they are not bullying others. It is best for parents to "befriend" their children on Facebook, and to "follow" them on Twitter.

In September 2010, SafetyWeb introduced a new subscription service for parents to help protect kids from common online dangers from sexting to cyber bullying [43]. Without the parents having to monitor every post, the service automatically scours the Internet and monitors a child's online activities and immediately red-flags for parent any and all potential threats to their child. The service goes a step further by helping parents keep tabs on their child's mobile calls and text messages. Although there is a delicate balance between children's privacy and parental awareness, a good parent should always be attentive to their children's activities and feelings. Rachel Ehmke's suicide note "I'm fine = I wish I could tell you how I really feel" pointed to deadly consequences of the lack of communication and parental awareness.

After all, parents play an epochal role in their children's behavior. In 1998, researchers from the University of Maryland and the National Institute of Child Health and Human Development found that "a proactive parental monitoring approach may be associated with less adolescent drinking" [44]. As a part of the 5 month Aware.Prepare.Prevent (A.P.P.) campaign, the Norfolk FBI in May 2012 held a program on parental awareness on innocent images, sexing, cyber bullying, and gangs [45]. In short, parental awareness and proper education are the keys to stop bullying.

13.4 Student Awareness and School Safety

April 16, 2007 was a truly sad day when I heard with disbelief in the news about the horrific school shooting at Virginia Tech, my alma mater. 23-year-old Seung Hui Cho, an English major at Virginia Tech murdered 32 and injured 17 students and faculty before taking his own life [46].

Although no one could have foreseen the tragedy, red flags and warning signs had been abundant for many years according to the 2007 Virginia Tech Review Panel report presented to then Virginia Governor Tim Kaine [47]. In 1999 when Cho was in his 8th grade, his middle school teachers identified suicidal and homicidal ideations in his writings referencing the Columbine High School massacre that occurred on April 20 that year. The school requested his parents to seek counseling for him. He received a psychiatric evaluation and was prescribed antidepressant medication.

In Fall 2005, as Cho started his junior year at Virginia Tech, his poetry professor Nikki Giovanni was concerned about violence in his writing. English Department Chair and Prof. Lucinda Roy removed Cho from Giovanni's class and tutored him one-on-one with assistance from Prof. Frederick D'Aguiar. When Cho refused to go to counseling, Roy notified the Division of Student Affairs, the Cook Counseling Center, the Schiffert Health Center, the Virginia Tech police, and the College of Liberal Arts and Human Sciences.

In Winter 2005, several female students filed reports with the Virginia Tech Police Department (VTPD) to complain about "annoying" contacts and "disturbing" instant messages from Cho. On December 13, Cho's suitemate received an instant message from Cho stating, "I might as well kill myself now". The suitemate alerted VTPD. Cho was taken to Carilion St. Albans Psychiatric Hospital for an overnight stay and mental evaluation. He was released after psychologists determined that he did not present an imminent danger to himself or others.

In Spring 2006, Cho wrote a paper in Prof. Bob Hicok's creative writing class, detailing a young man who hated the students at his school and planned to kill them and himself. In February 2007, Cho ordered his first handgun online from TGSCOM. In March, he purchased a second handgun at Roanoke Firearms. The store initiated the required background check by police, but found no record of mental health issues in the National Instant Criminal Background Check System. From March to April, Cho purchased several 10-round magazines and ammunition from eBay, Wal-Mart, and Dick's Sporting Goods.

About 7:15 in the morning of April 16, 2007, Cho entered West Ambler Johnston residence hall, a 2 min walk from his dormitory. He shot and killed Emily Hilscher in her dormitory room after she was dropped off by her boyfriend. Resident advisor Ryan Christopher Clark went to investigate noises in Hilscher's room and was also shot.

At 9:01 a.m., Cho mailed a package at the Blacksburg post office to NBC News in New York. The package contained pictures of him holding weapons, and 1,800-word rambling diatribe, and video recordings in which he expressed rage, resentment, and desire to get even with oppressors.

Two hours after the first double homicide, Cho entered Norris Hall, an engineering building, at 9:15 a.m. He chained the doors shut on the three main entrances from the inside. Around 9:30 a.m., he began a shooting spree that lasted about 11 min. He fired 174 rounds, killing 30 and wounding 17 students and faculty. Prof. Liviu Librescu barricaded his classroom door to give his students time to escape through the windows [48]. Librescu and one of his students were killed. The massacre finally ended at 9:51 a.m. when Cho shot himself in the head.

On April 19, the autopsy of Cho found no brain function abnormalities and no toxic substances, drugs, or alcohol that could explain the rampage. Furthermore, there was no evidence that he knew any of the 32 people whom he killed.

Dr. Roger Depue, a 21 year veteran of the Federal Bureau of Investigation (FBI), wrote in the Virginia Tech Review Panel report, "Experts who evaluate possible indicators that an individual is at risk of harming himself or others know to seek out many sources for clues, certain red flags that merit attention. ... When a cluster of indicators is present then the risk becomes more serious. Thus, a person who possesses firearms, is a loner, shows an interest in past shooting situations, writes stories about homicide and suicide, exhibits aberrant behavior, has talked about retribution against others, and has a history of mental illness and refuses counseling would obviously be considered a significant risk of becoming dangerous to himself or others" [49].

The report concluded, "Accurate and complete information on individuals prohibited from possessing firearms is essential to keep guns out of the wrong hands". However, privacy laws and social stigma of mental illness presented a huge obstacle in linking mental health data with criminal background check. "We need to do a much better job educating educators, [the] mental health community and law enforcement that they can, in fact, share information when a person's safety or a community's safety is in fact potentially endangered," said Health and Human Services Secretary Michael O. Leavitt after delivering the report to President George W. Bush [50].

Had Cho's mental history been added to the National Instant Criminal Background Check System, he would not have been able to purchase firearms. If school buildings had installed monitored security cameras, he might not have gotten away easily from the crime scene in West Ambler Johnston residence hall, he would not have had the time to chain the doors shut on the three main entrances of Norris Hall, and the police could have been dispatched after he fired the first few shots.

School safety is one of the topmost parental concerns for their kids. In February 2012, community leader Morris Grifton called for video surveillance in school after two teachers were arrested for lewd acts involving pupils at Miramonte Elementary School. "We're saying enough is enough," said Grifton at a rally with angry parents. "We want cameras in the classrooms, in the hallways and around the school" [51].

Virginia Tech President Charles W. Steger hinted towards the need for better information awareness in a written statement, "The [Virginia Tech Review Panel] report unearthed the deep complexities of the issues facing college campuses today. We believe that this will further inform the national and our state discussion on the nexus between societal safety and personal freedoms".

Better information awareness does not mean less personal freedoms. Feeling safe in school is a prerequisite for a conducive learning environment. Everyone should be free to express their opinions, voice their concerns, and become better informed. In the age of big data, correlating Cho's mental history and his purchase data from eBay could have alerted the authority, mental healthcare professionals, and university counselors that he really needed psychological help.

The 2007 Virginia Tech shooting prompted many universities to improve their emergency notification system and procedure in compliance with the Clery Act. Signed in 1990, the Clery Act is also known as the Crime Awareness and Campus Security Act—a law enacted after 19-year-old Lehigh University freshman Jeanne Clery was raped and murdered in her dorm room in April 1986 [52].

When gunshots erupted on the Virginia Tech campus again in December 2011, the university notified all 30,000+ students within minutes via text messages, emails, school website, Twitter, and campus-wide public address system. "We all knew immediately after it happened not to go to campus", said Virginia Tech sophomore Abby Lorenz. "All of my roommates and I got texts and e-mails, and they've sent us multiple updates" [53]. Timely notifications and crime awareness are essential to deterring violence on campus and minimizing potential causalities.

In addition to campus security, there are social apps designed for students to help one another in need. Winner of the White House "Apps Against Abuse" Technology Challenge, Circle of 6 is an iPhone app that uses GPS and pre-installed text messages to alert friends to the user's location if anything goes wrong [54]. Two weeks after its launch in March 2012, Circle of 6 already had 19,000 downloads [55].

In the Spring 2012 issue of *Virginia Tech Magazine*, Alumni Distinguished Professor Emeritus William E. Snizek wrote, "During almost 40 years on the Tech faculty, I was fascinated by the graffiti I found on desktops. … On one desktop, a student wrote, 'Why do I always want to cry?' And just below that, another responded, 'I know how you feel, trust me, talk to someone'" [56].

Without someone to talk to face-to-face openly, a troubled individual may rely solely on the Internet proliferated with information, misinformation, and disinformation. It is appalling that anyone can find on the Internet detailed instructions and user guides on school shooting, a horrific act of domestic terrorism. For instance, Lolokaust's school shooting guide laden with profanity, pornography, and erroneous information is the number one search result on Google for the search phrase "shoot up your school" (See Fig. 13.1).

Google Chrome's tagline is: "The web is what you make of it" [57]. The vile Lolokaust website might have a redeeming value if the Google search history—a part of user's digital footprint and exhaust data—would help identify those troubled individuals and provide them psychological counseling.

The prevalence of Facebook use also gives introverts an outlet to express their lonely feelings by reaching out to others. "By helping lonely people on the

+You   **Search**   Images   Maps   **Play**   **YouTube**   **News**   **Gmail**   **Documents**   **Calendar**   More ▾

shoot up your school   Sign in

Search   About 374,000,000 results (0.11 seconds)   ⚙

Everything   **SHOOT UP YOUR SCHOOL**! KILL EVERYONE!
                lolokaust.com/guides/**shooting**.html
Images   Lets be frank, **school** is shit right? You get **up** at stupid hours, walk through
                ridiculous weather, only to be beaten by the other students and mocked by overpaid ...
Maps

Videos   How to **shoot up your school** - Zoklet.net
                www.zoklet.net › Zoklet.net › Hobbies › Bad Ideas
News   47 posts · 26 authors - Oct 13, 2009
                Disclaimer: I've never done a **school shooting**, and I don't plan to go back to school
Shopping   just so I can **shoot** it **up**. What you do with this information is ...

More   How to Survive **a School Shooting**
                www.secretsofsurvival.com/survival/**school_shooting**.html
Los Angeles,   Apr 3, 2007 – You're sitting in class trying hard to pay attention, and keep **up** with
CA   your ... Escape **a School Shooting** - Know Your Surroundings in Advance ...

Change location
                Columbine High **School** massacre - Wikipedia, the free encyclopedia
Show search tools   en.wikipedia.org/wiki/Columbine_High_**School**_massacre
                Jump to **Shooting** begins: Killed by **a shot** to the chest on the West Staircase. 4.
                .... the cafeteria via **a** staircase leading **up** to the second floor of the **school**.
                → Eric Harris and Dylan Klebold - Bath School disaster - Rachel Scott

Fig. 13.1 Google search results on "shoot up your school"

periphery of a social network", said James H. Fowler of UC San Diego and Nicholas A. Christakis of Harvard University, "we can create a protective barrier against loneliness that will keep the whole network from unraveling" [58].

Facebook and other social media platforms can serve to increase student awareness and improve school safety. In March 2012, the American Civil Liberties Union sued Minnewaska Area Middle School over a search of Facebook and email accounts of a 12-year-old, sixth-grade female student [59]. Although the Minnesota middle school may have intruded on the student's privacy, the school should be commended for being proactive in the total awareness of its schoolchildren.

13.5 Crime Awareness and Video Surveillance

On the night of March 3, 1991, George Holliday was awakened in his apartment by police sirens and helicopter [60]. He grabbed his camera and recorded about 9 mins of video showing four LAPD officers beating up a drunk driver and parolee named Rodney King [61]. The video went viral on the national airwaves [62]. On April 29, 1992, a jury acquitted the officers accused in the beating, and Los Angeles erupted in weeklong riots that left 54 people dead and $1 billion in property damage [63]. The second trial of the four police offers began in February 1993. The jury found two of the officers guilty of civil rights violations, and the streets of Los Angeles remained quiet when the judge read the verdict on April 19, 1993 [64].

In some states such as Illinois, Massachusetts, and Maryland, it is illegal to record any on-duty police officer [65]. Under the existing wiretapping and eavesdropping laws, all parties must consent for a recording to take place. This restriction does not apply to property owner's video tapping in their own private residences or business premises for security purposes. There are many instances where secret recordings have saved lives and brought justices:

1. In 2003, a Florida couple Jennifer and Brett Schwartz installed a nanny-cam to keep an eye on their infant daughter who seemed unsettled being around their babysitter [66]. Among the hundreds of hours of video, 29-year-old babysitter Claudia Muro was seen shaking the child and slamming her to the floor. It was shocking because Muro was highly recommended by a local child care agency and she passed a series of background checks.
2. In 2010, another Florida couple noticed a black eye on one of their two children, and their nanny could not explain what happened. They installed a hidden camera, which caught the nanny swatting, slapping, and kicking an 11-month-old boy. 53-year-old nanny Jeannine Marie Campbell pleaded guilty to abuse charges [67].
3. In December 2011, Salvatore Miglino secretly recorded on his iPhone a verbal dispute with his estranged mother-in-law Cheryl Hepner. During the argument, Hepner pulled out a gun and shot Miglino. In a classic he-said, she-said, Hepner claimed self-defense; but the iPhone recording proved otherwise, and she was charged with attempted murder in the first degree [68].

In June 2012, American professional skateboarder Tony Hawk captured in his home security camera two thieves stealing a skateboard from his car. He posted several images on Instagram asking them to return the skateboard or else he would notify the police. Hawk said, "So much of our life is recorded on video now, including the worst parts" [69].

Fixed video surveillance, aka closed-circuit television (CCTV), has long been effective in reducing and deterring crime in shopping malls, convenience stores, gas stations, parking garages, airports, banks, casinos, and other public places. Public CCTV systems have been employed extensively in cities throughout Europe, and similar systems have been deployed in some major U.S. cities.

A Long Island, New York study found that serious crimes dropped 47 % after CCTV surveillance systems were installed by businesses and homeowners in 1993. There were 8,000 burglaries in 1994 compared to about 15,000 in 1975, and there were also fewer robberies in 1994 than in 1975 [70].

Researchers from UC Berkeley's Center for Information Technology Research in the Interest of Society studied the crime-deterrent effects of the San Francisco Community Safety Camera Program between January 2005 and January 2008. They found a statistically significant 22 % decline in property crime occurring within 100 feet of camera locations, but no statistically significant changes in crime beyond 100 feet from the site [71].

The City of Los Angeles is a California municipality in which law enforcement monitors video surveillance cameras in real time. Researchers from USC School of Policy, Planning, and Development reported in May 2008 that there was no statistical significance in the drop of violent crimes and property crimes along Hollywood Boulevard's "Walk of Fame" [72].

Despite the mixed results based on statistical analyses, video surveillance has shown effectiveness in solving crimes and apprehending suspects:

1. For 4 days between December 30, 2011 and January 2, 2012, there were 52 suspicious car and building fires across Los Angeles—a city that had not seen such a rash of fires since the 1992 Rodney King riots. LAPD was able to arrest the arsonist who resembled a man seen in a surveillance video near the scene of one fire [73].
2. When the anti-fraud and anti-money laundering (AML) systems identify suspicious bank transactions, it can:

   • Search on transactions in video surveillance system to find suspect's face.
   • Use correlated search to identify other potential suspects aiding criminal activity.
   • Use facial recognition to search across other transactions.
   • Find license plate of vehicle when person of interest uses a drive-up ATM.
   • Export video evidence for law enforcement.

13.6 Community Awareness and Neighborhood Watch

San Francisco's Community Safety Camera Program was launched by then Mayor Gavin Newsom in late 2005. The program placed more than 70 non-monitored cameras in mainly high-crime areas throughout the city. Researchers from UC Berkeley's Center for Information Technology Research in the Interest of Society found that the program resulted in over 20 % reduction in property crime within the view of the cameras [74]. Although the cameras were less effective in providing evidence for police investigations due to their choppy video quality (low frame rate and low resolution), Newsom spokesman Nathan Ballard told reporters, "We believe these cameras have a deterrent effect on crime. The neighbors appreciate them" [75].

Apart from citywide video surveillance, Neighborhood Watch is an organized group of citizens devoted to crime and vandalism prevention within a neighborhood. The modern practice began in 1964 as a response to the rape and murder of Catherine Susan (Kitty) Genovese in Queens, New York. In 1972, the National Sheriff's Association officially launched the nationwide Neighborhood Watch program that "counts on citizens to organize themselves and work with law enforcement to keep a trained eye and ear on their communities, while demonstrating their presence at all times of day and night" [76]. By 1982, 12 % of the U.S. population was involved in a Neighborhood Watch.

In February 2012, neighborhood watch leader George Zimmerman fatally shot 17-year-old Trayvon Martin at a gated community in Sanford, Florida. When Zimmerman first saw Martin walking inside the community, he called police to report Martin's behavior as suspicious. Zimmerman followed Martin and confronted him. Their altercation ended with Zimmerman shooting dead Martin who was unarmed. Sanford police did not arrest Zimmerman due to Florida's controversial Stand Your Ground law [77], which states that a person may use force in self-defense when there is a reasonable belief of a threat, without an obligation to retreat first. However, public outcry resulted in the government filing charges of second-degree murder against Zimmerman in April 2012. Nevertheless, documents and evidence began to surface, making the case more complicated for the state prosecutor [78].

In March 2012, President Barack Obama addressed the Trayvon Martin shooting in personal terms: "Obviously this is a tragedy. I can only imagine what these parents are going through. When I think about this boy I think about my own kids and I think every parent in America should be able to understand why it is absolutely imperative that we investigate every aspect of this and that everybody pulls together, federal, state and local to figure out exactly how this tragedy happened. ... If I had a son, he would look like Trayvon. I think they are right to expect that all of us as Americans are going to take this with the seriousness it deserves and we will get to the bottom of exactly what happened" [79].

If the gated community had installed video surveillance cameras, chances are that the truths would have been revealed or the altercation would not have occurred in the first place. In lieu of or in addition to community video cameras, homeowners can use their webcams to monitor their neighborhood on a volunteer basis.

SETI@home is a distributed computing program that involves 5 million at-home users in the Search for Extra Terrestrial Intelligence (SETI) [80]. Since its inception in 1999, SETI@home has been recycling the unused CPU cycles on home computers to help analyze data collected from radio telescopes in search of signals from other intelligent worlds.

Similarly, we can envision a distributed software program "STS@home" for Neighborhood Watch. The artificial intelligence system analyzes live video streams from webcams connected to the homeowner's computers in the Search for Trespassers and Suspects (STS) in their neighborhood. A suspicious activity triggers an alert, and a neighborhood-watch leader can forward the information to police after reviewing the video clip. A facial recognition feature in the software system can assist police in locating missing children, apprehending fugitives, and solving crimes. Technology exists today that uses video analytics to distill millions of hours of raw video footage into structured, searchable data [81]. It is a matter of time that "STS@home" will become a reality.

13.7 Location Awareness and Traffic Safety

Originally created by the U.S. Department of Defense (DoD) in 1973 for military applications, Global Positioning System (GPS) is a satellite-based navigation system that provides location and time information anywhere on Earth [82]. On September 1, 1983, a Soviet Su-15 interceptor aircraft shot down Korean Airlines

(KAL) Flight 007, killing all 269 crewmembers and passengers [83]. The civilian aircraft was en route from New York City to Seoul via Anchorage when it strayed into prohibited Soviet airspace. To avoid navigational errors like that of KAL 007, President Ronald Reagan ordered the U.S. military to make GPS available for civilian use.

GPS is one of the greatest inventions and one of the key components of Total Information Awareness. Smart phones, airplanes, boats, and modern cars have built-in GPS that has become an indispensable navigation tool. Furthermore, new Android and iOS applications such as Eco: Speed optimize GPS directions by factoring in fuel consumption, number of traffic stops, speed limits, and local traffic conditions [84].

John Leech, partner at auditing and advisory firm KPMG, contemplated a "car-to-infrastructure" future where "traffic systems can use vehicles as sensors to quickly identify congestion and divert drivers to clearer routes, saving time and reducing emissions". Leech also proposed a "car-to-car" technology that "lets drivers spontaneously network with each other to warn of road hazards or other traffic problems" [85].

The sci-fi future may arrive sooner than we think. In June 2011, Nevada became the first state in America to pass the robotic driver legislation [86]. After 200,000 miles of computer-led driving without accident in freeways and service streets, Google's self-driving car passed its Nevada driver's license test with flying colors in May 2012 [87].

On May 18, 2012, journalist Peter Valdes-Dapena rode with two Google engineers in a self-driving car on a loop around several blocks in Washington D.C. He wrote about his experience on *CNN*, "No Google engineer taught the car that a bunch of kids on a field trip would March out in front of it at an intersection. It stopped and waited for them on its own. And no-one told it that, right after that, another car would run the four-way stop sign right in front of it. It handled that, too, avoiding a collision all on its own" [88].

Until Google's self-driving cars become widely adopted, we will continue to see many drivers break traffic laws and create hazards to themselves and others. If everyone were to obey traffic safety rules, there would be no need for red light cameras installed in many busy intersections across America. A classmate of my wife was hit by a car as it was running a red traffic light. Fortunately, the classmate was not injured. The driver rushed to the pedestrian and helped her to the sidewalk. He kept apologizing and insisting that he had time to rush the yellow light. She eventually snapped out of her trance and snarled, "You obviously did not have time. The light was not yellow, it was red, and I had the right of way".

Invented in the Netherlands, red light cameras have been installed around the world [89]. A 2003 study revealed that camera enforcement reduced traffic violations 40-50 % [90]. While there were reports of an increase in rear-end crashes following camera installation, there was a 25–30 % reduction in injury crashes caused mostly by the more serious side-impact collisions.

In the city of Los Angeles, I personally witness every week at least one driver ignores a 4-way stop sign, runs a red light, or looks totally distracted talking on the cell phone. I thought, "Where are the police when we need them?"

Similar to a police cruiser's dashboard camera, some commercial dash cams allow drivers to record in high-definition video day or night of what is in front and on sides of their vehicles. If dash cams become more prevalent, drivers will be more cautious and not endanger themselves and others on the roads because of their road rage or aggressive driving habits. Dash cams can simplify investigations of auto accident claims, and may lower auto insurance premiums for most drivers.

Although there were stories about red light cameras catching cheating spouses and pot-smoking kids [91], privacy is not really an issue because we drive on public roads and our license plates are always in plain view. Both red light cameras and dash cams serve to heighten the awareness of our driving behaviors.

13.8 Location Awareness and Personal Safety

Researcher Amanda Lenhart at Pew Internet and American Life Project found that 75 % of 12–17years-old owned cell phones in 2010, up from 45 % in 2004 [92]. Some wireless phone companies offer family locator plans for parents to keep track of their kid's whereabouts using GPS programs. Jack McArtney of Verizon Wireless spoke of VZ Navigator, "Once you locate your child on a mobile device, you can press a button and get turn-by-turn directions to that location" [93].

For young children without cell phones, there are wearable or attachable GPS tracking devices such as the Amber Alert GPS. "Our priority is child safety and security", said Carol Colombo, CEO of Amber Alert GPS. "Kids should have the freedom to be kids, to run and play and ride their bike to their friend's house. The V3 device is designed to give parents the confidence to send their children into the world, knowing they have taken the right steps to keep them safe" [94].

GPS locator is not just for child safety. Emmy Anderson of Sprint said, "We're seeing adults using it with their elderly parents, just to make sure mom or dad didn't get lost when they were driving to their doctor's appointment, that kind of thing. … We're also seeing siblings using it, for example, if both of them are away at different colleges, and they just want to make sure the other is safe on a date" [95].

GPS also plays a role in search and rescue missions. Personal locator beacons (PLBs) have been available for satellite-aided search and rescue notification using geosynchronous and low earth orbit satellites. A more advanced system—MEOSAR (Medium Earth Orbit Search and Rescue satellites)—is adding search and rescue transponders to newer global navigation satellites including GPS (USA), GLON-ASS (Russia), and Galileo (ESA) [96]. The GPS version is dubbed the Distress Alerting Satellite System (DASS). According to the National Aeronautics and Space Administration (NASA) website, "NASA, in coordination with the Global Positioning System (GPS) Program Office and Sandia National Laboratories, has determined that the GPS constellation would be the best and most cost-effective MEO satellite constellation to host the search and rescue (SAR) instruments" [97].

Software companies are integrating geographic information systems (GIS) technology and social media to map people's tweets and other social media platforms with geospatial data. This pairing has been helpful in disaster response and crisis management. In the wake of the January 12th, 2010 earthquake in Haiti, a free phone number (4636) was established to allow people to text their requests for medical care, food, water, security, and shelter. According to the Mission 4636 report, "Tireless workers and volunteers translated, geolocated and categorized the messages via online crowdsourcing platforms which sorted the information by need and priority, and distributed it to various emergency responders and aid organizations. Initially, the focus was on search and rescue, but the service scaled up about 1 week after the earthquake to include a wide range of responses, including serious injuries, requests for fresh drinking water, security, unaccompanied children and clusters of requests for food, and even childbirths" [98].

In May 2012, researcher Laura Morris wrote in *Haiti Wired Blog*, "Not only is the ubiquity of mobile telephony globally coupled with the internet and GIS enabling the victims of crisis to become more active in their own recovery, making the delivery of aid a truly participatory process, semantic web tools such as Ushahidi are empowering the globally connected 'crowd' to engage in crisis response and support. Everywhere technology is being used in many different ways to help with disaster and conflict early-warning, management and resolution and for peace building in the aftermath of crisis" [99].

13.9 Information Awareness and Law Enforcement

In spite of high unemployment and economic recession in 2011, the Federal Bureau of Investigation (FBI) figures showed that murder, rape, robberies, and other serious crimes have fallen to a 48 year low across the United States [100].

Facebook has been involved in promoting public awareness of crime fighting. Since December 2009, Facebook has partnered with the AMBER Alerts [101]. Named after 9-year-old Amber Hagerman who was abducted and murdered in Arlington, Texas in 1996, the AMBER (America's Missing: Broadcasting Emergency Response) Alert Program is a voluntary partnership between law-enforcement agencies, broadcasters, transportation agencies, and the wireless industry, to activate an urgent bulletin in the most serious child-abduction cases [102]. The goal of an AMBER Alert is to galvanize the entire community, adding millions of extra eyes and ears to watch, listen, and help in the safe return of the child and apprehension of the suspect [103]. Since 2002, the AMBER Alert Program has been spreading internationally to Australia, Canada, France, Germany, Greece, the Netherlands, the United Kingdom, and others [104].

Facebook has contributed to many success stories in law enforcement:

1. To crack down on underage drinking, the La Crosse Police Department in Wisconsin created a Facebook account in 2009 under the name of "Jenny Anderson" and befriended University of Wisconsin-La Crosse college students. Many accepted the friend requests on Facebook. As a result, the police was able to obtain photos of underage drinkers and send them citations. Two of the students charged Adam Bauer and Cassandra Stenholt, did not upload the photos themselves, but rather were tagged by friends [105].
2. 26-year-old fugitive Maxi Sopo was on the run from charges of masterminding a bank fraud in Seattle. Sopo updated his Facebook from his hiding in Cancun, telling his friends that he was living in paradise and loving it. U.S. Secret Service agent Seth Reeg was able to track him down though one of his Facebook friends. Sopo was subsequently arrested in September 2009 [106].
3. In March 2012, detectives from the New York Police Department (NYPD) were attempting to find a shooter. The victim's brother pointed the detectives to Facebook. NYPD's Real Time Crime Center uploaded the Facebook photos into its facial recognition software, and matched them to a database of thousands of mug shots from arrest records. The police identified and arrested the shooter within a matter of days [107].

The U.S. government is increasing using social networking sites to aid law enforcement:

1. In a May 2008 memo, the U.S. Citizenship and Immigration Services (USCIS) wrote, "Social networking sites such as MySpace, Facebook, Classmates, Hi-5, and other similar sites are designed to allow people to share their creativity, pictures, and information with others. ... Narcissistic tendencies in many people fuel a need to have a large group of 'friends' link to their pages and many of these people accept cyber-friends that they don't even know. This provides an excellent vantage point for FDNS [Fraud Detection and National Security] to observe the daily life of beneficiaries and petitioners who are suspected of fraudulent activities. ... This social networking gives FDNS an opportunity to reveal fraud by browsing these sites to see if petitioners and beneficiaries are in a valid relationship or are attempting to deceive CIS about their relationship. Once a user posts online, they create a public record and timeline of their activities. In essence, using MySpace and other like sites is akin to doing an unannounced cyber 'site-visit' on a [sic] petitioners and beneficiaries" [108].
2. In a "privacy compliance review" issued in November 2011 by the U.S. Department of Homeland Security (DHS), the DHS National Operations Center has been operating a "Social Networking/Media Capability" since June 2010. The Center regularly monitors "publicly available online forums, blogs, public websites and message boards" in order to "collect information used in providing situational awareness and establishing a common operating picture". The list of monitored sites includes household names such as Facebook, MySpace, Twitter, Hulu, YouTube, Flickr, the Drudge Report, Huffington Post, and of course WikiLeaks [109]. Furthermore, *CNN* reported in March 2012 that DHS'

surveillance program looks for "words of interest" on Facebook and Twitter posts, and triggers investigations into suspicious profiles [110].

3. Around December 2011, computer hackers were targeting the Boston police website and a police union website. Boston law enforcement contacted Twitter to obtain information about a user for an official criminal investigation. After months of court battle behind closed doors between Boston and the American Civil Liberties Union, Twitter finally complied with the court order and handed over the data from one subscriber to Boston police in March 2012 [111].

13.10 Self-Awareness and Online Dating

English professor Mark Bauerlein at Emory University accused Facebook of killing love letters. Bauerlein wrote on *CNN*, "Back in the old days, love wasn't social, it was private. Communication, not to mention courtship, seemed to take a long time. Genuine love is anti-social". Reporter Samuel Axon at *Mashable* agreed, "Facebook makes dating far more complicated than it used to be. ... Overanalyzing [Facebook posts] will drive you crazy. ... You see all the action your ex is getting. ... Relationships and breakups are public. ... It's a record of every relationship mistake you've made. ... Other people's comments will make your date jealous" [112].

Contrary to Mark Zuckerberg's vision, Facebook not only does not cure loneliness, but it actually spreads loneliness among online friends. A December 2009 research study published in *Journal of Personality and Social Psychology* indicated that "loneliness occurs in clusters, extends up to 3 degrees of separation, is disproportionately represented at the periphery of social networks, and spreads through a contagious process. The spread of loneliness was found to be stronger than the spread of perceived social connections, stronger for friends than family members, and stronger for women than for men" [113]. The full network showed that participants are 52 % more likely to be lonely if a person they are directly connected to (at one degree of separation) is lonely. The size of the effect for people at two degrees of separation (the friend of a friend) is 25 % and for people at three degrees of separation (the friend of a friend of a friend) is 15 %. At four degrees of separation, the effect disappears (2 %). The research results confirmed the "three degrees of influence" rule of social network contagion that has been exhibited for obesity, smoking, and happiness.

Why do people feel lonely even when they are surrounded by hundreds of online friends? In her book *Alone Together: Why We Expect More from Technology and Less from Each* Other [114], MIT professor Sherry Turkle argues that people are increasingly functioning in the society without face-to-face contact. The ubiquity of texting, emailing, and social networking has pushed people closer to their machines and further away from each other. Dissatisfaction and alienation are often the result of the lack of face-to-face communication.

Some people put on facades when they meet people, for fear of revealing their true selves. The online world gives them even more power to hide their real personalities and create their own alter egos, which can lead to a bigger communication gap among friends and family. This is the same reason why some people fail to find true love, online and offline.

Self-awareness is a prerequisite to finding one's twin soul, avoiding karmic soul mates and codependent relationships that are painful and chaotic. "Cogito ergo sum," said René Descartes. Chinese philosopher Zhuangzi wrote an anecdote about himself, "Once Zhuangzi dreamt he was a butterfly, a butterfly flitting and fluttering around, happy with himself and doing as he pleased. He didn't know he was Zhuangzi. Suddenly he woke up and there he was, solid and unmistakable Zhuangzi. But he didn't know if he was Zhuangzi who had dreamt he was a butterfly, or a butterfly dreaming he was Zhuangzi. Between Zhuangzi and a butterfly there must be some distinction! This is a case of what is called the transformation of things" [115].

We are all transforming during different stages of our life, and yesteryears may seem like a dream. If we are true to ourselves at all times, online dating can be very effective. My wife and I met on an Internet dating website. I put up a profile that reflected my real self without exaggeration or sugarcoating. Among thousands of men on the website, she picked me and said, "This is the man I'm going to marry!" As a precaution, she had one of her friends at a law enforcement agency conduct an extensive background check on me just to be sure. We were engaged 2 days after we met in person. We share a similar taste in music, movies, books, fashion, food, philosophy, and even Betty Boop cartoons. The more we learn about each other in our years of marriage, the more we realize that we are twin souls (or twin flames)—one in a million among billions of cybercitizens and two of a kind complementing each other in a jigsaw puzzle.

In addition to online dating websites, mobile dating services use GPS technology to allow individuals in proximity of each other to chat and meet up [116]. Subscribers can use their cell phones as a homing device to find a date just a short distance away.

At the 2012 South by Southwest Interactive in Austin, Texas, Highlight's founder and CEO Paul Davison introduced a new service for matching likeminded people in their immediate area. Davison told an attentive audience, "Nothing affects our happiness more than the people in our lives. But the way we find these people and bring them into our lives always has been completely random and inefficient. We don't realize how bad it is because it's always been that way. Most people walk around like ants hoping that by randomness they'll intersect paths with the person of their dreams. Sometimes it happens, but many times you'll never meet" [117]. The Highlight app pulls data from the user's Facebook profiles to determine if there are matches in the physical proximity of the users.

Apart from mainstream dating websites such as Match.com and eHarmony, there are an increasing number of nontraditional dating sites: Survivalist Singles and PrepperDating for doomsdayer; Kwink for health nuts, germaphobic, and nerds, to name a few [118].

While all dating sites are trying to find people their best matches, there is one website that informs people about who not to date: Íslendingabók (the Book of Icelanders) enables users to avoid inbreeding by running a date's name through a genealogical database [119].

13.11 Pandora's Box of Total Information Awareness

In Francis Ford Coppola's *The Godfather* (1972), Michael Corleone said, "I'll make him an offer he can't refuse" [120]. Like it or not, the majority of us cannot refuse the temptation of social media and social networking services. As of June 2012, Facebook has 955 million active users worldwide [121], Google has over 1 billion unique visitors per month [122], and Twitter is on track for 500 million registered users [123]. With the massive amount of personal data on the Internet, Facebook nation has opened Pandora's Box of total information awareness in the age of big data. Fortunately, Pandora's Box released not only evil but also hope.

On one hand, total information awareness poses a risk in personal privacy and freedom as in "Big Brother is watching us", "companies know too much about us", or "parents and friends are prying into our private lives". In May 2006, *USA Today* reported that the National Security Agency (NSA) has been secretly collecting the phone call records of tens of millions of Americans without warrants [124]. Social critic Andrew Keen warned of future mind-reading predictive technology, "The computer 'server' and the 'server' in the bar will be indistinguishable.... They will both know what you want to drink before you know it yourself" [125].

On the other hand, total information awareness creates more transparency in governments, businesses, societies, and families. Proper use of information awareness offers substantial benefits in suicide prevention, child protection, school safety, crime prevention, neighborhood watch, traffic safety, personal safety, law enforcement, and even online dating.

The hope is that good will trump evil. The "precogs" in Steven Spielberg's *Minority Report* (2002) will be future artificial intelligence (AI) programs that employ biometric recognition technologies, correlate information from online and offline activities, and analyze video streams from live traffic cams, in-vehicle dash cams, ATM security cameras, Neighborhood Watch webcams, and public CCTV systems around town and in business establishments. The AI programs will help locate missing children and apprehend dangerous criminals, making our community a safer place to live.

Total information awareness affects all aspects of human lives, all levels of society, and all forms of government. As long as we are well prepared and well informed, total information awareness will prove to be more beneficial than harmful for everyone.

References

1. The Godfather: Part II. (December 20, 1974). Memorable Quotes for The Godfather: Part II. IMDb. http://www.imdb.com/title/tt0071562/quotes
2. Associated Press. (March 9, 2005). Mob leaders arrested after FBI infiltration. The New York Times. http://www.nytimes.com/2005/03/09/world/americas/09iht-web.0309mob.html
3. Zhao, Emmeline. (May 8, 2012). Rachel Ehmke, 13-Year-Old Minnesota Student, Commits Suicide After Months Of Bullying. Huffington Post. http://www.huffingtonpost.com/2012/05/08/rachel-ehmke-13-year-old-_n_1501143.html
4. CNN Wire Staff. (May 7, 2012). Indiana mom sends son to school with stun gun to confront bullies. CNN. http://www.cnn.com/2012/05/07/us/indiana-bullied-teen/index.html
5. Minority Report. (June 21, 2002). Minority Report. IMDb. http://www.imdb.com/title/tt0181689/
6. Facebook Data Team. (Retrieved May 4, 2012). About Facebook Data Team. Facebook. http://www.facebook.com/data/info
7. Smolan, Rick. (Retrieved May 3, 2012). What is 'big data'? Curiosity.com from Discovery. http://curiosity.discovery.com/question/what-is-big-data
8. Pachal, Peter. (May 22, 2012). A 'Leap' forward in gesture-control interfaces? CNN. http://www.cnn.com/2012/05/22/tech/innovation/leap-motion-control/index.html
9. Steel, Emily. (July 13, 2011). How a New Police Tool for Face Recognition Works. The Wall Street Journal. http://blogs.wsj.com/digits/2011/07/13/how-a-new-police-tool-for-face-recognition-works/
10. Walters, Ray. (December 14, 2011). Omni-directional 6-legged insect robot can save lives, do cartwheels. Geek.com. http://www.geek.com/articles/geek-cetera/omnidirectional-insect-robot-6-legged-20111214/
11. Efrati, Amir. (May 21, 2012). A New Home for Computer Screens: The Face. The Wall Street Journal. http://online.wsj.com/article/SB10001424052702303610504577418181348485336.html
12. Toor, Amar. (March 29, 2012). LG unveils flexible plastic e-paper display, aims for European launch next month. Engadget. http://www.engadget.com/2012/03/29/lg-flexible-e-paper-display-launch/
13. Cheng, Roger. (May 11, 2012). Ericsson could turn you into a human USB connection next year. CNet. http://reviews.cnet.com/8301-12261_7-57433025-10356022/ericsson-could-turn-you-into-a-human-usb-connection-next-year/
14. BBC News. (March 20, 2012). Vibrating tattoo alerts patent filed by Nokia in US. BBC News. http://www.bbc.co.uk/news/technology-17447086
15. Paul, Ian. (May 7, 2012). Disney Technology Turns Everything into a Touch Device. PC World. http://www.pcworld.com/article/255124/disney_technology_turns_everything_into_a_touch_device.html
16. Hay, Timothy. (May 29, 2012). The Wall Street Journal. http://online.wsj.com/article/SB10001424052702304707604577426251091339254.html
17. Dvorak, John C. (May 9, 2012). Google's Revolutionary Self-Driving Car. PC Magazine. http://www.pcmag.com/article2/0,2817,2404199,00.asp
18. Kaplan, Andreas M. (November 23, 2011). If you love something, let it go mobile: Mobile marketing and mobile social media 4x4. Elsevier. http://www.sciencedirect.com/science/article/pii/S0007681311001558
19. Thompson, Clive. (September 5, 2008). Brave New World of Digital Intimacy. The New York Time. http://www.nytimes.com/2008/09/07/magazine/07awareness-t.html?pagewanted=2
20. Warren, Frank. (April 24, 2012). How the world shares its secrets. CNN. http://www.cnn.com/2012/04/22/opinion/warren-post-secret/index.html

21. Dowd, Maureen. (March 12, 1984). 20 Years After The Murder Of Kitty Genovese, The Question Remains: Why? New York Times. http://www.nytimes.com/1984/03/12/nyregion/20-years-after-the-murder-of-kitty-genovese-the-question-remains-why.html
22. Darley, John M.; Latané, Bibb. (1968). Bystander intervention in emergencies: Diffusion of responsibility. Journal of Personality and Social Psychology 8: 377–383
23. Levine, M.; Crowther, S. (2008). The responsive bystander: how social group membership and group size can encourage as well as inhibit bystander intervention. Journal of Personality and Social Psychology 95(6): 1429-1439. http://www.ncbi.nlm.nih.gov/pubmed/19025293
24. Cacioppo, John T.; Fowler, James H.; Christakis, Nicholas A. (2009). Alone in the crowd: The structure and spread of loneliness in a large social network. Journal of Personality and Social Psychology 97(6): 977-991. http://psycnet.apa.org/journals/psp/97/6/977/
25. Keilman, John; McCoppin, Robert. (August 24, 2011). Study: Teen users of Facebook, Myspace more likely to drink, use drugs. Chicago Tribune. http://articles.chicagotribune.com/2011-08-24/news/ct-met-social-menace-20110824_1_social-media-teen-substance-abuse-teen-users
26. Pew Internet. (February 3, 2012). Why most Facebook users get more than they give. Pew Internet Press Release. http://www.pewinternet.org/Press-Releases/2012/Facebook-users.aspx
27. CNN Wire Staff. (December 12, 2011). Rutgers student's suicide reverberates 15 months later. CNN. http://www.cnn.com/2011/12/12/us/new-jersey-student-suicide/index.html
28. Parker, Ian. (February 6, 2012). The Story of a Suicide. The New Yorker. http://www.newyorker.com/reporting/2012/02/06/120206fa_fact_parker
29. Williams, Mary Elizabeth. (December 14, 2011). Can Facebook save your life? Salon. http://www.salon.com/2011/12/14/can_facebook_save_your_life/singleton/
30. McVeigh, Karen. (January 5, 2011). Facebook 'friends' did not act on suicide note. The Guardian. http://www.guardian.co.uk/technology/2011/jan/05/facebook-suicide-simone-back
31. Cellan-Jones, Rory. (March 7, 2011). Facebook adds Samaritans suicide risk alert system. BBC News. http://www.bbc.co.uk/news/technology-12667343
32. Facebook (Retrieved May 18, 2012). How do I help someone who has posted suicidal content on the site? Facebook Help Center. http://www.facebook.com/help/?faq=216817991675637
33. Codrea-Rado, Anna. (April 18, 2012). Using Social Media to Prevent Suicide. The Atlantic. http://www.theatlantic.com/health/archive/2012/04/using-social-media-to-prevent-suicide/256069/
34. CNN Wire Staff. (May 7, 2012). Indiana mom sends son to school with stun gun to confront bullies. CNN. http://www.cnn.com/2012/05/07/us/indiana-bullied-teen/index.html
35. Zhao, Emmeline. (May 8, 2012). Rachel Ehmke, 13-Year-Old Minnesota Student, Commits Suicide After Months Of Bullying. Huffington Post. http://www.huffingtonpost.com/2012/05/08/rachel-ehmke-13-year-old-_n_1501143.html
36. Brubaker, Elisabeth. (November 30, 2011). Anne O'Brien on the bullying her daughter suffered: "She didn't stand a chance". CNN Blogs. http://piersmorgan.blogs.cnn.com/2011/11/30/anne-obrien-on-the-bullying-her-daughter-suffered-she-didnt-stand-a-chance/
37. Cullen, Kevin. (January 24, 2010). The untouchable Mean Girls. Boston Globe. http://www.boston.com/news/local/massachusetts/articles/2010/01/24/the_untouchable_mean_girls/
38. Oliver, Kealan. (February 5, 2010). Phoebe Prince "Suicide by Bullying": Teen's Death Angers Town Asking Why Bullies Roam the Halls. CBS News. http://www.cbsnews.com/8301-504083_162-6173960-504083.html
39. Time Warner Inc. (September 19, 2011). Facebook and Time Warner Inc. Launch Stop Bullying: Speak Up App. Time Warner Press Releases. http://www.timewarner.com/newsroom/press-releases/2011/09/Facebook_and_Time_Warner_Inc_Launch_Stop_Bullying_Speak_Up_App_09-19-2011.php

40. Probst, Emily; Kaye, Randi. (March 31, 2012). Wanted: A bully to end bullying. CNN. http://www.cnn.com/2012/03/30/us/scary-guy/index.html
41. Gibson, Faye. (January 15, 2012). Am I Pretty or Ugly. YouTube. http://www.youtube.com/watch?v=WoyZPn6hKY4
42. Smith, Candace. (February 23, 2012). Teens Post 'Am I Pretty or Ugly?' Videos on YouTube. ABC News. http://abcnews.go.com/US/teens-post-insecurities-youtube-pretty-ugly-videos/story?id=15777830
43. SafetyWeb. (September 9, 2010). Forget Spying! SafetyWeb Offers A Smart New Way To Protect Kids Online. SafetyWeb Press Releases. http://www.safetyweb.com/forget-spying-safetyweb-offers-a-smart-new-way-to-protect-kids-online
44. Beck, Kenneth H.; Shattuck, Teresa; Haynie, Denise; Crump, Aria Davis; Simons-Morton, Bruce. Associations between parent awareness, monitoring, enforcement and adolescent involvement with alcohol. Health Education Research 14(6): 765-775. http://her.oxfordjournals.org/content/14/6/765.full
45. FBI. (May 2012). Federal Bureau of Investigation. http://www.fbi.gov/norfolk/news-and-outreach/in-your-community/aware.prepare.plan-campaign
46. Massacre at Virginia Tech. (2007). CNN. http://www.cnn.com/SPECIALS/2007/virginiatech.shootings/
47. Virginia Tech Review Panel. (August 2007). Mass Shootings at Virginia Tech. Report of the Virginia Tech Review Panel. Presented to Governor Kaine, Commonwealth of Virginia. Virginia.gov. http://www.governor.virginia.gov/TempContent/techPanelReport.cfm
48. Virginia Tech. (April 16, 2008). Liviu Librescu. Virginia Tech. http://www.remembrance.vt.edu/biographies/librescu.html
49. Depue, Roger. (August 2007). Red Flags, Warning Signs and Indicators. Virginia.gov. http://www.governor.virginia.gov/tempcontent/techPanelReport-docs/28%20APPENDIX%20M%20-%20RED%20FLAGS%20WARNING%20SIGNS%20AND%20INDICATORS.pdf
50. CNN Special Report. (June 13, 2007). Virginia Tech report: Share mental health data. CNN. http://www.cnn.com/2007/US/06/13/virginia.tech/index.html
51. Hurtado, Jaqueline. (February 6, 2012). Superintendent: All of L.A. school's teachers to be replaced. CNN. http://www.cnn.com/2012/02/06/justice/california-teacher-bondage-photos/index.html
52. Kassa, Jonathan. (November 8, 2010). The Jeanne Clery Act, Twenty Years Later: From Admitting to Addressing Campus Crime. Now What? Huffington Post. http://www.huffingtonpost.com/jonathan-kassa/the-jeanne-clery-act-twen_b_779989.html
53. Dorell, Oren. (December 8, 2011). Va. Tech's quick alerts to shootings in contrast to 2007. USA Today. http://www.usatoday.com/news/nation/story/2011-12-08/virginia-tech-shooting-swift-alerts/51750854/1
54. Circle of 6. (Retrieved May 20, 2011). Circle of 6. http://www.circleof6app.com/
55. Swift, James. (April 11, 2012). New Smartphone App Aims to Prevent Date Rape. Youth Today. http://www.youthtoday.org/view_article.cfm?article_id=5236
56. Snizek, William E. (Spring 2012). Virginia Tech Magazine. http://www.vtmag.vt.edu/spring12/we-remember.html
57. Google Chrome Channel. (Retrieved May 21, 2012). YouTube. http://www.youtube.com/playlist?list=PL5308B2E5749D1696
58. Landau, Elizabeth. (December 4, 2009). Loneliness spreads in social networks. CNN. http://articles.cnn.com/2009-12-04/health/loneliness.social.network_1_loneliness-lonely-people-social-networks
59. CNN Wire Staff. (March 10, 2012). Minnesota girl alleges school privacy invasion. CNN. http://www.cnn.com/2012/03/10/us/minnesota-student-privacy/index.html
60. Myers, Steve. (March 3, 2011). How citizen journalism has changed since George Holliday's Rodney King video. Poynter. http://www.poynter.org/latest-news/top-stories/121687/how-citizen-journalism-has-changed-since-george-hollidays-rodney-king-video/

61. Phillips-Sandy, Mary. (March 3, 2011). Rodney King Revisited: Meet George Holliday, the Man Who Shot the Infamous Video. AOL News. http://www.aolnews.com/2011/03/03/rodney-king-revisited-meet-george-holliday-the-man-who-shot-th/

62. Jmackfaragher (Uploaded on November 15, 2010). Rodney King tape on national news. YouTube. http://www.youtube.com/watch?v=SW1ZDIXiuS4

63. Wilson, Stan. (April 25, 2012). Riot anniversary tour surveys progress and economic challenges in Los Angeles. CNN. http://www.cnn.com/2012/04/25/us/california-post-riot/index.html

64. The Baltimore Sun. (April 19, 1993). Just About a Perfect Verdict. The Baltimore Sun. http://articles.baltimoresun.com/1993-04-19/news/1993109024_1_verdict-rodney-king-law-enforcement

65. Mcelroy, Wendy. (June 2, 2010). Are Cameras the New Guns? Gizmodo. http://gizmodo.com/5553765/are-cameras-the-new-guns

66. Good Moring America. (October 13, 2003). Nanny-Cam Leads to Babysitter Arrest. ABC News. http://abcnews.go.com/GMA/story?id=128269

67. KTLA News. (August 30, 2010). Nannycam Video Lands Sitter in Prison – Graphic Content. KTLA. http://www.ktla.com/news/landing/ktla-nannycam-arrest,0,7859954.story

68. (December 9, 2011). Cheryl Hepner, Angry Grandma, Shoots Son-In-Law Who Records Attack On iPhone. Huffington Post. http://www.huffingtonpost.com/2011/12/09/video-cheryl-hepner-angry_n_1139459.html

69. Zeidler, Sari. (June 23, 2012). Viral vigilantism, Tony Hawk style. CNN. http://news.blogs.cnn.com/2012/06/23/viral-vigilantism-tony-hawk-style/

70. Nieto, Marcus. (June 1997). Public Video Surveillance: Is it an Effective Crime Prevention Tool? California Research Bureau. California State Library. http://www.library.ca.gov/crb/97/05/crb97-005.pdf

71. King, Jennifer; Mulligan, Deirdre; Raphael, Steven; Richardson, Travis; Sekhon, Jasjeet. (March 17, 2008) Preliminary Findings of the Statistical Evaluation of the Crime-Deterrent Effects of The San Francisco Crime Camera Program. ACLU of Northern California. https://www.aclunc.org/issues/government_surveillance/asset_upload_file796_7024.pdf

72. Cameron, Aundreia; Kolodinski, Elke; May, Heather; Williams, Nicholas. (May 5, 2008). Measuring the Effects of Video Surveillance on Crime in Los Angeles. The California State Library. http://www.library.ca.gov/crb/08/08-007.pdf

73. CNN Wire Staff. (January 2, 2012). Man charged with arson in case of California fires. CNN. http://www.cnn.com/2012/01/02/us/california-arson/index.html

74. Center for Information Technology Research in the Interest of Society. (January 9, 2009) CITRIS study on SF public cameras released. CITRIS News. http://citris-uc.org/news/2009/01/09/citris_study_sf_public_cameras_released

75. Bulwa, Demian. (January 28, 2008). San Francisco security cameras' choppy video. San Francisco Chronicle. http://www.sfgate.com/cgi-bin/article.cgi?f=/c/a/2008/01/27/MN37TKH6O.DTL

76. National Crime Prevention Council. (Retrieved May 22, 2012). Neighborhood Watch. Ncpc.org. http://www.ncpc.org/topics/home-and-neighborhood-safety/neighborhood-watch

77. Debate Club. (Retrieved May 22, 2012). Are 'Stand Your Ground' Laws a Good Idea? US News and World Report. http://www.usnews.com/debate-club/are-stand-your-ground-laws-a-good-idea

78. Leger, Donna Leinwand; Dorell, Oren. (May 18, 2012). New documents show complexity of Trayvon Martin case. USA Today. http://www.usatoday.com/news/nation/story/2012-05-18/George-Zimmerman-Trayvon-Martin-police-documents/55061830/1

79. Deshishku, Stacia. (March 23, 2012). President Obama statement on Trayvon Martin case. White House Blogs. http://whitehouse.blogs.cnn.com/2012/03/23/president-obama-statement-on-trayvon-martin-case/

80. SETI@home. (Retrieved May 23, 2012). SETI@home. The Search for Extra Terrestrial Intelligence at UC Berkeley. http://seti.berkeley.edu/setiathome

81. 3VR Inc. (Retrieved May 28, 2012). Use Video Analytics and Data Decision Making to Grow Your Business. Digital Signage Today. http://www.digitalsignagetoday.com/whitepapers/4891/Use-Video-Analytics-and-Data-Decision-Making-to-Grow-Your-Business

82. Glasscoe, Maggi. (August 13, 1998). What is GPS. NASA. http://scign.jpl.nasa.gov/learn/gps1.htm

83. Fischer, Benjamin B. (March 19, 2007). A Cold War Conundrum: The 1983 Soviet War Scare. U.S. Central Intelligence Agency (CIA). https://www.cia.gov/library/center-for-the-study-of-intelligence/csi-publications/books-and-monographs/a-cold-war-conundrum/source.htm#HEADING1-12

84. Clarian Labs. (Retrieved May 23, 2012). Eco:Speed. http://www.goecospeed.com/

85. Leech, John. (February 2, 2012). OEMs must drive the connected car - or get left behind. AutomotiveWorld.com   http://www.automotiveworld.com/news/oems-and-markets/91682-oems-must-drive-the-connected-car-or-get-left-behind

86. Lee, Kevin. (June 24, 2011). Nevada Passes Robotic Driver Legislation. PC World. http://www.pcworld.com/article/231105/nevada_passes_robotic_driver_legislation.html

87. Paul, Ian. (May 8, 2012). Google's Self-Driving Car Licensed to Hit Nevada Streets. PC World.   http://www.pcworld.com/article/255204/googles_selfdriving_car_licensed_to_hit_nevada_streets.html

88. Valdes-Dapena, Peter. (May 18, 2012). Thrilled and bummed by Google's self-driving car. CNN Money. http://money.cnn.com/2012/05/17/autos/google-driverless-car/index.htm

89. GATSO. (Retrieved May 28, 2012). GATSO Road Safety Enforcement. GATSO. http://www.gatso.com/road-safety-solutions/enforcement.html

90. Rettinga, Richard A.; Fergusona, Susan A.; Hakkertb, A. Shalom. (2003). Effects of Red Light Cameras on Violations and Crashes: A Review of the International Literature. Traffic Injury Prevention. 4(1):17-23. http://www.tandfonline.com/doi/abs/10.1080/1538958030 9858

91. Photo Enforced. (October 18, 2011). Red Light Cameras Catch Cheating Spouses & Pot Smoking Kids. Photo Enforced. http://blog.photoenforced.com/2011/10/red-light-cameras-catch-cheating.html

92. Lenhart, Amanda. (April 20, 2010). Teens, Cell Phones and Texting. Pew Research Center Publications. http://pewresearch.org/pubs/1572/teens-cell-phones-text-messages.

93. Choney, Suzanne. (August 25, 2008). A good find: GPS to locate the kids. MSNBC. http://www.msnbc.msn.com/id/26318777/ns/technology_and_science-tech_and_gadgets/t/good-find-gps-locate-kids/

94. AT&T. (October 11, 2011). New Tracking Device Delivers Peace Of Mind To Parents. AT&T News. http://www.att.com/gen/press-room?pid=21658&cdvn=news&newsarticleid=33047&mapcode=wireless-networks-general|consumer

95. Choney, Suzanne. Ibid

96. Reich, Jesse. (February 14-16, 2012). MEOSAR Overview. SAR Controllers Training 2012. United States Coast Guard. http://www.uscg.mil/hq/cg5/cg534/EmergencyBeacons/2012SarsatConf/Presentations/SAR2012_Feb16_MEOSAR_Overview_Reich.pdf

97. Morris, Christopher. (December 22, 2008). Distress Alerting Satellite System (DASS). NASA. http://searchandrescue.gsfc.nasa.gov/dass/index.html

98. Mission 4636. (Retrieved May 25, 2012). Mission 4636. http://www.mission4636.org/

99. Morris, Laura. (May 10, 2012). ICT in Conflict & Disaster Response and Peacebuilding Crowdmap. Haiti Wired Blogs. http://haitirewired.wired.com/profiles/blogs/ict-in-conflict-disaster-response-and-peacebuilding-crowdmap

100. McGreal, Chris. (August 21, 2011). America's serious crime rate is plunging, but why? The Guardian. http://www.guardian.co.uk/world/2011/aug/21/america-serious-crime-rate-plunging

101. AMBER Alert. (December 30, 2009). Facebook. http://www.facebook.com/AMBERalert

102. U.S. Department of Justice. (Retrieved May 24, 2012). AMBER Alert. http://www.amberalert.gov/

103. FCC. (Retrieved May 24, 2012). Amber Plan (America's Missing Broadcast Emergency Response). Federal Communications Commission. http://www.fcc.gov/guides/amber-plan-americas-missing-broadcast-emergency-response
104. National Center for Missing & Exploited Children. (Retrieved May 24, 2012). International AMBER Alert Plans. National Center for Missing & Exploited Children. http://www.missingkids.com/missingkids/servlet/PageServlet?LanguageCountry=en_US&PageId=1422
105. Anderson, Jonathan. (December 7, 2009). Do you know who your (Facebook) friends are? The UWM Post. University of Wisconsin-La Crosse. http://www.uwmpost.com/2009/12/07/do-you-know-who-your-facebook-friends-are-2/
106. Topping, Alexandra. (October 14, 2009). Fugitive caught after updating his status on Facebook. The Guardian. http://www.guardian.co.uk/technology/2009/oct/14/mexico-fugitive-facebook-arrest
107. Kemp, Joe. (March 16, 2012). Police nab Queens suspect using hi-tech face-detector. New York Daily News. http://articles.nydailynews.com/2012-03-16/news/31202755_1_facial-recognition-cops-real-time-crime-center
108. Lynch, Jennifer. (October 12, 2010). Applying for Citizenship? U.S. Citizenship and Immigration Wants to Be Your "Friend". Electronic Frontier Foundation. https://www.eff.org/deeplinks/2010/10/applying-citizenship-u-s-citizenship-and.
109. Hosenball, Mark. (January 11, 2012). Homeland Security watches Twitter, social media. Reuters. http://www.reuters.com/article/2012/01/11/us-usa-homelandsecurity-websites-idUSTRE80A1RC20120111
110. Obeidallah, Dean. (March 9, 2012). The government is reading your tweets. CNN. http://www.cnn.com/2012/03/09/opinion/obeidallah-social-media/index.html
111. Ellement, John R. (March 1, 2012). Twitter gives Boston police, prosecutors data from one subscriber in criminal inquiry. Boston.com. http://www.boston.com/Boston/metrodesk/2012/03/twitter-provides-boston-police-and-suffolk-prosecutors-with-subscriber-information-for-criminal-probe/DfoELIrEBPzx4KCVbLZo8L/index.html
112. Axon, Samuel. (April 10, 2010). 5 Ways Facebook Changed Dating (For the Worse). Mashable. http://mashable.com/2010/04/10/facebook-dating/
113. Cacioppo, John T.; Fowler, James H.; Christakis, Nicholas A. (December 2009). Alone in the crowd: The structure and spread of loneliness in a large social network. Journal of Personality and Social Psychology. Vol. 97(6). pp. 977-991
114. Turkle, Sherry. (January 11, 2011). Alone Together: Why We Expect More from Technology and Less from Each Other. Basic Books
115. Wikipedia. (August 7, 2011). Zhuangzi. Wikipedia. http://en.wikipedia.org/wiki/Zhuangzi#The_butterfly_dream
116. Kim, Ryan. (July 23, 2005). Hey, baby, want a date? New mobile dating services allow people to browse profiles via cell phone and message potential matches – even on the spot. San Francisco Chronicle. http://www.sfgate.com/cgi-bin/article.cgi?f=/c/a/2005/07/23/BUGKMDSB4P1.DTL
117. Gustin, Sam. (March 12, 2012). Highlight Aims to Alert You To Like-Minded Folks in Your Immediate Vicinity. Time Magazine. http://business.time.com/2012/03/12/sxsw-highlight-founder-aims-to-build-sixth-sense-for-mobile-web/
118. Ellis, Blake. (March 29, 2012). Doomsday dating sites: 'Don't face the future alone'. CNN Money. http://money.cnn.com/2012/03/29/pf/doomsday-dating/index.htm
119. Grossman, Samantha. (February 9, 2012). Icelanders Avoid Inbreeding Through Online Database. Time Magazine. http://newsfeed.time.com/2012/02/09/icelanders-avoid-inbreeding-through-online-incest-database/
120. The Godfather. (March 24, 1972). Memorable Quotes for The Godfather. IMDb. http://www.imdb.com/title/tt0068646/quotes
121. Facebook. (Retrieved August 11, 2012). Facebook Newsroom. http://newsroom.fb.com/content/default.aspx?NewsAreaId=22

122. Efrati, Amir. (June 21, 2011). Google Notches One Billion Unique Visitors Per Month. The Wall Street Journal. http://blogs.wsj.com/digits/2011/06/21/google-notches-one-billion-unique-visitors-per-month/.

123. Barnett, Emma. (February 22, 2012). Twitter 'to hit 500 million registered users'. The Telegraph. http://www.telegraph.co.uk/technology/twitter/9098557/Twitter-to-hit-500-million-registered-users.html

124. Cauley, Leslie. (May 11, 2006). NSA has massive database of Americans' phone calls. USA Today. http://www.usatoday.com/news/washington/2006-05-10-nsa_x.htm

125. Keen, Andrew. (June 19, 2012). Should we fear mind-reading future tech? CNN. http://www.cnn.com/2012/06/18/tech/predictive-technology-future/index.html

Part V
Epilogue

Chapter 14
From Total Information Awareness to 1984

Google, Facebook would not exist, had it not been for investments that we made as a country in basic science and research.
—President Barack Obama (April 2012)

Facebook in particular is the most appalling spying machine that has ever been invented.
—WikiLeaks founder Julian Assange (May 2011)

One of my heroes, Edwin Land of Polaroid, said about the importance of people who could stand at the intersection of humanities and sciences, and I decided that's what I wanted to do.
—Apple and Pixar co-founder Steve Jobs (2009)

Every major technological innovation propels humanity forward to the point of no return.
—Newton Lee (2012)

14.1 Brave New World of Total Information Awareness

On May 18, 2012, Facebook offered the largest technology IPO in history and the third largest U.S. IPO ever, trailing only Visa in March 2008 and General Motors in November 2010 [1]. Selling 421.2 million shares to raise $16 billion, Facebook has a $104.2 billion market value and is more costly than almost every company in the Standard & Poor's 500 Index [2]. Former U.S. Treasury secretary Lawrence H. Summers called Facebook's offering "an American milestone" comparable to Ford and IBM's, "Many companies provide products that let people do things they've done before in better ways. Most important companies, like Ford in its day or I.B.M. in its, are those that open up whole new capabilities and permit whole new connections. Facebook is such a company" [3]. However, the Facebook IPO was also one of the biggest opening flops in stock market history. The stock was down by 16.5 % at the end of its first full week of trading.

On May 19, 2012, a day after the bumpy IPO, 28-year-old Facebook co-founder and CEO Mark Zuckerberg added a life event on his timeline: Married Priscilla Chan [4]. Within a week, the wedding picture that he uploaded to Facebook had received 1.5 million "Likes" and 800 comments from his 14 million subscribers.

N. Lee, *Facebook Nation*, DOI: 10.1007/978-1-4614-5308-6_14,
© Springer Science+Business Media New York 2013

In addition, Zuckerberg and Chan's Hungarian Sheepdog named "Beast" is also a "Public Figure" on Facebook with a respectable 575,000 "Likes," but he is far behind the Pomeranian named "Boo" who has garnered 4.4 million "Likes" as of May 2012 [5].

Back on April 11, 2012, when a hoax spread on Twitter about Boo's death in a duck pond, Boo's owner quickly addressed the rumors on Facebook, saying, "hi friends! i heard the rumors, and i would like all my friends to know that i am happy and kickin'! i asked human if i could do a press conference to reassure everyone on camera, but she reminded me that i can't talk" [6]. As Mark Twain said about his obituary mistakenly published in the *New York Journal* in May 1879, "The report of my death was an exaggeration" [7].

To some, Facebook is a self-published tabloid and a public relations gem. To others, Facebook is a communication tool for families and friends around the world to stay in touch. From a macroscopic point of view, Facebook offers insights into public sentiments and national trends. In a microscopic view, Facebook allows people to reach out and connect on a very personal level. Zuckerberg told ABC's Robin Roberts in a 2012 interview that the idea of the organ donation initiative came to him during a dinner conversation with his then girlfriend and future wife Priscilla [8]. Increasingly for many users, Facebook has become an indispensible platform for spreading messages of anti-bullying, AMBER Alerts, organ donation, political activism, and world peace.

Whatever Facebook is or is not, the massive volume of photos, biometric data, and personally identifiable information (PII) on Facebook has raised serious privacy concerns. Some people have deactivated their Facebook for privacy reason as well as relationship problems, job issues, or simply freeing up their time for face-to-face interpersonal connections with the people whom they really care about [9]. A June 2012 survey of 1,032 Facebook users in the U.S. found that 34 % of them spend less time on the site than they did half a year ago [10]. There are also reports indicating that Facebook is getting "uncool" for 18–24 years old—a mindset tantamount to "parents turn up at the party, the party's over" [11].

Nonetheless, the majority of 955 million users cannot envision life without Facebook. Indeed, the new Generation C of digital omnivores has largely accepted Facebook's norm of information sharing in lieu of the traditional norm of privacy. In January 2010, Zuckerberg told the audience at the Crunchie awards in San Francisco, "People have really gotten comfortable not only sharing more information and different kinds, but more openly and with more people. That social norm is just something that has evolved over time."

At one end of the social spectrum, we have an Arizona man using carrier pigeons to communicate with his business partner in the year 2012 [12]. At the other end, we have blogger Robert Scoble of Rackspace's Building 43 who said, "Facebook is good at a lot of things. It is a new kind of new media company that personalizes the media. The more Zuckerberg knows about you, the better the user experience will be. … Everybody has a freaky line. I am way over the freaky line. I want the Internet to know everything about me because that way it can really help me. In that way, Facebook is way ahead and I get more for my efforts that way" [13].

Notwithstanding privacy concerns, having our real identity rather than anonymity online has an advantage of keeping people honest and courteous in the Internet space. *Forbes Magazine* contributor Anthony Wing Kosner observed, "Instead of the anonymous trolls of the early web, Zuckerberg's social web reinforced us for being ourselves online and revealing as much (or more) about ourselves as possible. And the Facebook revolution worked. People do act more civil when their real name is attached to a comment. People do think twice (sometimes) about posting questionable photos that may come back to haunt them. And it has become much easier to find people, not only through Facebook, but LinkedIn, Google+ and other real-name networks" [14].

The same psychology applies to the offline world long before the existence of Facebook and Google. Drivers think twice about running a red traffic light when the red light camera is present at an intersection. Although red light camera continues to be a topic of fierce debate in cities like Houston, Texas [15], reports have shown that there has been an overall 25–30 % reduction in injury crashes at intersections following camera installation [16].

Around the world, public closed-circuit television (CCTV) systems help deter crimes in shopping malls, convenience stores, gas stations, parking garages, airports, banks, casinos, and other public places. Although the proliferation of CCTV cameras has created some unease about the erosion of civil liberties and individual human rights, the majority of people have accepted the presence of CCTV in public places.

Prof. Amitai Etzioni of George Washington University observed, "Facebook merely adds to the major inroads made by the CCTV cameras that are ubiquitous in many cities around the globe, along with surveillance satellites, tracking devices, spy malware and, most recently, drones used not for killing terrorists but for scrutinizing spaces heretofore considered private, like our backyards" [17].

Back in the 60s, Defense Advanced Research Projects Agency (DARPA) initiated and funded the research and development of Advanced Research Projects Agency Network (ARPANET) that went online in 1969. The success of ARPANET gave rise to the global commercial Internet in the 90s and the new generation of Fortune 500 companies today such as Amazon.com, Google, eBay, and Yahoo!.

President Barack Obama said at a campaign fundraiser in April 2012, "I believe in investing in basic research and science because I understand that all these extraordinary companies ... many of them would have never been there; Google, Facebook would not exist, had it not been for investments that we made as a country in basic science and research" [18]. Another good example is the talking, question-answering Siri application on Apple's iPhone [19]. Siri originated from a DARPA-funded project known as PAL (Personalized Assistant that Learns)—an adaptive artificial intelligence program for data retrieval and data synthesis [20].

As if life comes full circle in the 21st century, private businesses and the ubiquity of social networks such as Facebook, Google +, Twitter, and YouTube are creating the technologies and infrastructures necessary for the DARPA-proposed Total Information Awareness program. Facial recognition, location tracking, ambient social apps on GPS-enabled devices, Google Street View, digital footprints, and data mining are some key elements in information awareness.

WikiLeaks founder Julian Assange told RT's Laura Emmett in a May 2011 interview, "Facebook in particular is the most appalling spying machine that has ever been invented. Here we have the world's most comprehensive database about people, their relationships, their names, their addresses, their locations and their communications with each other, their relatives, all sitting within the United States, all accessible to US intelligence" [21]. Assange further alleged that, "Facebook, Google, Yahoo—all these major US organizations have built-in interfaces for US intelligence. It's not a matter of serving a subpoena. They have an interface that they have developed for US intelligence to use."

Total Information Awareness requires efficient and effective data mining. On March 29, 2012, the Obama administration announced more than $200 million in funding for "Big Data Research and Development Initiative" [22]. One of the beneficiaries of the initiative is Centers for Disease Control and Prevention (CDC). Using the funding, CDC runs a BioSense program to track health problems as they evolve and to safeguard the health of the American people [23].

The U.S. government has also been learning from private businesses who often share customers' data to make a profit or a future sale. Letitia Long, Director of the National Geospatial-Intelligence Agency (NGA) described the shift across the post-9/11 intelligence community as the transition from a "need-to-know" atmosphere to a "need-to-share and need-to-provide" culture. "In solving intelligence problems, including diversity of thought is essential," said Long, "[In] the Osama bin Laden operation, the intelligence community witnessed the true value of merging many thoughts and perspectives, and we must continue to replicate this kind of integration across the enterprise in the future" [24].

The quest for information awareness has also resulted in biosurveillance systems such as Argus—an artificial intelligence program that monitors foreign news reports and other open sources looking for signs that would trigger an early warning of an epidemic, nuclear accident, or environmental catastrophe. Eric Haseltine, former director of research at NSA and then associate director for science and technology at ODNI, said in a 2006 *U.S. News & World Report* interview, "I sleep a little easier at night knowing that Argus is out there" [25].

The brave new world of Total Information Awareness is a connected world that benefits individuals as well as society as a whole. Mark Zuckerberg wrote in his IPO letter, "At Facebook, we're inspired by technologies that have revolutionized how people spread and consume information. We often talk about inventions like the printing press and the television—by simply making communication more efficient, they led to a complete transformation of many important parts of society. They gave more people a voice. They encouraged progress. They changed the way society was organized. They brought us closer together. Today, our society has reached another tipping point. We live at a moment when the majority of people in the world have access to the internet or mobile phones—the raw tools necessary to start sharing what they're thinking, feeling and doing with whomever they want. Facebook aspires to build the services that give people the power to share and help them once again transform many of our core institutions and industries. There is a huge need and a huge opportunity to get everyone in the world connected, to give everyone a voice and to help transform society for the future. The scale of the technology and infrastructure that must be built is unprecedented, and we believe this is the most important problem we can focus on" [26].

14.2 George Orwell's 1984

In February 2012, a reader by the name of Helen Corey left a one-line comment on a *Wall Street Journal* report on Google's iPhone tracking, "Orwell's 1984 novel has become reality" [27]. It was her response to Google and other advertising companies bypassing Apple's Safari browser settings for guarding privacy on the users' iPhones and computers [28].

George Orwell's novel *Nineteen Eighty-Four* (first published in 1949)[29] portrays pervasive government surveillance, incessant public mind control, disinformation, and manipulation of the past in a "Big Brother" society or a dystopian future. It tells a terrifying story of a world without privacy. Orwell coined the terms Big Brother, doublethink, thoughtcrime, Newspeak, and memory hole that have become contemporary vernacular.

In the year 2012, from ATMs to parking lots to shopping malls, there are approximately 30 million cameras in the world capturing 250 billion hours of raw footage annually [30]. Since the 1970s, the proliferation of CCTV cameras in public places has led to some unease about the erosion of civil liberties and individual human rights, along with warnings of an Orwellian "Big Brother" culture.

In the United Kingdom, CCTV is so prevalent that some residents can expect to be captured by a camera at least 300 times a day [31]. With more than 1.85 million cameras operating in the U.K. [32], the security-camera cordon surrounding London has earned the nickname of "Ring of Steel" [33]. The U.K. first introduced the security measures in London's financial district in mid-1990s during an Irish Republican Army (IRA) bombing campaign. After the terror attacks in the United States on September 11, 2011, the "Ring of Steel" was widened to include more businesses [34].

In the U.S., New York, Los Angeles, San Francisco, and Chicago are among the major cities that have implemented citywide CCTV monitoring systems. Disney theme parks, Six Flags, and other public attractions also use video surveillance systems that can see in the dark.

In January 2008, Pulitzer Prize-winner Lawrence Wright wrote in *The New Yorker*, "The fantasy worlds that Disney creates have a surprising amount in common with the ideal universe envisaged by the intelligence community, in which environments are carefully controlled and people are closely observed, and no one seems to mind" [35].

Tourists not only love to visit Disneyland but also flock to Las Vegas casinos and resorts, another fantasy world, where security cameras are in ample use. In March 2012, Mirage Resort in Las Vegas became the 50th casino to install facial recognition software as part of the surveillance suite of Visual Casino loss-reduction systems [36].

Video surveillance is not always associated with crime prevention. SceneTap, for example, allows consumers to get a real-time snapshot of 50 bars and clubs in Chicago [37]. Facial detection and "people-counting" technologies automatically inform customers about the crowd size and male-to-female ratio in each venue. Without encroaching on individual privacy, the system does not store the videos or identify the faces. SceneTap takes barhopping into the 21st century.

In the future, private citizens will join Big Brother in "watching us." An Intel-commissioned white paper in May 2012 summarized, "While the future is never certain, a future where humans are infused with mobile technology where we are part of the device, our own bodies and brains part of the technology, and where there are no barriers to pure capability, is becoming more believable by the day" [38].

We have already seen a glimpse of that future. In 2009, Canadian filmmaker Rob Spence called himself an "Eyeborg" when he replaced his prosthetic eye with a battery-powered, wireless video camera that records everything that he sees in real time to a computer. "In today's world, you have Facebook and camera eyes," he said. "Tomorrow, we'll have collective consciousness and the Borg. It's a collective robot consciousness. I believe that's a genuine modern concern" [39].

In November 2010, controversial professor Wafaa Bilal at New York University implanted a camera in the back of his head for a yearlong art project [40]. The camera snapped a picture every minute, published the image on a website, and displayed it on monitors labeled "The 3rd I" at Mathaf: Arab Museum of Modern Art in Doha, Qatar.

We may begin to wonder how many Rob Spence's and Wafaa Bilal's will be living among us in the future. They too have their own personal rights to take pictures and record videos in public. Dictatorship of the majority over the minority would be an encroachment on the rights of the individual and their prerogative to personal freedom.

A saying commonly attributed to Benjamin Franklin goes like this, "Any society that would give up a little liberty to gain a little security will deserve neither and lose both." The question is: Did we give up any personal freedom because of public CCTV, red light cameras, Google social search, or Facebook privacy settings? The answer is: No, not really. We do not hesitate to go to public places, drive around town, search for information on Google, and socialize with friends on Facebook and other social networks.

Pete Cashmore, founder and CEO of *Mashable,* has commented that the world of 2012 is both reminiscent of George Orwell's *Nineteen Eighty-Four* and radically at odds with it. Cashmore wrote in a January 2012 *CNN* article, "The online world is indeed allowing our every move to be tracked, while at the same time providing a counterweight to the emergence of Big Brother. ... Unlike in Orwell's dystopian world, people today are making a conscious choice to do so. The difference between this reality and Orwell's vision is the issue of control: While his Thought Police tracked you without permission, some consumers are now comfortable with sharing their every move online" [41].

14.3 Aldous Huxley's Brave New World

Will the "Big Friend" of Facebook replace the "Big Brother" of government? Will human beings have their lives recorded from birth to death on the pages of Facebook?

In fact, some parents have been posting the sonograms of their unborn babies on Facebook [42]. Some families and friends have been leaving posts on the deceased's Facebook Timeline in remembrance [43]. Our future may be one step closer to Aldous Huxley's *Brave New World* (1932) rather than George Orwell's *Nineteen Eighty-Four* (1949).

Social critic Neil Postman contrasted the worlds of Orwell and Huxley in his 1985 book *Amusing Ourselves to Death: Public Discourse in the Age of Show Business.* Postman wrote, "What Orwell feared were those who would ban books. What Huxley feared was that there would be no reason to ban a book, for there would be no one who wanted to read one. Orwell feared those who would deprive us of information. Huxley feared those who would give us so much that we would be reduced to passivity and egotism. Orwell feared that the truth would be concealed from us. Huxley feared the truth would be drowned in a sea of irrelevance. Orwell feared we would become a captive culture. Huxley feared we would become a trivial culture, preoccupied with some equivalent of the feelies, the orgy porgy, and the centrifugal bumblepuppy. As Huxley remarked in *Brave New World Revisited*, the civil libertarians and rationalists who are ever on the alert to oppose tyranny 'failed to take into account man's almost infinite appetite for distractions.' In *1984*, Orwell added, 'people are controlled by inflicting pain.' In *Brave New World,* they are controlled by inflicting pleasure. In short, Orwell feared that what we fear will ruin us. Huxley feared that our desire will ruin us" [44].

What a surprise it is that Postman's discourse about television in the age of show business is equally applicable to the Internet and social networks in the age of big data.

14.4 Point of No Return

Every major technological innovation propels humanity forward to the point of no return. Hardly anyone would seriously consider giving up the Internet, cell phones, automobiles, and everyday comfort and convenience. Instead of turning back, we continue to innovate and push humanity towards the next point of no return. It is a good thing.

X PRIZE Foundation founder and CEO Peter Diamandis spoke at the TED2012 conference in February, "The future is going to be better than many of us think … We will live in a world of abundance made possible by new technology" [45].

Time Magazine named Facebook co-founder and CEO Mark Zuckerberg its Person of the Year 2010 for connecting more than half a billion people and mapping the social relations among them, for creating a new system of exchanging information and for changing how we live our lives. *Time* summarized Facebook's mission in an idealistic description: "Facebook wants to populate the wilderness, tame the howling mob and turn the lonely, antisocial world of random chance into a friendly world, a serendipitous world. You'll be working and living inside a network of people, and you'll never have to be alone again. The Internet, and the whole world, will feel more like a family, or a college dorm, or an office where your co-workers are also your best friends" [46].

Such a grand vision is a tall order indeed. We will know in the future whether Facebook or a new breed of social networks will accomplish such a noble goal. Media theorist Douglas Rushkoff shared his optimism on *CNN*, "This new form of media—social networking—will not only redefine the Internet, change human relationships, create a new marketing landscape, and challenge Google, but it will now rescue and alter the economy itself. Like virtual kudzu, it will infiltrate the financial markets, creating new sorts of opportunities for this peer-to-peer 'social' economy to take root. We will all make our living playing Farmville, or designing new versions of it, or investing in companies that do" [47].

An old English proverb says, "If you can't beat them, join them." There is another saying, "If you can't beat them, join them, and then beat them."

Perhaps decentralized Internet will create the utopia for privacy protection and personal freedom in the age of big data and total information awareness. Isaac Wilder and Charles Wyble co-founded the Free Network Foundation (FNF) in 2011 to investigate peer-to-per communications infrastructure that is resistant to government censorship and corporate influence [48]. NFN deployed nine-foot-tall FreedomTowers at Occupy Wall Street in September and Occupy Austin in October 2011, in order to provide secured WiFi connectivity to activists on the ground [49].

As affordable computing power and data storage capacity continue to increase, we can envision a new peer-to-peer social networking application in the future that combines Skype's VoIP (voice over Internet Protocol) and Facebook's Timeline. We will not upload personal information for storage in some central servers or public clouds that are subject to the exploitation by businesses. Instead, each tight-knitted community of family and friends will form its own circle of peer-to-peer social network, secured from prying eyes.

14.5 Facebook Questions

In July 2010, Facebook introduced "Facebook Questions." Akin to Yahoo! Answers, the question-and-answer feature allows users to pose their questions to the entire Facebook community [50].

In April 2011, Google launched "A Google a Day" trivia. User experience researcher Dan Russell wrote in the official Google blog, "As the world of information continues to explode, we hope 'A Google a Day' triggers your imagination and helps you discover all the types of questions you can ask Google – and get an answer" [51].

The "Deep Thought" supercomputer in Douglas Adams' *The Hitchhiker's Guide to the Galaxy* (first broadcasted in 1978) took seven and a half million years to compute the answer to the ultimate question of life, the universe, and everything. The answer turned out to be 42, but the ultimate question itself was unknown [52].

Billions of cybercitizens on Facebook, Google, Twitter, Yahoo!, and other social networks are giving us many different answers to every difficult question. Nevertheless, if we ask the right question, we will get the correct answer.

References

1. Pepitone, Julianne. (May 18, 2012). Facebook trading sets record IPO volume. CNN. http://money.cnn.com/2012/05/18/technology/facebook-ipo-trading/index.htm
2. Spears, Lee; Frier, Sarah. (May 18, 2012). Facebook Advances in Public Debut After $16 Billion IPO. *Bloomberg.* http://www.bloomberg.com/news/2012-05-17/facebook-raises-16-billion-in-biggest-technology-ipo-on-record.html
3. Sengupta, Somini, and Rusli, Evelyn M. (January 31, 2012). Personal Data's Value? Facebook Is Set to Find Out. The New York Times. http://www.nytimes.com/2012/02/01/technology/riding-personal-data-facebook-is-going-public.html
4. Zuckerberg, Mark. (May 19, 2012). Facebook Timeline. *Facebook.* http://www.facebook.com/zuck
5. Zuckerberg, Mark. (Retrieved May 27, 2012). Beast. *Facebook.* http://www.facebook.com/zuck#!/beast.the.dog
6. Boo's owner. (April 11, 2012). Boo. *Facebook.* http://www.facebook.com/Boo/
7. Twainquotes.com. (Retrieved May 28, 2012). Directory of Mark Twain's maxims, quotations, and various opinions. *Twainquotes.com.* http://www.twainquotes.com/Death.html
8. Good Morning America. (May 1, 2012). Zuckerberg's Dinners with Girlfriend Help Spur Life-Saving Facebook Tool. *ABC News.* http://abcnews.go.com/blogs/headlines/2012/05/zuckerbergs-dinners-with-girlfriend-help-spur-life-saving-facebook-tool/
9. Imam, Jareen. (May 18, 2012). The anti-social network: Life without Facebook. CNN. http://www.cnn.com/2012/05/18/tech/social-media/facebook-deactivation-ireport/index.html
10. Whitney, Lance (June 6, 2012). 1 in 3 users are tuning out Facebook. CNet. http://asia.cnet.com/1-in-3-users-are-tuning-out-facebook-62216195.htm
11. Mcclellan, Steve. (November 16, 2009). Is Facebook Getting Uncool for 18-24 s? *Adweek.* http://www.adweek.com/news/technology/facebook-getting-uncool-18-24s-100908

12. Ellis, Blake. (March 9, 2012). Craziest tax deductions: Carrier pigeons. http://money.cnn.com/galleries/2012/pf/taxes/1203/gallery.wacky-tax-deductions/
13. Israel, Shel. (May 3, 2012). Is Facebook Larry Page's Moby Dick? *Forbes*. http://www.forbes.com/sites/shelisrael/2012/05/03/is-google-larry-pages-moby-dick/2/
14. Kosner, Anthony Wing. (May 26, 2012). Facebook Fails Us, Why Mark Zuckerberg's Revolution Will Not Be Fully Monetized. *Forbes*. http://www.forbes.com/sites/anthonykosner/2012/05/26/facebook-fails-us-the-revolution-will-not-be-monetized/
15. Shay, Miya. (August 24, 2011). Houston City Council votes to turn off red light cameras. ABC 13. http://abclocal.go.com/ktrk/story?section=news/local&id=8323624
16. Rettinga, Richard A.; Fergusona, Susan A.; Hakkertb, A. Shalom. (2003). Effects of Red Light Cameras on Violations and Crashes: A Review of the International Literature. *Traffic Injury Prevention*. 4(1):17-23. http://www.tandfonline.com/doi/abs/10.1080/15389580309858
17. Etzioni, Amitai. (May 27, 2012). Despite Facebook, privacy is far from dead. *CNN*. http://www.cnn.com/2012/05/25/opinion/etzioni-facebook-privacy/index.html
18. Lucas, Fred. (April 6, 2012). Obama: 'Google, Facebook Would Not Exist' Without Government. *The Washington Times*. http://times247.com/articles/obama-google-facebook-would-not-exist-without-big-government
19. Ackerman, Spencer. (October 5, 2011). The iPhone 4S' Talking Assistant Is a Military Veteran. *Wired*. http://www.wired.com/dangerroom/2011/10/siri-darpa-iphone/
20. SRI International. (Retrieved May 28, 2012). PAL (Personalized Assistant that Learns). *SRI International*. https://pal.sri.com/Plone
21. RT. (May 2, 2011). WikiLeaks revelations only tip of iceberg – Assange. *RT News*. http://www.rt.com/news/wikileaks-revelations-assange-interview/
22. Kalil, Tom. (March 29, 2012). Big Data is a Big Deal. *The White House*. http://www.whitehouse.gov/blog/2012/03/29/big-data-big-deal
23. CDC BioSense Program. (February 8, 2012). *Centers for Disease Control and Prevention*. http://www.cdc.gov/biosense/
24. Young, Denise. (Spring 2012). Letitia Long: A Global Vision. Alumna leads intelligence agency in new era of collaboration. *Virginia Tech Magazine*. http://www.vtmag.vt.edu/spring12/letitia-long.html
25. U.S. News & World Report. (November 3, 2006). Q&A: DNI Chief Scientist Eric Haseltine. *U.S. News & World Report*. http://www.usnews.com/usnews/news/articles/061103/3qahaseltine_6.htm
26. Facebook. (February 1, 2012). Form S-1 Registration Statement. *United States Securities and Exchange Commission*. http://sec.gov/Archives/edgar/data/1326801/000119312512034517/d287954ds1.htm
27. Corey, Helen. (Retrieved February 17, 2012). Google's iPhone Tracking. *The Wall Street Journal Readers' Comments*. http://online.wsj.com/article_email/SB10001424052970204880404577225380456599176-lMyQjAxMTAyMDEwNjExNDYyWj.html#articleTabs%3Dcomments
28. Angwin, Julia; Valentino-Devries, Jennifer. (February 17, 2012). Google's iPhone Tracking. *The Wall Street Journal*. http://online.wsj.com/article/SB10001424052970204880404577225380456599176.html
29. Orwell, George. (1949). *Nineteen Eighty-Four*. Secker and Warburg (London).
30. 3VR Inc. (Retrieved May 28, 2012). Use Video Analytics and Data Decision Making to Grow Your Business. *Digital Signage Today*. http://www.digitalsignagetoday.com/whitepapers/4891/Use-Video-Analytics-and-Data-Decision-Making-to-Grow-Your-Business
31. Fussey, Pete. (2007). An Interrupted Transmission? Processes of CCTV Implementation and the Impact of Human Agency, Surveillance & Society. *Surveillance and Criminal Justice*. 4(3): 229-256. http://www.surveillance-and-society.org
32. Reeve, Tom. (March 2011). How many cameras in the UK? Only 1.85 million, claims ACPO lead on CCTV. *Security News Desk*. http://www.securitynewsdesk.com/2011/03/01/how-many-cctv-cameras-in-the-uk/
33. Hope, Christopher. (August 25, 2009). 1,000 CCTV cameras to solve just one crime, Met Police admits. *The Telegraph*. http://www.telegraph.co.uk/news/uknews/crime/6082530/1000-CCTV-cameras-to-solve-just-one-crime-Met-Police-admits.html

34. BBC News. (December 18, 2003). 'Ring of steel' widened. *BBC News*. http://news.bbc.co.uk/2/hi/uk_news/england/london/3330771.stm

35. Wright, Lawrence. (January 21, 2008). The Spymaster. Can Mike McConnell fix America's intelligence community? *The New Yorker* http://www.newyorker.com/reporting/2008/01/21/080121fa_fact_wright?currentPage=all

36. Viisage Technology, Inc. (March 29, 2012). Viisage Technology and Biometrica Systems Achieve 50th Facial Recognition Installation at Mirage Resort, Las Vegas. *PR Newswire*. http://www.prnewswire.com/news-releases/viisage-technology-and-biometrica-systems-achieve-50th-facial-recognition-installation-at-mirage-resort-las-vegas-73268177.html

37. Murph, Darren. (June 12, 2011). SceneTap app analyzes pubs and clubs in real-time, probably won't score you a Jersey Shore cameo. *Engadget*. http://www.engadget.com/2011/06/12/scenetap-app-analyzes-pubs-and-clubs-in-real-time-probably-won/

38. Goldman, David. (May 3, 2012). Intel wants to plug a smartphone into your brain. *CNN Money*. http://money.cnn.com/2012/05/03/technology/smartphone-in-your-brain/index.htm

39. Hornyak, Tim. (June 11, 2010). Eyeborg: Man Replaces False Eye with Bionic Camera. *IEEE Spectrum*. http://spectrum.ieee.org/automaton/biomedical/bionics/061110-eyeborg-bionic-eye

40. Orden, Erica. (December 3, 2010). His Hindsight Is 20-20. *The Wall Street Journal*. http://online.wsj.com/article/SB10001424052748703377504575651091530462742.html

41. Cashmore, Pete. (January 23, 2012). Why 2012, despite privacy fears, isn't like Orwell's 1984. *CNN*. http://www.cnn.com/2012/01/23/tech/social-media/web-1984-orwell-cashmore/index.html

42. Bartz, Andrea; Ehrlich, Brenna. (May 8, 2012). Baby-pic overload! Social media advice for parents. *CNN*. http://www.cnn.com/2012/05/09/tech/social-media/social-media-parents-netiquette/index.html

43. Kelly, Max. (October 26, 2009). Memories of Friends Departed Endure on Facebook. *The Facebook Blog*. http://www.facebook.com/blog.php?post=163091042130

44. Postman, Neil. (November 4, 1986). Amusing *Ourselves to Death: Public Discourse in the Age of Show Business*. Penguin.

45. Diamandis, Peter. (May 6, 2012). The future is brighter than you think. *CNN*. http://www.cnn.com/2012/05/06/opinion/diamandis-abundance-innovation/index.html

46. Grossman, Lev. (December 15, 2010). Person of the Year 2010. Mark Zuckerberg. *Time Magazine*. http://www.time.com/time/specials/packages/article/0,28804,2036683_2037183_2037185,00.html

47. Rushkoff, Douglas. (February 22, 2012). Facebook IPO's meaning: Zuckerberg faces reality. *CNN*. http://www.cnn.com/2012/01/31/opinion/rushkoff-facebook-ipo/index.html

48. FNF. (Retrieved May 30, 2012). The Free Network Foundation. http://freenetwork foundation.org/

49. Anderson, Brian A.; Carr, Erin Lee. Movement aims to decentralize the Internet. *CNN*. http://www.cnn.com/2012/03/28/tech/web/vice-free-the-network/index.html

50. Ross, Blake. (July 28, 2010). Searching for Answers? Ask Facebook Questions. *The Facebook Blog*. http://blog.facebook.com/blog.php?post=411795942130

51. Russell, Dan. (April 11, 2011). A trivia game where using Google is allowed. Google *Official Blog*. http://googleblog.blogspot.com/2011/04/trivia-game-where-using-google-is.html#!/2011/04/trivia-game-where-using-google-is.html

52. Adams, Douglas. (April 30, 2002). The Ultimate Hitchhiker's Guide to the Galaxy. Del Rey.

Facebook Timeline

2003

October

- Mark Zuckerberg releases Facemash, the predecessor to Facebook. It was described as a Harvard University version of Hot or Not.

2004

January

- Zuckerberg begins writing Facebook.
- Zuckerberg registers thefacebook.com domain.

February

- Zuckerberg launches Facebook on February 4. 650 Harvard students joined thefacebook.com in the first week of launch.

March

- Facebook expands to MIT, Boston University, Boston College, Northeastern University, Stanford University, Dartmouth College, Columbia University, and Yale University.

April

- Zuckerberg, Dustin Moskovitz, and Eduardo Saverin form Thefacebook.com LLC, a partnership.

June

- Facebook receives its first investment from PayPal co-founder Peter Thiel for US$500,000.
- Facebook incorporates into a new company, and Napster co-founder Sean Parker becomes its president.
- Facebook moves its base of operations to Palo Alto, California.

N. Lee, *Facebook Nation*, DOI: 10.1007/978-1-4614-5308-6,
© Springer Science+Business Media New York 2013

August

- To compete with growing campus-only service i2hub, Zuckerberg launches Wirehog. It is a precursor to Facebook Platform applications.

September

- ConnectU files a lawsuit against Zuckerberg and other Facebook founders, resulting in a $65 million settlement.

October

- Maurice Werdegar of WTI Partner provides Facebook a $300,000 three-year credit line.

December

- Facebook achieves its one millionth registered user.

2005
February

- Maurice Werdegar of WTI Partner provides Facebook a second $300,000 credit line and a $25,000 equity investment.

April

- Venture capital firm Accel Partners invests $12.7 million into Facebook. Accel's partner and President Jim Breyer also puts up $1 million of his own money.

July

- News Corp acquires MySpace, spurring rumors about the possible sale of Facebook to a larger media company. Zuckerberg stated he did not want to sell Facebook.

August

- Facebook acquires Facebook.com domain for $200,000.

September

- Facebook launches a high school version of the website.

October

- Facebook expands to universities in the United Kingdom, Mexico, Puerto Rico, and U.S. Virgin Islands.

December

- Facebook expands to universities in Australia and New Zealand.

2006
January

- Facebook rebuffs an offer from Viacom that gives Facebook a valuation of $750 million.

March

- A potential acquisition of Facebook is reportedly under negotiations. Facebook reportedly declined an offer of $750 million.

April

- Greylock Partners, Meritech Partners, the Founders Fund, and Accel invests $27.5 million into Facebook.

June

- Interpublic invests $5 million in Facebook.

September

- Facebook and Yahoo! discussed possible acquisition of Facebook for $1 billion. Facebook eventually turned down the offer.
- Facebook is open to everyone aged 13 and over with a valid email address.

2007

May

- Facebook launches the Facebook Platform to enable third-party developers to integrate with the Facebook Open Graph.

September

- Google expressed interest in buying a portion of Facebook.

October

- Microsoft invests $240 million into Facebook.

November

- Li Ka-Shing Foundation in Hong Kong invests $60 million into Facebook.
- Facebook launches Beacon.

2008

January

- European Founders Fund invests $15 million in Facebook.

March

- Li Ka-Shing invests a second $60 million into Facebook.

June

- Facebook settles both lawsuits, ConnectU vs. Facebook, Mark Zuckerberg et al. and intellectual property theft, Wayne Chang et al. over The Winklevoss Chang Group's Social Butterfly project. The settlement effectively had Facebook acquiring ConnectU for $20 million in cash and over $1.2 million in shares, valued at $45 million based on $15 billion company valuation.

August

- Employees reportedly privately sell their shares to venture capital firms, at a company valuation of between $3.75 billion to $5 billion.
- Facebook has 100 million registered users with a monthly growth rate of 178.38 %.

October

- Facebook sets up its international headquarters in Dublin, Ireland.

2009
January

- Facebook surpasses MySpace to become top social network site for the first time.

April

- Facebook has 200 million registered users with a monthly growth rate of 13.33 %.

May

- Digital Sky Technologies invests $200 million into Facebook.

August

- Facebook acquires social media real-time news aggregator FriendFeed.

September

- Facebook claims that it has turned cash flow positive for the first time.
- Facebook has 300 million registered users with a monthly growth rate of 9.38 %.
- Facebook shuts down Beacon.

December

- Facebook partners with the AMBER Alerts.

2010
February

- Facebook acquires Malaysian contact-importing startup Octazen Solutions.
- Facebook has 400 million registered users with a monthly growth rate of 6.99 %.

April

- Facebook announces the acquisition of photo-sharing service called Divvy-shot for an undisclosed amount.

- Facebook introduces Community Pages that are populated with articles from Wikipedia.
- Facebook introduces Instant Personalization, starting with Microsoft Docs, Yelp, and Pandora.

June

- Facebook employees sell shares of the company on SecondMarket, a U.S. financial marketplace online, at a company valuation of $11.5 billion.

July

- Facebook has 500 million registered users with a monthly growth rate of 4.52 %.
- Facebook introduces "Facebook Questions."

October

- *The Social Network*, a film about the beginnings of Facebook directed by David Fincher is released. The film is met with widespread critical acclaim as well as commercial success. However, Mark Zuckerberg says that the film is a largely inaccurate account of what happened.

2011
January

- Facebook receives $450 million investment from Goldman Sachs, $50 million from Digital Sky Technologies, and $1 billion from Goldman's overseas clients.
- Facebook has 600 million registered users with a monthly growth rate of 3.57 %.
- President Barack Obama, in his 2011 State of the Union Address, called America "the nation of Edison and the Wright brothers" and "of Google and Facebook."

February

- Facebook becomes the largest online photo host. Facebook application and content aggregator Pixable estimates that Facebook will host 100 billion photos by summer 2011.
- Facebook adds new "civil union" option for gay partnerships.
- Kleiner Perkins Caufield & Byers invest $38 million in Facebook.

March

- Mutual fund company T. Rowe Price invests $190.5 million in Facebook.
- Yahoo! files a lawsuit against Facebook for infringing on ten of its patents covering advertising, privacy controls and social networking.

May

- Facebook has 700 million registered users with a monthly growth rate of 3.45 %.

August

- Facebook overtakes Orkut as top social networking site in Brazil.

September

- Facebook partners with Heroku for Facebook application development using the Facebook Platform.
- Facebook collaborates with Cartoon Network in launching the "Stop Bullying: Speak Up" social pledge application.
- Facebook has 800 million registered users with a monthly growth rate of 3.73 %.

October

- Facebook launches iPad app.

December

- Facebook launches its new profile user interface, Facebook Timeline.

2012
February

- Facebook files for an initial public offering (IPO) seeking to raise $5 billion.

March

- Facebook introduces sponsored stories.

April

- Facebook acquires picture sharing and social network, Instagram, for $1 billion, the largest acquisition to date.
- Facebook has 900 million registered users with a monthly growth rate of 1.74 %.

May

- Facebook unveils organ donation initiative.
- Facebook acquires ambient location app Glancee.
- Facebook sets IPO price at $38 a share, giving the company a $104.2 billion market value.
- Facebook IPO raises $16 billion, making it the third largest in U.S. history, trailing only Visa in March 2008 and General Motors in November 2010.
- Facebook stock ends its first full week of trading at $31.91, a 16.5 % decline.
- In a dozen of lawsuits, Facebook shareholders sue Facebook and its underwriters for misleading private investors in the purchase of Facebook's stock.

June

- Facebook acquires facial recognition company Face.com for between $55 and $100 million.

- Facebook announces real-time ad bidding Facebook Exchange.
- Facebook tests Find Friends Nearby feature.
- Facebook and its underwriters file a motion in New York to consolidate the outstanding shareholder lawsuits against them.
- Facebook has 955 million monthly active users, 81% of whom are outside the U.S. and Canada.

About the Author

Newton Lee is CEO of Newton Lee Laboratories LLC, president of the Institute for Education, Research, and Scholarships, and founding editor-in-chief of ACM Computers in Entertainment. Previously, he was a research scientist at Bell Laboratories, senior producer and engineer at The Walt Disney Company, and research staff member at the Institute for Defense Analyses. He earned a B.S. and M.S. degree in Computer Science from Virginia Tech, and received an A.S. degree in Electrical Engineering and honorary doctorate from Vincennes University. He is the co-author of *Disney Stories: Getting to Digital.*

N. Lee, *Facebook Nation*, DOI: 10.1007/978-1-4614-5308-6,
© Springer Science+Business Media New York 2013

Index

N. Lee, *Facebook Nation*, DOI: 10.1007/978-1-4614-5308-6,
© Springer Science+Business Media New York 2013

CPSIA information can be obtained at www.ICGtesting.com
Printed in the USA
LVOW072346240513

335521LV00008B/184/P